Chinese and Soviet Aid to Africa

edited by
Warren Weinstein

The Praeger Special Studies program—
utilizing the most modern and efficient book
production techniques and a selective
worldwide distribution network—makes
available to the academic, government, and
business communities significant, timely
research in U.S. and international economic, social, and political development.

Chinese and Soviet Aid to Africa

PRAEGER SPECIAL STUDIES IN INTERNATIONAL POLITICS AND GOVERNMENT

Praeger Publishers   New York   Washington   London

Library of Congress Cataloging in Publication Data

Weinstein, Warren.
    Chinese and Soviet aid to Africa.

    (Praeger special studies in international politics
and government)
    Includes bibliographies.
    1. Economic assistance, Chinese—Africa—Addresses,
essays, lectures.   2. Economic assistance, Russian—
Africa—Addresses, essays, lectures.   I. Title.
HC502.W44   338.91'6'047   74-3512
ISBN 0-275-09050-7

PRAEGER PUBLISHERS
111 Fourth Avenue, New York, N.Y. 10003, U.S.A.
5, Cromwell Place, London SW7 2JL, England

Published in the United States of America in 1975
by Praeger Publishers, Inc.

Printed in the United States of America

To my Wife and Daughters

CONTENTS

LIST OF TABLES, FIGURES, AND MAP

Table   Page

Figures

Map

This volume grew out of a joint seminar held at the City Graduate Center of the City University of New York in late May 1973. It was sponsored by the African American Labor Center (AALC) and the State University College at Oswego, New York. Our purpose was to review and analyze the role Chinese and Soviet aid plays in Africa's political and economic development, and to provide for an exchange of views between academic and nonacademic specialists. The selection of papers presented here includes some read at this conference, and others later solicited by the editor. The essays cover a variety of topics and many aspects of recent Chinese and Soviet involvement with Africa.

As one reads through the selections, several broad trends emerge. First is the important fact that the 1970s is not the 1960s! The naive enthusiasm for Africa in the earlier period has turned to hard cynicism among many American and Soviet officials in dealing with that continent. Ten years of experience with tropical African states has shown their regimes to be weak, ephemeral, and unpredictable. Expected payoffs for economic, technical, and military aid have failed to materialize. The Chinese appear to be less disillusioned, but they too have taken a harder and more pragmatic approach to their relations with African states.

The superpowers of the 1960s, the United States and the Soviet Union, have downgraded their interest in Africa as the region is now peripheral to their major preoccupations. Each has become more involved with internal problems, East-West trade, detente, and the Middle East. As Bruce Larkin has stated in his chapter, the potential power centers in the world have abdicated in the African aid field to those other states prepared to fill this void. Larkin included the United States, the Soviet Union, the Common Market (EEC), and Japan in this first group. As a result, the Chinese have been able to expand their activities on the continent with little difficulty. But the Chinese have not been overly hasty and have confined their involvement to small-scale projects and a few larger ones such as the TanZam Railway.

China in 1970 is a new international actor. Its leaders now follow a pragmatic course in their relations with Africa in contrast to their highly politicized approach in the early 1960s. The new Chinese policy builds upon several factors: China has entered the United Nations and has, at least in the short run, indicated a desire to work within the formal international system and not against it; China is searching for assurances against possible Soviet attack along their long common border and is wooing support among all Third World states whatever their proclaimed ideological leanings; and China ia a developing industrial state searching for secure sources for needed primary materials as well as potential markets for her products. There is some question whether China can fulfill its desire to become the leader of a Third World common front against the superpowers, and the Chinese leadership will have to prove continuously to Third World governments that China is sincerely not interested in hegemony. Because China has global interests, its leaders, like those of the United States and the Soviet Union, may increasingly subordinate interests of clients to their own national needs. It is more probable that China will increasingly act like a superpower if it sustains its growth in power. The pragmatic approach discerned in Sino-African relations so far in the 1970s appears to support such predictions.

An apparent convergence in Chinese, Soviet, and American policies stems from the now more businesslike outlook characteristic of the policies each one is pursuing toward Africa. This point is part of the conclusions drawn in the contributions made by Valerie Plave Bennett, Helen Desfosses, and John D. Esseks. However, there are some basic differences. The United States has moved increasingly toward multilateralization of aid, an approach that both the Soviets and Chinese eschew. The United States is heavily committed to support the position of the Portuguese and South African regimes, which handicaps their dealings elsewhere in tropical Africa. The decision to concentrate on a select group of target countries while ignoring the wider substantive and psychological needs of Africa has placed the United States somewhat at a disadvantage--but since the Nixonian policy is one of a general low profile in Africa this does not concern very many Americans. Indeed, the growing interest in turning the Indian Ocean into a strategic zone could play against increased American interest in Black Africa since it would buttress those voices in American politics who view a stable, pro-West South Africa as an important partner in any U.S. posture in this area. The U.S. response to

the Sahelian drought or to Burundi's gross violation of
basic human rights shows the very low level of U.S. interest in sub-Saharan Africa.[1]

SOVIET AID AND TRADE: PATTERNS AND ACHIEVEMENTS

The Soviet Union has veered somewhat closer to the
U.S. position in revising its views of aid to Africa and
Africa's importance to Soviet foreign policy. Although
the Soviets have not openly slashed aid funding as did the
United States in 1973/74, they have reduced their commitments. In 1971 Soviet aid to Africa dipped to a low point
and its aid to LDCs (Less Developed Countries) in general
fell 30 percent below 1971 levels in 1972.[2] No new aid
was committed to any African state in 1972. The Soviets
have also followed a policy of aiding target states. An
example of this is their concentrated involvement in
Somalia on the Horn of Eastern Africa. Desfosses points
out that this does not lead the Soviets to have the political or even economic clout they may have once expected.
She lists rather the dilemmas that a superpower faces in a
country of concentrated aid efforts: "how to have leverage without responsibility, how to advise without becoming
involved in Somalia's border disputes, how to give enough
assistance to impress . . . without intensifying the fears
of anti-Soviet factions, and how to keep the level of Great
Power competition in the Horn from threatening the general
thrust of peaceful coexistence."

The Soviet involvement in Africa is now restricted
mainly to pragmatic business deals and strict terms. Both
Bennett and Esseks raise serious questions about Africa's
profit in this new relationship; this theme is put cogent-
ly by Angela Stent in Chapter 6. Stent concludes that the
Soviet Union, "like other developed nations has become
disillusioned with aid as a political lever."

The shift to an emphasis on trade and economic payoffs carries potential costs for Africa. Esseks has
sketched some of these: "Net decreases in the supply of
goods for domestic use, through export surpluses to the
Soviet Union which are not later compensated for in import surpluses; through less attractive terms of trade;
and/or through deficiencies in quality--of the goods,
themselves, of the speed and regularity of deliveries, of
the provision of spare parts, and of other aspects of the
trading relationship." The same costs may occur in Chinese aid involvement with Africa, a point raised in the
chapters by George Yu and myself.

Other potential drawbaks are income and employment
dislocations caused by irregular Soviet purchases and the
generally accepted dangers inherent in economic dependence:
vulnerability to economic sabotage, and balance of payments
difficulties. These costs are not all limited to Soviet-
African trade—many, if not all, are present in economic
relations and trade with Peking as well as with the industrialized states of the West. There are also benefits
that accrue to African states, but in terms of overall development, international price change structures may be
more productive for developing states than aid per se.
The 1973 annual report of Barclays Bank International Limited, concluded: "The World Bank Group is doing great
work in trying to reduce the extremes of poverty but in
fact world commodity prices have, over the past year, done
much more . . . . [To] pay better prices for the products
of the less developed countries, assisting them to stand
on their own economic feet, is so much better than a succession of charity handouts."

dependence

The Soviets have continued to exploit their support
to African liberation movements as a propaganda tool
against the United States and the EEC countries. In part
continued Soviet military and financial support to liberation movements in Southern Africa and Guinea-Bissau arises
from the Soviets' desire to maintain their image as a revolutionary state and to limit China's role in this domain.
Sino-Soviet rivalry has prompted much Soviet support to
these movements; a fact which has led our contributors--
Michael H. Glantz and Mohamed A. El-Khawas--to question
the sincerity of the USSR. In fact, none of the movements
has received support in a magnitude that would allow them
quick victory and their dependence on the Soviets has exacerbated internal dissensions between different liberation groups of the same state as well as among competitive
factions or personalities within any particular movement.
Glantz and El-Khawas conclude that the Soviets "have sought
to further their own ideological interests at the cost of
national liberation." The Soviet conflict with China has
been deflected by each of the disputants to competition
with the other in Southern Africa. Desfosses has raised
this same point in her analysis of Soviet involvement in
the Horn.

?

To some extent, the Soviet presence in Africa for
more than ten years puts them together with Americans as
deja-vu for many Africans, and talk of a Soviet-American
detente fosters a twinning of these superpowers in the
minds of African statesmen. Soviet generosity is ques-

tioned for its sincerity since it is a superpower which
has acted on a basis of realpolitik in its international
dealings. Moreover, the Soviets themselves have, like the
Americans, stated bluntly their interest in maintaining
and exploiting the "existing [world] division of labor"
between the industrialized rich states and the raw material
producing states.[3] The Soviets have been grouped with the
Americans as global capitalists interested in keeping the
underdeveloped states poor by neo-marxist scholars like
Immanuel Wallerstein and revisionists like Johan Galtung.[4]

CHINA: THE CHALLENGER AND POTENTIAL RIVAL

China, as a world power, has just entered the world
arena and whether or not it becomes and acts like a superpower it is too early to qualify it as such. The Chinese
leadership disclaim any hegemonistic desires identified
with superpower status, and it is too soon to know how sincere they are or will be. The fact that China has not
reached the level of development achieved by the United
States and the Soviet Union makes it appear less overwhelming and threatening and shows it as a potential leader
since it is the most powerful have-not state. The advent
of a highly visible Chinese presence in Africa has not
sparked renewed Soviet or American interest as some had
anticipated--and even hoped. The limited physical capabilities of China's economy have led it to emphasize self-
reliance, small-scale industry, and agricultural development. These themes come much closer to African realities
than the American or Soviet experience.
China has a major advantage over the United States
and the Soviet Union: from 1965 to 1970 there was almost
no Chinese presence in Africa and so China is something
new--certainly it's not deja-vu. China has also made the
most of an argument employed by the Soviets during the
period of political decolonization of Africa: we are in
no way responsible for your plight, indeed we too were
subject to the (neo-) colonialism of the developed states
and excolonial powers. The Soviets can now be lumped together with Americans and West Europeans as white and as
one of the "industrialized states." The Chinese hint
subtly at the fact that they are not, and in the 1970s
where the have-nots are nonwhite states this provides the
Chinese with a definite psychological advantage. All over
Africa, where the Chinese share a presence with Soviets
and East Europeans, the Chinese are quick to point out to

their host Africans that the behavior and life-style of
these "Europeans" is similar to that of Westerners while
the Chinese wear local clothes and live at the indigenous
level. This noticeable difference in style has not been
lost on Africans, and it has often provided the Chinese
with a psychological victory. This has boomeranged at
times, since the Chinese behavior and their tendency to
keep strictly apart from the locals has led some Africans,
as Thomas Kanza has remarked, to view the Chinese to be as
"paternalistic and race-conscious toward Africa as the
European Communists."

The Chinese have had to live down their pre-1965 reputation for supporting oppositionist movements within independent Black African states. The Soviets were never as
reckless about this, and even if they were, since 1965
their activity in Africa has been pragmatic and correct.
China has, since its renewed activity in Africa beginning
in 1970, established relations with almost every African
regime and sweetened some with offers of generous aid on
favorable terms. They have deliberately avoided the
rhetoric of opposition voiced in the early 1960s.

The Chinese willingness to finance and construct the
TanZam railway was, as George Yu submits, a benchmark
achieved in Sino-African relations: the Chinese proved
the West, including the Soviets and East Europeans, have
no monopoly on technological superiority and dominance;
the behavior and living patterns of Chinese technicians
and laborers demonstrated that they identified with and
were willing to live at an African level; and the decision
to undertake a project refused by all other potential aid
donor states demonstrated a genuine interest in providing
support to the African states in the front line of the
struggle against minority-ruled South Africa, Rhodesia,
Angola, and Mozambique. Most of all the progress in constructing the railway has demonstrated China's capabilities
and powers. However, it has also placed a serious burden
on China's limited resources in trained manpower, transportation, construction industrial output, and hard currency holdings.

The TanZam Railroad may stand as an eloquent example
of just how much China can provide, but it is doubtful
whether China can sustain more major projects of this
magnitude--at least not at the same time. China has
global interests and some African states may be disappointed if not disillusioned if they request such major
projects and find Chinese commitments do not permit it.
In fact, as Bruce Larkin has pointed out, China's commit-

ments to Africa are meager in contrast to those of the
Soviet Union, the United States, or the EEC countries.
Furthermore, Chinese commitments will run for another
thirty years and there may be little new forthcoming during this time.

Once repayments begin and Africa has a broader experience with China, the glitter of newness may wear off,
leaving China standing closer to the U.S.-USSR image than
presently. There is some supporting evidence. Those Tanzanians who have spent the longest time in China have the
most serious doubts about its drab, regimented life-style.
In 1973 Sino-Zambian relations began to sour as China
acted more like a big power imposing its will on the weaker African state. It was reported in early 1973 that four
Zambian students had been ordered from China. The influential journal, Jeune Afrique, commented candidly that China
is a big power "in gestation" with its own interests to defend. This is nowhere more evident than in China's policy
toward African liberation movements. Glantz and El-Khawas
document that China has encouraged splits by offering support to spin-off movements, and insisted groups sign a
statement condemning Soviet revisionism. The concern has
been less with liberating Southern Africa and more with
responding to earlier Soviet initiatives.

It is still too soon to make any definitive statement
about Chinese aid and China's potential role among Third
World states. But the experience of both the Soviets and
Chinese goes against those theories of dependence which
assume an aid donor's expectations constitute self-
fulfilling prophecies helped by donor intervention. As
several of our contributors put it, there is some question
about the benefits Africans derive from Soviet aid. The
Soviets have faced a problem of debt rescheduling as well
as accusations that they, like the West, are insensitive
to Africa's needs while their expected political payoffs
have not materialized and most regimes they supported for
political reasons have been overthrown. The Chinese also
face this problem, and recognize it, as Mao is reported to
have told President Mobutu of Zaire (see Chapter 3).

CONCLUSION

Neither the Soviet Union nor China act alone in Africa; there is a very strong American and EEC presence as
well as growing Japanese involvement. Therefore, it is
difficult to foresee China's renewed interest as creating

a serious challenge to either the older external interests
or to the African states themselves. Nor are the Chinese
interested necessarily in presenting themselves as such.
Since both U.S. and Soviet policymakers view Africa as
peripheral, it is doubtful they view China as a challenge
so much as a newcomer to share the burden of aid to the
developing states. To be sure, in Southern Africa the interaction is more politicized and there is an element of
competition. This competition is working to the detriment
of the African liberation effort, and few African states
appear to be all that committed to the liberation in the
south by violent means. The Soviets and Chinese have
shifted away from direct support somewhat and have channeled their funds and arms through African governments in
whose territory liberation movements exist. By doing this,
both states have indicated the greater value they place on
correct relations with independent African governments--
all part and parcel of the businesslike, pragmatic approach
which characterizes U.S. behavior toward Africa as well.

It is difficult to predict foreign policy of states
such as the Soviet Union, the United States, and China,
but the style and direction described and analyzed in the
chapters which follow present a picture that is likely to
continue to dominate the interaction these states have
with Africa.

In addition to the collection of original essays presenting the views of noted African and American scholars,
I have added an appendix with statistical data and documents that bear on Chinese and Soviet aid to Africa. In
selecting papers for publication, I have been careful to
include only those written by academics. Since the AALC
participated in the coordination of the May 1973 conference, where several of the papers were presented, I felt
it only fair to include a statement by them. This statement reflects the views of the AALC alone, and does not
reflect those of the editor or of the various authors
whose work appears in this volume.

I also wish to acknowledge the role played by David
Brombard of the AALC in planning the conference and his
collaboration in providing me with source materials for
our use. The free exchange and discussion among participants at the conference contributed to sharpening the
focus and direction of a number of papers revised for this
publication. I would like to express my appreciation to
the many conference participants.

I would like to express my deep gratitude to Dean
Richard Soter, Dean of Arts and Sciences at the State

University College at Oswego, whose encouragement and support helped to make the conference and this book a reality. His comments on papers proved quite useful, and his provision of secretarian and xeroxing facilities helped greatly in getting this manuscript into print. My gratitude also goes to my colleague, Professor Mab Huang, who read and provided useful comments on many of the papers. Thanks are also due to my research assistant, Carl Hausman, who spent endless hours proofreading manuscripts and verifying references. Most of all I am indebted to my charming wife, Elaine, who put up with my long hours at the office working on the manuscript, and who kept my spirits up throughout this project.

NOTES

1. Roger Morris, "The Triumph of Money and Power," New York Times, March 3, 1974, section 4, p. 13.

2. U.S. Department of State Memorandum, "Communist Governments and Developing Nations: Aid and Trade," RSE-65, 14.

3. L. Zevin, "Voprosy povysheniia ustoichivosti i effektivnosti ekonomicheskikh sviazei SSSR s Razvivaiushchimisia stranami" (Problems of Increasing the Stability and Effectiveness of Economic Relations between the USSR and the Developing Countries), Planovoe Khoziaistvo, no. 7 (1971): 26. Cited by Helen Desfosses, "USSR and Africa: Specialization of Interests and Influence," Background Paper #4, presented at the Sino and Soviet Aid to Africa Seminar, May 30-31, 1973 at the City University of New York Graduate Center.

4. Immanuel Wallerstein, "Dependence in an Interdependent World: The Limited Possibilities of Transformation Within the Capitalist World Economy," paper delivered at the Conference on Dependence and Development in Africa sponsored by the Canadian African Studies Association at the School of International Affairs, Carleton University, Canada, February 16-18, 1973; Johan Galtung, "A Structural Theory of Imperialism," The African Review 1, no. 4 (April 1972): 81-117, and his remarks to the plenary session of the Conference on Dependency and Development, supra.

Chinese and Soviet
Aid to Africa

Tunisia

Morocco

Spanish
Sahara

Algeria

Libya

Egypt

Mauritainia

Mali

Niger

Chad

Sudan

Terr. of
the Afars
& Issas

Senegal

Upper
Volta

Gambia
Port
Guinea

Guinea

Nigeria

Central
African
Rep.

Ethiopia

Somalia

Sierra
Leone

Ghana

Liberia

Ivory
Coast

Togo
Dahomey

Cameroon

Rwanda
Burundi

Uganda

Kenya

Equitorial
Guinea

Gabon

Zaire

Rep. of
Congo

Tanzania

Malawi

Mozambique

Angola

Zambia

South
West
Africa

Botwana

Malagasy
Rep.

Rhodesia

South
Africa

Swaziland

Lesotho

CHINESE AID IN POLITICAL
CONTEXT: 1971-73
Bruce D. Larkin

Chinese aid activities received fresh impetus in 1970 when Peking set out to establish more political contacts.* It is not that Peking was inactive during the Great Proletarian Cultural Revolution as the largest Chinese aid effort, building the Tanzania-Zambia Railway, was then set in motion. But the African states with which China had diplomatic relations fell from 18 to 13 and few other aid commitments were made. The object of this paper is to show the extent of commitments since 1970 and something of the policy context from which they have sprung.

From May 1966 until the 9th Congress of the Chinese Communist Party in April 1969 China's leadership was consumed with the Great Proletarian Cultural Revolution. Of all China's ambassadors, only one remained at his post in 1967, Huang Hua, then ambassador to Cairo and later China's first representative in the UN Security Council. In mid-1967 the Foreign Ministry itself was beset by sharp factional conflicts; for a brief period an unauthorized group sought to act for China in foreign affairs. It is not

---

*Material on Chinese-African relations prior to 1971 can be found by using the Bibliographic Note and Bibliography in Bruce D. Larkin, China and Africa: 1949-1970 (Berkeley: University of California Press, 1971), pp. 245-56. Particularly appropriate to this subject are George T. Yu, "China and Tanzania: A Study in Cooperative Interaction" (Berkeley: University of California Center for Chinese Studies, 1970), China Research Monograph No. 5; W. Scott Thompson, Ghana's Foreign Policy 1957-1966 (Princeton: Princeton University Press, 1969); and a soon to be published volume by Alaba Ogunsanwo, China's Policy in Africa 1958-1971.

correct to say that China's foreign relations were suspended in the 1966-69 period, but it is true that the attention given foreign relations was unusually scant, that China was preoccupied by internal politics, and that her representation abroad was delegated in almost every capital to a charge d'affaires.

Since the 9th Party Congress, and even more so since Sino-Canadian diplomatic relations were established on October 13, 1970,[1] China has negotiated many new ties. Henry Kissinger's visit of mid-1971, the United Nations decision of October 25, 1971 "to restore all its rights to the People's Republic of China," and the Nixon and Tanaka pilgrimages to Peking in 1972 are the most dramatic of these events. But there has also occurred a gradual extension of China's foreign relations, including her relations with Africa.

We can discern an identity among Chinese aims near her borders and far away: security--especially from Soviet attack; economic advantage--through trade; and freedom of action--to sustain the control of her own resources yet enable her to act in the world and achieve a major role in world affairs. Similar ends are sought by leaderships everywhere. China's assessment of the world, however, is distinctive.

THE POLITICAL CONTEXT

On January 1, 1973 China's three principal organs editorialized that "the present international situation is excellent." They stressed change:

> The whole world is undergoing changes
> through a process of great turbulence,
> great division and great realignment.
> The revolutionary struggles of the
> people of various countries are develop-
> ing in depth. The small and medium-
> sized countries are uniting on a broader
> scale in opposition to the hegemonism
> and power politics of the two super-
> powers, the United States and the Soviet
> Union. . . .

Moreover, China commits herself to

> resolutely support the revolutionary
> struggles of the people of various

countries, [and] strive for peaceful coexistence with countries of different
social systems on the basis of the Five
Principles. . . .[2]

In short, China supports revolutionary war in some countries. She also believes that force may be required in
international affairs, arguing that nonuse of force can
"only be conditional, not unconditional." In the present
world

imperialism, colonialism and neo-colonialism
of various descriptions are still using
force to enslave, commit aggression against,
control and threaten a majority of the countries of the world. . . .[3]

War is a "barbarous way of settling disputes" but is "inevitable so long as society is divided into classes and
the exploitation of man by man still exists." In the
words of China's ambassador to the United Nations China
opposes unjust wars, but supports just wars. Nonetheless,
a country's having a "different social system" is no bar
to relations if the Five Principles of Peaceful Coexistence govern: (1) mutual respect for sovereignty and territorial integrity, (2) mutual nonaggression, (3) nonin-
terference in each other's internal affairs, (4) equality
and mutual benefit, and (5) peaceful coexistence.
    On August 24, 1973, addressing the 10th Congress of
the Chinese Communist Party, Premier Chou En-lai briefly
summarized:

The present international situation is
one characterized by great disorder on the
earth. "The wind sweeping through the
tower heralds a rising storm in the moun-
tains." This aptly depicts how the basic
world contradictions as analysed by Lenin
show themselves today. Relaxation is a
temporary and superficial phenomenon, and
great disorder will continue. Such great
disorder is a good thing for the people,
not a bad thing. It throws the enemies
into confusion and causes division among
them, while it rouses and tempers the
people, thus helping the international
situation develop further in the direction

3

favourable to the people and unfavourable
to imperialism, modern revisionism and
all reaction.
    The awakening and growth of the
Third World is a major event in contemporary international relations. The
Third World has strengthened its unity
in the struggle against hegemonism and
power politics of the superpowers and is
playing an ever more significant role in
international affairs.[4]

"Relaxation is a temporary and superficial phenomenon,
and great disorder will continue." So reads the most important public Chinese statement on the world situation
in 1973, a year which otherwise found Chou En-lai premier
of a down-to-work Chinese government which also sponsored
the creation of a United States Liaison Office in Peking
and diplomatic relations with the reactionary stalwarts
of Franco's Spain. The readiness to mount state-to-state
relations and expand foreign trade seems to contradict
revolutionary commitment. Perhaps Chou En-lai is protect-
ing detente, or--quite a different possibility--anticipat-
ing that detente cannot but be temporary. "World intran-
quillity," he goes on to say, is caused by "U.S.-Soviet
contention for hegemony." We can infer that if a "rising
storm" falls upon us, its sources shall not be in Peking.

SMALL AND MEDIUM-SIZED STATES

    The main theme of Chinese foreign policy since early
1970 is that the small and medium-sized states must unite
against the Soviet Union and United States, twinned as
superpowers. Ch'iao Kuan-hua told the United Nations in
his maiden speech

        . . . we are opposed to the power politics
        and hegemony of big nations bullying small
        ones or strong nations bullying weak ones.
        We hold that the affairs of a given country
        must be handled by its own people. . . .[5]

and that China forever renounces "aggression, subversion,
control, interference and bullying."
    Chinese spokesmen have voiced this position repeat-
edly. As An Chih-yuan told the UN Economic Commission
for Asia and the Far East on April 11, 1973:

> We hold that the people of each country
> have the right to choose the social sys-
> tem of their own country according to
> their own will and to safeguard the inde-
> pendence, sovereignty and territorial in-
> tegrity of their country, and that no
> country has the right to subject another
> country to its aggression, subversion,
> control, interference or bullying. We
> are opposed to the power politics and
> hegemonism of the big bullying the small
> and the strong bullying the weak. . . .[6]

Two other distinctions appeared in Chinese comment during
1973: a distinction between rich and poor, and the identification of China as a Third World member. Peking Review reproduced UN speakers' remarks on exploitation, saying many not only spoke of the rich-poor division, "but
actually went into the root cause of why this is so and
elaborated on how the rich countries exploit the poor
ones."[7] That China is a Third World country was declared
by no less authoritative a spokesman than Mao Tse-tung,
speaking to visiting Malian president Moussa Traore: "We
all belong to the third world, we are developing countries."[8] Others, including Premier Chou En-lai and Foreign Minister Chi P'eng-fei, also made this point.[9]
Though this does violence to many understandings of the
notion of a Third World, it gives an old name to the new
united front which China is endeavoring to gather. In
short, China is poor, Third World, developing, and cham-
pion of the small and medium-sized states.
    A thumbnail assessment of Africa formed part of
Chinese UN ambassador Ch'iao Kuan-hua's speech to the
General Assembly on October 2, 1973.

> An excellent situation prevails in Africa.
> In the past year, the African people have
> achieved a series of new victories in
> their struggle to win and safeguard na-
> tional independence and oppose racism,
> colonialism, neo-colonialism, imperialism
> and hegemonism. Through their struggle,
> they have come to realize more and more
> the necessity of armed struggle and mutual
> support. . . .[10]

He proceeds to spell out a few specifics: the racist regimes use more insidious and brutal means, the superpowers

are sowing dissension, African people face a protracted,
complicated and tortuous struggle. China recognized the
Republic of Guinea-Bissau. But for a more detailed statement we shall have to turn to an earlier source, a _Peking
Review_ article of January 26, 1973.

The article treats six subjects: armed struggle, the
"mass movement in Southern Africa," extra-African intervention in Africa, developing national economy and culture,
cooperation among African states, and African participation in world affairs.

The discussion of armed struggle is confined to actions against Portuguese colonialism and the "racist regimes" in South Africa and Rhodesia. A quarter of Mozambique, a third of Angola, and three-quarters of Guinea
(Bissau) are reported liberated. The article quotes a
resolution of the 8th Summit Conference of East and Central African Countries: "The armed struggle is the only
way through which colonialism, apartheid and racial discrimination in southern Africa and Guinea (Bissau) can be
eliminated." It observed that the people of Namibia,
Zimbabwe, and "other areas" are in armed struggle against
Rhodesia and South Africa. "The concept of winning national independence through armed struggle," the article
asserts, "has become increasingly accepted in Africa."

The second section simply cites strikes, mass rallies,
and student boycotts of classes in Rhodesia and South Africa in 1971 and 1972. In the third, the authors cite instances of non-African states intervening in Africa. Portugal (in Guinea, Tanzania, Congo, and Senegal), Spain (in
Equatorial Guinea), Israel (in Uganda), and by inference
the United States, Soviet Union, and France are the tar-
gets of attack. The "superpowers" are charged with naval
activity in the Mediterranean and the Indian Ocean. Former French colonies' demands to revise "unequal" cooperation agreements are lauded. Egyptian action--presumably
against the Soviet Union--is reported to have won "wide
acclaim."

The brief discussion of national economy reports
(a) takeovers from foreign control, (b) refusal to extend
petroleum concessions, (c) agricultural promotion and
steps against monoculture dependence, (d) setting up small
and medium-sized industries, and (e) speeding economic development on the basis of self-reliance. These themes--
self-reliance, small-scale industry, stress on agricul-
ture--mirror major themes in the Chinese press directed
to China's own development.

On mutual support, China notes the role of states
bordering southern Africa and other colonies as the

"immediate rear bases of the national-liberation movements." On the other hand, she cites with approval settlements of disputes between independent African states by
peaceful negotiations: Guinea and Senegal, Tanzania and
Uganda. On international action, China observes that

> The African countries are playing an increas-
> ingly prominent rolé in the present interna-
> tional arena, and the superpowers' attempt
> to manipulate and control international af-
> fairs will no longer work.

Through the Chinese commentator does not spell out
what "great turbulence, great division and great realignment" might mean for Africa, he does make it clear that
vast changes are taking place. "The day when the African
people will decide their own destiny is approaching."
Revolutionary struggle is developing, and African states
do oppose the hegemonism of Washington and Moscow. China
supports a specific short list of African revolutionary
struggles, and emphasizes that the African states themselves declare their support for those struggles. Toward
other states, China professes a readiness to conduct relations on the basis of the Five Principles, and applauds
"peaceful negotiations" to settle interstate differences.
This image of Africa is therefore very much in keeping
with the categories of the 1973 New Year's Day editorial,
and is reinforced later in 1973. China reproduced the
full text of the Solemn Declaration on General Policy of
the 10th Assembly of the Heads of State and Government of
the Organization of African Unity (May 27-29, 1973) which
states, in part, that "armed struggle is the main form
that efforts to achieve liberation must take."[11] Peking
also applauded mutual aid and cooperation among African
states to achieve economic development and economic independence.[12]

Sino-African relations in the early 1970s display
five key characteristics. First, China's diplomatic relations with African states have increased from a low of
13 in 1967--five states had broken or suspended relations
with China--to a high at the start of 1974 of 30. Second,
China has entered the United Nations; there in the specialized agencies and sponsored conferences, China now
meets with African delegates and must declare herself on
the floor and in roll-call votes. Third, the Tanzania-
Zambia Railway, just begun in 1970, is now well toward
completion; moreover, China has renewed her readiness to
commit aid to African states. Fourth, African opposition

to Portuguese, Rhodesian, and South African rule has persisted; it is expressed in the language, and to some extent the action, of armed struggle; and China continues to voice support. Fifth, China's leaders have conceived a new dichotomy in the world--that between "the superpowers" and the "small and medium-sized countries"--and declared their commitment to the cause of the weaker against the stronger, denying any intention on China's part to become a superpower.

DIPLOMATIC RELATIONS

Table 1.1 lists the African states now maintaining diplomatic relations with China and the date on which relations were established or resumed. It is perhaps easier to list those not maintaining diplomatic relations with China: South Africa and the three former High Commission Territories--Botswana, Lesotho, and Swaziland; four among the French succession states--Gabon, Ivory Coast, Niger, and the Central African Republic; and Gambia, Malawi, Liberia, and Libya.

TABLE 1.1

African States Maintaining Diplomatic
Relations with China

Algeria	Dec 58	Mauritius	Apr 72
+Burundi	Oct 71	Morocco	Nov 58
Cameroon	Mar 71	Nigeria	Feb 71
Chad	Nov 72	Rwanda	Nov 71
Congo	Feb 64	Senegal	Dec 71
+Dahomey	Dec 72	Sierra Leone	Jul 71
Egypt	May 56	Somalia	Dec 60
Equatorial Guinea	Oct 70	Sudan	Feb 59
Ethiopia	Nov 70	Tanzania	Dec 61
+Ghana	Feb 72	Togo	Sep 72
Guinea	Oct 59	+Tunisia	Oct 71
Kenya	Dec 63	Uganda	Oct 62
Malagasy	Nov 72	Upper Volta	Sep 73
Mali	Oct 60	Zaire	Nov 72
Mauritania	Jul 65	Zambia	Oct 64

Note: Cases marked "+" show the date of resumption of relations.

Relations once broken or suspended have been resumed with minimum fanfare. In the Tunisian case, China published no communique, but merely an article noting that after friendly consultations with Tunis "the Chinese government has decided that the Chinese Embassy in Tunis will resume its work." The late-1972 resumption of relations with Dahomey, however, was agreed in a joint communique closely following the formula for new relations.

The typical communique formula has four paragraphs: the first states that the two sides have decided to enter diplomatic relations at ambassadorial level; the second that China "supports," "respects," "firmly supports," or "resolutely supports" the African government in some task or commitment, perhaps "in its struggle against all forms of foreign aggression and domination" or against "imperialism, colonialism and neo-colonialism"; the third that the African state recognizes China, either as the "sole legal government representing the entire Chinese people" or as the "sole legal Government of China"; and the fourth that diplomatic relations, friendship, and cooperation shall be developed in accord with the Five Principles of Peaceful Coexistence.

There are variations among the communiques. The Chinese-Cameroon statement makes a unique reference to the "frankness" of their talks, hinting at the differences between the two countries, and China's committing herself to oppose "all forms of foreign aggression and domination" doubtless recalling the onetime Chinese support for Cameroon oppositionists. In the Nigerian case, China makes the sole reference to supporting efforts to safeguard "territorial integrity," which reminds us of reported Chinese support to the Biafran separatist movement only a few years before. Although some African signers are prepared to accept China's support for opposition to imperialism, others apparently insisted on milder terms. Finally, China appears to pick and choose in according degrees of support: that Chad, Malagasy, and Togo are merely "supported," and Senegal and Dahomey "respected" in the positions which follow, acknowledges the somewhat more slender bond of common views joining those countries with China. Though the language is very formal, it does provide a measure of China's readiness to associate herself with the policies of the several African governments.

CHINA ON AFRICAN ISSUES

China's entry into the United Nations forces her to take stands on resolutions concerning Africa as well as offering opportunities. In January 1972, when the Security Council agreed to hold a meeting in Addis Ababa, China made a point of her support for the move, and portrayed the United States and Soviet Union as opposed to the initiative.[13]

On December 14, 1972 China was called to vote on a resolution concerning Namibia in the Fourth Committee of the UN General Assembly. While stating that a "considerable number" of prior UN resolutions on Namibia had been "correct," the Chinese delegate criticized recently concluded discussions between South African authorities and a representative of the UN Secretary-General as producing "no positive result," creating confusion "within and outside the United Nations," and permitting the South Africans to "extricate themselves from their political isolation and mollify their condemnation by the people of various countries."[14]

On March 10, 1973 China voted for a Security Council resolution which affirmed the "right of the people of Zimbabwe to self-determination" and called on Britain to take "all effective measures" to enable them to exercise that right. Before the vote Huang Hua explained that China had consistently held that Britain should "immediately put an end to the colonialist rule by the Rhodesian white racist regime," but would vote for the resolution because China understood that it "in the main reflected the legitimate desire of the African countries and people to defend their national independence."[15] Elsewhere, however, China has observed that the United Nations record concerning Rhodesia and South West Africa is one of failure. In the UN Security Council, China's delegate declared that she opposed sending an Emergency UN Military Force to the Middle East, but, rather than veto, would not participate in the vote out of respect for the expressed wishes of "victims of Israeli aggression." China would not, however, pay for such a force.[16] In short, China has encouraged use of the United Nations, but cautioned that Chinese policy retains distance from the organization and from policies which have been erroneous.

As Donald Klein has observed, any fear that China would undertake a wrecking operation in the United Nations, or treat it with contempt, was dispelled by the dispatch of able and informed personnel to New York. Their reservoir of experience in Africa and African affairs is substantial. Huang Hua, Ambassador and Chinese representative to the Security Council, was ambassador in Accra and Cairo. His first deputy in the Security Council, Ch'en Ch'u, had been head of the West Asian and North African Affairs Department of the foreign ministry. Kao Liang, a secretary who serves also as press officer, was very active as a Hsinhua correspondent in East Africa in the early and mid-1960s. Two other secretaries, Chou Nan and Chao Wei, have also served in Africa.[17]

The political context of aid to Africa incorporates some other specific themes that merit mention. China asserts that the "Mediterranean belongs to Mediterranean countries," citing the position of Algeria, Libya, Morocco, and Tunisia that the Mediterranean should be a "sea of peace." China quotes Algerian Foreign Minister Bouteflika, with apparent approval, who said "The current situation of foreign military presence in the Mediterranean runs counter to the liberation of our peoples and their aspirations for progress and advancement" citing "the real danger represented by foreign military presence which is exemplified by bases and fleets."[18] Condemning the "superpowers' contention for hegemony in the Mediterranean," China has located an issue on which coastal nationalism and Chinese dichotomization converge. China also supports Ceylon's drive to declare the Indian Ocean a peace zone and claims Zambian support.[19]

China's specific interest motivating her Mediterranean and Indian Ocean comments is to deny the United States and Soviet Union their present freedom of movement; her secondary aim is to make political capital from a verbal effort at denial. But China is also a prospective competitor with advanced industrial states in the looming contest for natural resources. Arrival of a Chinese technical delegation in the Sudan to do geological survey work in search of chrome deposits[20] underscores a report that chromium is one of two minerals which China can obtain only from abroad.[21]

Peking's interest in copper and the politics of copper is evidenced by the TanZam Railway. In December 1972 China was one of five observers attending a meeting of the Inter-Governmental Committee of the Conference of Copper Exporting Countries in Santiago, Chile.[22] The Committee took up themes favorable to China, for example that acts impeding the sovereign right of a country to dispose freely of its own natural resources constituted economic aggression. The coup against President Salvador Allende may deny Chinese access to Chilean copper. But Zambia sells to China, and the overthrow of Allende reverberated in Zambia in a way which confirmed themes China has insisted upon. "There is a bitter lesson to be learnt from all of this," commented the Times of Zambia,

> which is that we should never allow foreign capitalist or other companies, which are known to be hostile to Zambia, to have a strangle-hold on our country. What has happened in Chile should afford us an opportunity to root out all undesirable foreign concerns whose interests are as far apart from ours as the North Pole is to the South Pole.[23]

This brief list in no way exhausts the issues relevant to Africa on which China has now taken a position, but it indicates typical views, and China's care to define her particular position.

AID COMMITMENTS

Ch'iao Kuan-hua reaffirmed China's long-standing aid policy in his speech to the UN General Assembly in October 1972.[24] Of aid, he said "our capabilities in this respect are limited and the aid we can give is not much." Emphasis continues to be placed on self-reliance.

From 1965 until 1969 China made few commitments of aid to Africa. Steps toward the TanZam Railway credits were made, but this period--roughly coinciding with the Great Proletarian Cultural Revolution--was otherwise slack. More than half of the credits and grants China has authorized for use by African countries, totaling $1,218 million through 1971, were made in the years 1970 and 1971, including the TanZam commitments. In 1971-73 China made seventeen aid commitments in Africa, summarized in Table 1.2.

China ceased to publish the formal terms of credits and grants in 1966. New commitments, however, follow the pre-1966 pattern. Typically they are available over several years--four, five, eight--and interest-free; repayment is projected to take place in equal installments over, say, ten years, but not beginning until a few years after the end of availability. Actual utilization is still a different matter. Some grants made in the early

1960s remain unutilized, or partially utilized. For example China's 1971 agreement with Algeria reportedly specified uses of a credit authorized in 1963. China and Ghana have agreed that the remainder of a large credit granted during Nkrumah's rule, only a fraction of which had been utilized, will be reopened. If a high degree of inaccuracy were tolerated, a set of informed guesses would show that less than half of China's pre-Cultural Revolution aid was actually utilized. For the period from 1967 we can anticipate that a greater proportion will be drawn upon, not only because the TanZam Railway is well underway, but because the ambiance of this period seems to promise more opportunities to match China's offered assistance to specific development projects.

The most recent grants are largely of two kinds. Some are credits to countries whose relations with the Soviet Union have gone awry, such as Sudan and Egypt. Others seem to sweeten the opening or reestablishment of diplomatic relations: Burundi, Mauritius, Cameroon, Togo, Tunisia, Zaire. Economic and technical cooperation agreements also exist between China and several other countries which have not received large-scale aid. Projects are reported underway, for example, in Sierra Leone.

It remains, however, to explain the commitments China has made to Ethiopia ($85 million) and Somalia ($110 million). Customary explanations note the geographic significance of the Horn and adjacent waters, China's interests in the southern Arabian Peninsula, Soviet activities in Somalia, and a Chinese sense that some "balancing" of commitments between Ethiopia and Somalia is now desirable. The 1973 protocol between Ethiopia and China listed four rural development projects to be carried out: a highway, 20 water wells, a veterinary station, and eight diesel power stations for provincial towns.[25] While Chinese aid to Ethiopia will strengthen the writ of the Emperor in the countryside, the chief Chinese project in Somalia will provide readier Somali access to a vast stretch of hinterland lying along the Ethiopian border. Some $65 million of the sum committed to Somalia is to be spent on a 1,045 km road, to run from Beledwein, north of Mogadishu and already connected by a tarmac road to the capital, to Burao, in Somalia's north, which is in turn linked to Berbera. Begun in 1973, the road is to be finished in 1976. In August 1973 Chinese were reported already on site and working in camps spread down the length of the road.[26]

TABLE 1.2

Major Chinese Aid Commitments to Africa, 1971-73

Recipient	Year	Sum in U.S. $ (millions)	Terms and Comments
Algeria	1971	40	Given by Tansky[k] as a new credit, but elsewhere described as a 250 million franc credit from sums previously authorized in 1963; to be used for an irrigation project.[a]
Burundi	1972	20	Loan available 1972-76; repayable 1982-91 in Burundi exports to China.[b]
Cameroon	1973	78.3	Interest-free loan; 10-year grace period before repayment begins. Also given as 18 billion francs CFA.[c] Conversion at U.S. $1 = 230 francs CFA yields $78.26 million.
Chad	1973	56	100 million Yuan, about 13,000 million francs CFA; by terms of agreement signed in Peking September 20, 1973.[o] Also given as 13,000 million francs CFA = $65 million.[p]
Dahomey	1973	47.8	Sum given as 220 million French francs,[q] conversion at $1 = 4.6 francs. Also reported as $45 million, immediately available, interest-free, 15-year grace period, repayable in exports over 30 years.[r] Elsewhere given as $44 million.[t]
Ethiopia	1971	84	Long-term, probably to be used for agricultural development.[ek]
Malagasy	1973	10.7	$8 million promised in November 1972, announced January 1973, repayable over 15 years; to be used to pay off indebtedness to South African creditors.[d] Also reported as 2 billion FMG, interest-free, long-term loan; in addition, China gave 10,000 tons of rice as a grant.[f] Total given elsewhere as 4,000 million francs.[s] Figure of 12.8 generated by converting 2,000 million FMG at 230 FMG = $1, yielding $8.7 million; plus a nominal U.S. $0.20/kilo for the rice.
Mauritania	1971	20	The Mauritanian Minister of Foreign Affairs, though not announcing the amount, said China had given an interest-free, long-term loan to finance a deep water port for Nouakchott and other projects.[gk]

14

Country	Year	Amount	Notes
Mauritius	1972	33.8	Available 1972-77; repayable interest-free in installments 1987-97, either in "Mauritius export commodities" or convertible currency. Primarily for an airport and highway to the airport. Local costs--materials, wages, transport, etc.--will be met by buying general goods from China.[h] Given as $34 million in another source. Yet another writes of a loan of $175 million for construction of a modern airport, to be repaid over 30 years with interest only after 5 years.[u] That appears erroneous; cf. W. A. C. Adie, who puts it at Rs. 175 million = £13 million,[v] which was $33.8 million.
Rwanda	1972	22	Sources report $20 million, interest-free, repayable in commodities over 15 years;[w] and $22 million.[t]
Senegal	1973	47.8	Reported as 11 million francs CFA. On March 28, 1973 Senegal decided not to renew its cooperation agreement with Taiwar. Peking then replaced the 56 Taiwanese experts who had been withdrawn. In November 1973 the economic and technical cooperation agreements underlying this loan were signed in Peking. Conversion at U.S. $1 = 230 francs CFA.
Somalia	1971	110	Diverse projects.[kl] Among them the most important is a $65 million project to build a 1,045 km road from Beledwein to Burao, skirting some distance behind the Ethiopian border from above Mogadishu to the northern section of Somalia. Started in 1973.[x] Completion expected in 1976.[y]
Sudan	1971	40[k]	$35 million loan for roads, bridges, textile factory, and international conference center.[i] Tansky gives $40 million.[k]
Togo	1972	44.9	Reported as 100 million Yuan = 11.5 billion francs CFA, interest-free.[j] Converting at U.S. $1 = 256 francs CFA, 11.5 billion yields $44.92 million. Another source reports $45 million.[t]
Tunisia	1972	40[m]	Given as $36 million elsewhere.[t]
Zaire	1972	100[n]	
Zambia	1973	10.9	A grant of K7 million in February 1973 to aid Zambia's rerouting of trade.[z] Conversion at Kwacha .643 = U.S. $1.

Notes to Table 1.2

[a]Marches Tropicaux et Mediterraneens, July 24, 1971, cited in Africa Research Bulletin (Economic), pp. 2110-11.

[b]Africa Research Bulletin (Economic), July 24, 1971, citing news agency reports of March 10, 1972.

[c]Africa, no. 21 (May 1973): 45; no. 22 (June 1973): 12.

[d]Le Moniteur Africain du Commerce et de l'Industrie, no. 635, November 29, 1973.

[e]Uganda Argus, October 11, 1971, cited in Africa Research Bulletin (Economic), p. 2167.

[f]Le Moniteur Africain du Commerce et de l'Industrie, February 22, 1973.

[g]Afrique Nouvelle (Dakar), April 28, 1971, cited in Africa Research Bulletin (Economic), p. 2030.

[h]Johannesburg Star, December 30, 1972.

[i]Radio Omdurman, August 24, 1971, cited in Africa Research Bulletin (Economic), p. 2140.

[j]Jeune Afrique, no. 614, p. 16.

[k]Leo Tansky, "China's Foreign Aid: The Record," in Current Scene 10, no. 9 (September 1972), originally published in People's Republic of China: An Economic Assessment, compiled by the Joint Economic Committee of the Congress of the United States, Washington, D.C., 1972. Current Scene is published by the U.S. Information Service.

[l]See also "Somalia," in Africa, no. 21 (May 1973): 48-50, summarizing Soviet and Chinese aid to that country.

[m]L'Action (Tunis), September 9, 1972, cited in Africa Research Bulletin (Economic), p. 2482.

[n]Jeune Afrique, no. 632 (February 17, 1973): 19.

[o]Le Moniteur Africain du Commerce et de l'Industrie, no. 633 (November 15, 1973): 7.

[p]Africa Research Bulletin (Economic), p. 2909C, citing news agency dispatches, November 8, 1973.

[q]Le Monde, March 18-19, 1973.

[r]Africa, no. 19 (March 1973): 24.

[s]Paul Bernetel, Africa, no. 22 (June 1973): 17.

[t]U.S. Government, Department of State, Bureau of Intelligence and Research, RECS-10, released June 15, 1973; August 1973, Table 4.

[u]Africa Research Bulletin (Economic), p. 2763B, citing news agency dispatches.

[v]W. A. C. Adie, "China's Year in Africa," in Africa Contemporary Record, 1972-73, ed. Colin Legum.

[w]New York Times, September 4, 1972.

[x]African Development, August 1973, cited in Africa Research Bulletin (Economic), p. 2823C.

[y]African Development (August 1963): 513.

[z]Times of Zambia, May 28, 1973, in Africa Research Bulletin (Economic), p. 2745C.

How is Chinese aid received? One journal, reporting the Beledwein-Burao road project and installation of Hargeisa water supplies in Somalia, commented that Chinese aid is "discreet, effective and practical with concentration on projects much appreciated by the rural population."[27] Recipients are constrained to speak well of gifts received, but their comments merit reporting. Mali's Moussa Traore told a Peking banquet that

> China's disinterested assistance, based on the eight principles which you set forth during your visit to Bamako in 1964 and concretized and supplemented by the Chinese delegation to the conference of the UNCTAD held in Santiago, Chile, is all the more appreciated because we are in a world dominated by the egoism and hegemonic desire of the imperialist big powers, who impose their will on international trade, resulting in the constant deterioration of trading terms to the detriment of the developing countries.[28]
>
> In the name of the Malian people, I wish to convey through you our thanks to the Chinese people for this co-operation which is suited to our convenience and is assuredly always effective.
> I am glad to point out in particular China's participation in the execution of the Three-Year Development Plan which we worked out within the framework of our policy of economic and financial rehabilitation. . . .
> . . . the aid and assistance made available by your country to developing countries are also generous and disinterested.[29]

Sierra Leone President Siaka Stevens, also in Peking, spoke of

> the great assistance we have received and are receiving from the government and people of this great republic. We also want to thank you for the invaluable help you have been giving to our brothers and sisters in other parts of the continent of Africa, such as the Tanzam Railway. . . .[30]

17

A grant of 7 million kwach to help Zambia reroute trade in early 1973[31] was the largest grant then received by Zambia to help ease her through the border crisis. Peking also was a major donor of aid to drought-stricken West African states: her contribution of 50,000 tons of grain was about 11 percent of that reported received from all sources by July 1973.[32] A judicious choice of aid and a wish to be known as a disinterested donor promise China political effect.

The TanZam Railway is treated more fully elsewhere in this volume,* but it is the most ambitious and most expensive of China's aid projects, dwarfing all others, and must be borne in mind when considering China's aid as a whole. The maximum credit China has undertaken to extend is $402 million; if the costs exceed that amount, China will bear the overrun. Repayment is to begin in 1983 and extend for 30 years. The loan, too, is interest-free. Much of the local cost is to be met by importing Chinese goods, but the governing agreement provides that if earnings from local sales are inadequate China will accept the deficit; reportedly, Tanzania invoked this provision in 1970-71.[33] Observers make various predictions concerning completion of the Railway. David Martin anticipates opening to the Copper Belt in 1974, with ancillary works requiring a bit longer.[34]

Kenneth Kaunda and Julius Nyerere marked the line's crossing into Zambia in ceremonies at the border on August 27, 1973. Then 606 miles of track was laid in Tanzania, and 556 miles remained to be laid on the Zambian side.[35] Estimates of the number of Chinese working on the project range from 14,000 to 17,000 of the estimated 40,000 to 50,000 total personnel. The significance of this project as a demonstration is evident. It shows not only China's capacity to perform a large-scale engineering work, but also her ability to do so with minimum abrasion on the host country. And the political significance of the line, gracing Zambia with an alternate rail path to the sea, is well understood.

In addition to economic aid, African states have received some military aid from China. Leo Tansky estimates that Tanzania has received $40 million in military aid commitments from China since 1964, citing MIG jets, light tanks, patrol boats, infantry and support equipment. Furthermore, China is constructing naval and air facilities

---

See Chapter 2, "Chinese and Soviet Aid to Africa: The Tanzania-Zambia Railway," in this volume.

in Tanzania. Smaller amounts of military aid have been
committed to the Congo People's Republic, Ghana, Guinea,
and Mali.[36] Guinea reportedly received four Shanghai-
class gunboats, accompanied by a 40-member Chinese training group, and Sudan received six MIG 19s. Sixty Sierra
Leonese have reportedly trained in China to use gunboats,
the nucleus of a coast guard.[37] According to other dispatches, Siaka Stevens, in a public appearance, made special mention of the training of army and other personnel
in the use of equipment from China.[38] Although the total
value of arms is small by comparison to the value of development aid, it may be particularly welcome.

LIBERATION MOVEMENTS

During the 1960s China extended some financial assistance and political support to national liberation movements in Africa. Excluding those which failed to unseat
independent African governments, some of which now enjoy
diplomatic relations with China, our attention focuses on
colonial and white-supremacist rule in the Portuguese colonies, Rhodesia, and South Africa. The Spanish Sahara
might be added.[39] Chou En-lai recently reaffirmed China's
"full support" of the "national-liberation movement in
South Africa."[40]
A few years ago we would have said that China extended evident or probable support to one set of movements,
the Soviet Union to another, with two movements receiving
assistance from both:

	China	Both	USSR	Neither
ANGOLA	UNITA		MPLA	GRAE
MOZAMBIQUE	COREMO	FRELIMO		
ZIMBABWE	ZANU		ZAPU	FRELIZI
SOUTH AFRICA	PAC		ANC	
NAMIBIA	SWANU		SWAPO	
GUINEA (BISSAU)		PAIGC		FLING

To judge from China's public references to groups among
the liberation movements, she is prepared today to acknowledge the greater activity of FRELIMO, MPLA, and SWAPO, in
the last case more often describing activity but mentioning no group by name.
Amilcar Cabral visited China a few months before he
was assassinated.[41] China, reporting the assassination,
credited Cabral with "outstanding contributions to Africa's
national-liberation struggle," and quoted from the PAIGC

communique pledging "determination to revenge the ignoble
crime 'by exterminating the colonialists and their cor-
rupted agents on its sacred soil.'"[42]

China gave UNITA priority in specific references to
UNITA and MPLA in early 1971,[43] gave little emphasis to
Angola in 1972, and in 1973 reported the agreement to
unite MPLA and FNLA, without comment.[44] Holden Roberto,
leader of FNLA, visited China in December 1973 and his
visit was given modest reportage by Hsinhua.[45] The agreement between ZANU and ZAPU was also reported, with a quotation from the agreement that "the two organizations
should wage more effective revolutionary armed struggle
through combined action. . . ."[46] Nonetheless, it is ZANU
to which China gives attention, and a very recent report
underscored that "a guerrilla unit led by the Zimbabwe
African National Union fired the first shot against the
white racist regime" seven years earlier, but made no mention of the ZANU-ZAPU agreement.[47]

China also continues to give currency to statements
by PAC representatives.[48] In the case of Namibia (South
West Africa), a Peking Review summary titled "Namibian
People's Struggle" fails to mention any organization by
name,[49] although Huang Hua, speaking before the UN Security Council, had earlier mentioned restrictions on the
political activity of the Acting President of SWAPO, to
illustrate wrongful South African actions there.[50]

China reported with apparent satisfaction the decision of the 10th Assembly of Heads of State and Government
of the OAU meeting in Addis Ababa in May 1973 to "increase
the moral support and material assistance to the fight"
for liberation (while not mentioning, of course, the OAU
Liberation Committee's actual receipts).[51] A few days
earlier the OAU Council approved sending missions to non-
African countries to obtain material and financial support
for African liberation movements. First among states
listed in the proposal to the Council were the Soviet
Union and China. Accompanying those specifics are plans
for further unity among competing organizations, and to
emphasize armed struggle.[52]

Although Chinese aid to specific movements, in cash
and training, is widely reported, it is limited in extent.
Leo Tansky believes that "the volume of Chinese arms moving clandestinely to 'liberation groups,' particularly in
Africa, has not been significant."[53] The emphasis of
China's published views also suggests that direct Chinese
assistance must be limited. A Chinese discussion of national liberation, the most "theoretical" statement in

recent months, places emphasis on two quotes from Mao Tse-
tung which stress self-reliance:

> In the fight for complete liberation the
> oppressed people rely first of all on their
> own struggle and then, and only then, on
> international assistance. (Talk with Afri-
> can friends in August 1963)
>   On what basis should our policy rest?
> It should rest on our own strength, and
> that means regeneration through one's own
> efforts.

The article goes on to extend this theme:

> Self-reliance means relying on the man-
> power and resources of one's own country
> to continually overcome difficulties that
> will inevitably arise in the course of
> the revolution. . . .

And although Mao Tse-tung is quoted as saying that "The
revolutionary storm in Asia, Africa and Latin America is
sure to deal the whole of the old world a decisive and
crushing blow," the tenor of the article is to stress a
broad united front built upon the common interests of two
intermediate zones: the Third World, and the industrialized states not "socialist" in form.[54]
China will continue to tender support to liberation
movements. With formal OAU support and the hospitality of
friendly African states, the movements can use modest
amounts of Chinese aid. To the extent that African aid is
not forthcoming, Chinese aid assumes greater importance to
those groups. The Liberation Committee's efforts to
achieve at least formal unification of hitherto contending
groups may not yield important gains, but it could alter
the pairing off into China-supported and Soviet-supported
groups. In the early 1960s, it should be noted, China
spoke approvingly of unity in national liberation struggles,
correctly perceiving that divided peoples work at cross-
purposes or dissipate their energies. There is therefore
precedent for China's viewing with approval the initiatives
recently undertaken to unite groups in Rhodesia and Angola.
From the emphasis in Chinese statements, however, it can be
inferred that China will rest her judgments on the extent
to which the combined organizations actually conduct armed
struggle.

CONCLUSION

A revolutionary future, or a future of persuasion, interest, incremental change, and conventional relations?

The correct model, in my view, remains that of short-term preparation and long-term transformation, a sustained commitment to social revolution in the long term. In the short term, China will seek small contributions to immediate needs: insurance against the Soviet Union (which she perceives as a threatening neighbor, posing an urgent and serious threat), advantage in her leadership contest with the Soviet Union, access to markets, and a role in shaping world settlements.

The best forums for settlements are those which combine broad representation--and therefore legitimacy--with an opportunity to upset those rules which have hitherto defined world order in the interest of yesterday's Establishment. Correct relations with independent states are therefore essential to settlement, trade, and insurance against Moscow. Correct relations also permit China to display her wares.

China's middle term aim may be to confine the United States and the Soviet Union, restrict their freedom of movement, and ultimately sharpen their internal and external difficulties. As resources shrink, the growth societies will feel the hurt more strongly because of their reliance on consumption of energy. Several consequences could follow. Among growth societies, jealousies may divide the large, well-endowed superpowers--the United States and Soviet Union--from their more vulnerable cousins. Signs of such division appeared in late 1973, as oil politics struck with particular savagery against the exposed economies of England, Japan, and the Netherlands. Though the United States was a target of the Arab boycott, it enjoyed--with the Soviet Union--insulation from the most severe consequences. The category of "small and medium-sized states" speaks to this prospect. Second, the contradiction between high-consumption societies and low-consumption, Third World, underdeveloped states could become acute. The dichotomy between rich and poor could become a struggle for resources. Sources once reliable would dry up, or prices be raised--as the Organization of Petroleum Exporting Countries (OPEC) has raised prices-- to command a larger share of the production of advanced industrial countries. Third, China's themes of self-reliance, frugality, invention, and intensive agricultural production will be increasingly relevant as populations

grow and food imports become more costly, or unobtainable.
A particular style of aid and demonstration, one in which
China is practiced, would be the only viable form of external assistance available. Fourth, mutual cooperation
among the poor, low-consumption societies could be shown
to promise special practical benefits; and the lessons of
unity to be drawn from OPEC activities, for example, will
be lively antidotes to national chauvinism and disunity.
To the extent that China offers convincing political explanations of the aims of high-consumption industrial
states and can identify strategies which enhance the common capacity of the less developed, China's political position could become central. China's leaders may hope that
some changes of this kind will be part of the "great turbulence, great division and great realignment" through which
the world is now passing.

Less speculatively, we should specify how Africa's
leaders view China today. Some inferences can be drawn
from known facts. First, as a Security Council permanent
member China can exercise the veto: Africans may believe
that China will, on some occasions, wield the veto, and
the threat of its use, in their interest. Moussa Traore
spoke in this vein:

> the presence of the People's Republic of
> China in the United Nations as a permanent
> member of the Security Council [will] con-
> tribute notably to the strengthening of
> the capacity of this organization in main-
> taining peace and international security
> and . . . at the same time it [will] con-
> stitute a guarantee for the small coun-
> tries, which are often victims of direct
> imperialist aggression or aggression in-
> stigated by imperialism. . . .[55]

Second, China's aid in 1971, 1972, and 1973 is running at
about $300 million authorizations per annum to Africa;
China is a model, a contributor, and an anticipated future
contributor (who may withhold aid, as well as renew it).
Third, China does perform some military aid and training;
it may also be that China is perceived capable of unauthorized training. Fourth, China is a trading partner, now at
very modest levels, prospectively one among a group of important customers and sources. Fifth, China is a large
state, a nuclear state, and a state ready to take a lead;
China's offer of a lead to states sharing weakness may be

declined, or accepted selectively, by African states; but
the African states also give form and content to China's
leadership, because few among all possible issues are
salient at any one time, and salience rests on how non-
Chinese perceive the world.

Although other states have greater resources than
China to provide aid to Africa, they may abdicate to China.
Each faces other claims on resources. With growing population and resource depletion, those claims may intensify,
and they may not be prepared to contest China's politico-
economic style employing both small rural projects and
large-scale construction schemes. Nyerere has made it
clear that China's offer to finance the TanZam Railway was
originally accepted because it was the only offer. Will
the other four veto powers be willing to serve African purposes in the Security Council? Will regional and func-
tional bodies--for example, OPEC--or African statesmen provide a comprehensive rationale for the weak to constrain
economic intervention by the strong? The growing decrepi-
tude of the United States and the persistent difficulties
of the Soviet Union limit their capacity to act; the former
metropoles will gradually diversify their attentions, plac-
ing less importance on Africa; and Japan is carving a very
special role for herself in which commerce is paramount and
politico-military activity shunned. Therefore there will
be greater scope for Chinese action than could be expected
were the other four centers--Moscow, Tokyo, Washington, and
the EEC capitals--more ready to act.

In the early 1960s China helped movements against
African-led independent governments. In 1973 she is conducting formal diplomatic relations with some of those
same governments. Will she once again subsidize and encourage armed social revolution, or even armed action
against governments simply because she opposes their policies? In my view, that will depend on the extent to which
Peking perceives its freedom of action constrained by
those governments, and most sharply if they appear in collusion with other centers against China.

Dialectics suggest that growing Third World acceptance
of Chinese leadership would provoke other centers to resist,
and that internal contradictions within those African states
now socially "reactionary" would also sharpen in a microform
of the sharpening world situation. Under such circumstances
China could select encouragement of social revolution as a
rational response.

A second possibility: that the language of China's
assessment would become commonplace, but China be kept at

a distance. Leaders of small and medium-sized states would denounce rich nations, superpower hegemony, and neocolonialism. Nevertheless, their practical ties to the United States, Soviet Union, and other advanced industrial states would look much like those of today. Such states might insist on more favorable terms for trade and investment, but in no important respect would China's world-view command policy. China could achieve sought for trade and some prestige and political credits. She could interpret the visible currency of her symbols as a sign that political consciousness was rising.

There is a third path, though in my view an unlikely one: that China would remain simply one participant among many. If China's view of the world were simply refused—if Africans' choices failed to presume at least an important symbolic role for China—Peking would have three choices: to work again with small conspiratorial groups, or cast about for a more persuasive focus for the "broadest possible united front," or accept trade and practical benefits as a sufficient reason for relations, not rocking the boat.

Today China is not a major participant in African affairs. Africa will remain a tertiary concern to Peking. The Soviet Union and United States, because of their wealth and military power, and Asia, because of its proximity, will continue to be more important to China. China's position is that of the second possibility: as a source of some symbols, donor of some valued economic aid, and occasional political support, but far from being leader of a movement or a bloc of states. Only if events seemed to confirm Chinese analyses, and if Chinese leads were to be accepted by Africans with increased frequency, would the first possibility capture the situation more accurately. Chinese aid is particularly salient because it is important in the two most turbulent scenarios readily imagined: large-scale war in Southern Africa (Chinese aid to national liberation movements conducting armed struggle) and efforts by high-consumption states to sustain access to resources (Chinese "self-reliance" offering a model to resist dependence on advanced industrial states).

In any case, much will hinge on whether China can reassure the African states, and others as well, that her rejection of negemonism is real and reliable, that she will share both wealth and poverty, and that she has devised realistic policies enabling poor states to achieve their national goals. The evidence of her performance on African aid projects suggests that she recognizes the importance of such reassurance and takes it very seriously.

NOTES

1. Joint Communique, <u>Peking Review</u> (hereafter referred to as <u>PR</u>), no. 42 (October 16, 1970): 12. It is
significant because a formula was agreed which displayed
Chinese readiness to enter into relations.
2. <u>PR</u>, no. 1 (January 5, 1973): 11.
3. Ch'iao Kuan-hua,,speech to the UN General Assembly,
October 3, 1972, in <u>PR</u>, no. 41 (October 13, 1972): 8.
4. <u>PR</u>, nos. 35-36 (September 7, 1973): 22.
5. <u>PR</u>, no. 47 (November 19, 1971): 5-9.
6. <u>PR</u>, no. 16 (April 20, 1973): 15. Also see "Third
World Struggle Against Hegemony," in <u>PR</u>, no. 38 (September
21, 1973): 13-15.
7. <u>PR</u>, no. 43 (October 26, 1973): 10-11. "It may be
recalled," wrote a Hsinhua correspondent, "that before and
during the Algiers summit conference of nonaligned countries, the Soviet press raised a hue and cry to forbid the
use of such terminology as 'rich countries' and 'poor countries,' and ban talk that 'the world is divided into rich
and poor countries.'" Clearly, the Soviet Union, in
China's version, is a rich country.
8. <u>PR</u>, no. 26 (June 29, 1973): 3.
9. Chou En-lai, ibid., p. 8, at the banquet for
Traore. Chi P'eng-fei, at a reception on May 25, 1973
marking the 10th anniversary of African Liberation Day
and the founding of the Organization of African Unity,
<u>PR</u>, no. 22 (June 1, 1973): 6. And Chou En-lai several
months later speaking at a banquet welcoming Sierra Leonese
president Siaka Stevens, who himself incorporates the same
phrase into his own speech: <u>PR</u>, no. 46 (November 16, 1973):
8-9.
10. <u>PR</u>, no. 40 (October 5, 1973): 15.
11. <u>PR</u>, no. 23 (June 8, 1973): 14.
12. <u>PR</u>, no. 39 (September 28, 1973): 14-15.
13. <u>PR</u>, no. 4 (January 28, 1972): 12-13.
14. <u>PR</u>, no. 51 (December 22, 1972): 14-15.
15. <u>PR</u>, no. 11 (March 16, 1973): 11.
16. <u>PR</u>, no. 44 (November 2, 1973): 44.
17. Donald W. Klein, "The Men and Institutions Behind
Chinese Foreign Policy," <u>Sino-American Relations, 1949-1971</u>,
ed. Roderick MacFarquhar (New York: Praeger Publishers,
1972), pp. 50-52.
18. Bouteflika, <u>Rose El Youssef</u>, September 24, 1972,
cited in <u>PR</u>, no. 41 (October 13, 1972): 21-22.
19. <u>PR</u>, no. 4 (January 28, 1972): 15, titled "Medium-
Sized and Small Nations Unite to Oppose Two Superpowers'

Hegemony." Also see "US-Soviet Scramble for Hegemony in South Asian Subcontinent and Indian Ocean," in <u>PR</u>, no. 2 (January 14, 1972): 16-17; and "Third World Role in International Affairs," ibid., no. 1 (January 5, 1973): 18-20.

20. Sudan News Agency, September 12, 1973, in <u>Africa Research Bulletin (Economic)</u>, p. 2887B.

21. <u>Far Eastern Economic Review</u> (August 27, 1973): 44, citing a study of Chinese raw materials by the German Institute of Economic Research in West Berlin. China's present source of chrome, states the report, is Cuba.

22. The Inter-Governmental Committee is composed of Chile, Peru, Zambia, and Zaire. The other observer states were Algeria, Rumania, Yugoslavia, and Mexico. <u>PR</u>, no. 51 (December 22, 1972): 19.

23. <u>Africa Research Bulletin (Political)</u>, September 14, 1973, p. 3001A.

24. "We hold that all countries which are sincere in providing aid . . . should help the recipient countries and not exploit them. Their loans should be interest-free or, at least, low in interest. They must not press for repayment but should allow its postponement. When providing a loan or other forms of aid, they should strictly respect the sovereignty of the recipient countries, attach no conditions and ask for no privileges. . . ," October 3, 1972, in <u>PR</u>, no. 41 (October 13, 1972): 7-8.

25. <u>Ethiopian Herald</u>, February 21, 1973, cited in <u>Africa Research Bulletin (Economic)</u>, p. 2669B.

26. <u>African Development</u>, August 1973, cited in <u>Africa Research Bulletin</u> (Economic), p. 2823C. Also <u>African Development</u>, November 1973, p. 513.

27. <u>African Development</u>, November 1973, p. 513.

28. Hsinhua, Peking, June 24, 1973; in Hsinhua News Agency, London, June 25, 1973. Traore also noted the Malian people's esteem for the slogans "relying on one's own efforts" and "walking on two legs" from Chairman Mao Tse-tung's writings.

29. <u>PR</u>, no. 26 (June 29, 1973): 9.

30. <u>PR</u>, no. 46 (November 16, 1973): 9.

31. <u>Times of Zambia</u>, May 28, 1973, cited in <u>Africa Research Bulletin</u> (Economic), p. 2745C.

32. <u>Africa Research Bulletin (Economic)</u>, p. 2780B, citing European Economic Community sources. At about the same time China published figures of her grain donations since April 1973, totaling by Peking's count 35,000 tons: 8,000 to Mauritania, 8,000 to Mali, 5,000 each to Senegal, Niger and Upper Volta, and 4,000 to Chad. <u>PR</u>, no. 29 (July 20, 1973): 18.

33. <u>African Development</u>, December 1972, p. T. 15.

34. Ibid., p. T. 13.

35. <u>East African Standard</u>, July 27, 1973; <u>Times of Zambia</u> and <u>Daily News</u> (Tanzania), July 28, 1973; cited in <u>Africa Research Bulletin</u> (Economic), p. 2839BC.

36. Leo Tansky, "China's Foreign Aid: The Record," in <u>Current Scene</u> 10, no. 9 (September 1972), originally published in <u>People's Republic of China: An Economic Assessment</u>, compiled by the Joint Economic Committee of the Congress of the United States, Washington, D.C., 1972. <u>Current Scene</u> is issued by the U.S. Information Service in Hong Kong.

37. Associated Press, June 4, 1973.

38. <u>Africa Research Bulletin (Political)</u>, p. 2890C.

39. Chou En-lai spoke, though before China and Spain established diplomatic relations, of struggle by the people of the Spanish Sahara. <u>PR</u>, no. 38 (September 22, 1972), speech welcoming Zambian President Kaunda, September 17, 1972.

40. <u>PR</u>, no. 51 (December 22, 1972): 23, paraphrasing Chou En-lai's remarks.

41. <u>PR</u>, no. 31 (August 4, 1972): 7.

42. <u>PR</u>, no. 5 (February 2, 1973): 18-20.

43. <u>PR</u>, no. 7 (February 12, 1971): 22.

44. <u>PR</u>, no. 3 (January 19, 1973), 23.

45. Hsinhua, Peking, December 18, 1973.

46. <u>PR</u>, no. 13 (March 30, 1973): 20.

47. <u>PR</u>, no. 19 (May 11, 1973): 14.

48. <u>PR</u>, no. 46 (November 17, 1972): 18-19.

49. <u>PR</u>, no. 51 (December 22, 1972): 15-16.

50. <u>PR</u>, no. 32 (August 11, 1972): 16.

51. <u>PR</u>, no. 23 (June 8, 1973): 14.

52. <u>Africa Research Bulletin (Political)</u>, p. 2844BC.

53. Tansky, op. cit., p. 9.

54. <u>PR</u>, no. 45 (November 10, 1972): 6-9.

55. Hsinhua, Peking, June 24, 1973; in Hsinhua News Agency, London, June 25, 1973.

CHINESE AID TO AFRICA:
THE TANZANIA-ZAMBIA RAILWAY
George T. Yu

The ceremonies inaugurating the formal construction of the Tanzania-Zambia Railway on October 26, 1970 marked another page in the annals of Chinese-African interaction and Chinese foreign policy and international behavior. Tanzania and Zambia perceived the railway as the realization of a long and frustrating dream come true, which would contribute both to the economic and political development of the two countries and Eastern Africa and to the support of "the liberation struggle in Southern Africa." It was not unexpected, therefore, that the railway took on the aura of a crusade, real and symbolic, and was referred to as The Great Uhuru Railway. For China the $401 million plus project represented the largest single foreign aid and technical assistant commitment to date, a demonstration of her capabilities and power. The railway signified China's continued support to the economic and political goals of Tanzania and Zambia, thereby contributing to the further cohesiveness of China's relationship with the two countries; and it symbolized China's increased level of international activism in Africa and the world.

This is a revised version of "Working on the Railroad: China and the Tanzania-Zambia Railway," which originally appeared in <u>Asian Survey</u> 11, no. 11 (November 1971). Copyright 1971 by the Regents of the University of California. Reprinted by permission.

The author wishes to acknowledge support for this research from the Center for International Comparative Studies, University of Illinois, Urbana-Champaign and the Joint Committee on Contemporary China, Social Science Research Council, New York.

In short the Tanzania-Zambia Railway constituted both a bench mark in Chinese-African interaction and a new departure in Chinese foreign policy and behavior.

Within the general frame of reference of China's commitment to finance, construct, and equip the Tanzania-Zambia Railway, this study will focus upon the following: (1) A brief review of the events leading to China's commitment; (2) the stages of China's commitment; (3) the financial terms of the rail project; (4) the manpower and technical requisites; (5) the rail link's construction; and (6) a tentative assessment of the significance of the railroad as a case study in Chinese-African interaction and Chinese foreign policy and international behavior.

THE HISTORY

The idea of a rail link between Tanzania (and East Africa) and Zambia dates back to the British colonial era. The possible implementation of the project was not seriously considered until the 1960s following Tanzania's and Zambia's independence, and the impetus for the actual construction of the railroad developed in 1965 following Rhodesia's independence, which was perceived as a threat to Zambia's economic and political existence. One of the earliest surveys for the rail link was commissioned by the British Colonial Office in 1952. Since both Tanzania (then Tanganyika) and Zambia (then Northern Rhodesia) were under British jurisdiction, a primary objective of the survey was to investigate the possibility of linking the then Rhodesia Railway and the East African Railway (which consisted of the rail systems of Tanzania, Kenya, and Uganda). Such a linkage would have contributed to the further consolidation of British political and economic interests in Africa. One of the findings of the report was that, from the engineering viewpoint, there were no apparent difficulties. No decision was forthcoming on the survey, however. In part, this was due to the existing patterns of political development and economic linkages. Politically, while Tanzania constituted part of British East Africa, Zambia, which had been largely explored and administered until 1924 by the British South Africa Company, was much more a part of British southern Africa. Economically, the single most important event was the development of the Zambian copper belt by the British South Africa Company beginning in 1924. The copper mines became a primary supplier of the mineral to the world market; in turn, copper constituted Zambia's chief export. However, Zambia is landlocked which raised the question of the transportation of the copper from Zambia to the world market. Three main rail routes were developed: through Rhodesia to the ports of Beira and Lourenco Marques in Portuguese Mozambique; across Zaire to Lobito in Portuguese Angola; and (though with less frequency) through South African ports.* The same routes were used for Zambia's imports. These and other economic linkages undoubtedly contributed further toward Zambia's "southern" dependency and orientation. In short, political and economic factors combined to deter consideration of a rail link between Tanzania and Zambia.

The independence of Tanzania (1961) and Zambia (1964) altered the traditional political and economic patterns; Rhodesia's independence in 1964 further aggravated the breakdown. It was within the context of the newly emerging political divisions that a renewed interest was expressed in a rail link between Tanzania and Zambia. (The 1952 British report was reexamined unilaterally by East African Railways in 1963; however, nothing came of the review.) The project had its origins in several considerations. First, by 1964 the vast majority of the African colonies had been given independence by the European powers. The movement had reached the Zambezi with Zambia's independence. However, it soon became clear that neither the white minority regimes of South Africa and (later) Rhodesia nor the Portuguese were going to follow the patterns of Africa for the Africans, nor were the major Western powers inclined to put pressure upon them. Those African states committed in principle to the liberation of all Africa were confronted with the difficult question of how to combat the new situation, both to preserve their newly won political independence and to promote Africa's total liberation. Tanzania and Zambia were in the forefront of those states dedicated to the liberation of all of Africa.

Second, the political divisions had a profound effect upon the new African states economically, since most of them had been dependent upon and integrated into economic

---

*Other routes technically available were the following: (1) Via Zaire to Port Francquie and on to Matadi; (2) via Zaire, across Lake Tanganyika and on to Dar es Salaam, Tanzania; (3) via the Great North Road to Dar es Salaam and Mtwara, Tanzania; and (4) via the Great East Road to Salima, Malawi, and on to Beira and Nacala.

systems dominated by the colonial powers. Independence
had left the new states with little or none of the institutional and resource requisites. Yet, one of the foremost
goals of the African states was the achievement of economic
independence, both in terms of gaining control over internal development and forging new economic linkages. This
would serve the dual objectives of breaking traditional
economic patterns and establishing economic priorities according to indigenous requisites. Tanzania's and Zambia's
economic development had followed the traditional colonial
pattern; both sought to reorient their economic systems
following independence. Finally, its landlocked status
and geographical proximity to the last vestiges of white
rule made the development of alternative economic linkages
vital to Zambia's political and economic survival. Zambia
was concerned that, without new communication lines, its
economic dependency upon the traditional sources would
compromise its political independence. From Tanzania's
viewpoint, the reorientation of Zambia's economic linkages
would strengthen Zambia and therefore strengthen the forces
of African freedom. In short, Zambia's determination to be
politically and economically independent converged with
Tanzania's commitment toward the freedom of all Africa.

Thus a variety of economic, political, and security
considerations prompted a renewed interest in the Tanzania-
Zambia rail link. Appeals by Tanzania (and Zambia) for
financial and other support for the project led to a series
of surveys on the economic and engineering merits of the
rail link beginning in 1963. The proposal was rejected by
the World Bank Mission in 1963 on the grounds that the
likely economic benefits would be negligible, that the existing rail lines were sufficient to handle the traffic,
and that development in Tanzania and Zambia would be better served by other projects.[1] The Seers Report, made
under the auspices of the United Nations in 1964, also rejected the idea of the rail link. The report argued that
the reasons put forward for the railway were speculative,
that the existing rail systems had spare capacity, and
that the likely developmental benefits measured in terms
of stimulating Zambian agricultural growth were invalid.[2]
The rail link, concluded the Seers Report, would be an
"expensive mistake." An appeal to the Soviet Union also
failed to elicit a favorable response in 1964.

Still another survey was conducted by the Anglo-
Canadian Consortium in 1966 (the Maxwell Stamp survey).[3]
This was the most detailed of the studies, taking the
project up to a final design stage. The survey concluded

that the railway was feasible and would be more profitable
than originally thought, namely, the costs per ton-mile
from Zambia through Tanzania would be less than through
Mozambique and Angola or the South African ports.* Notwithstanding the encouraging words of the Anglo-Canadian
survey, the surveys shared one thing in common: Tanzania's
and Zambia's appeals went unanswered. In large part this
was due to a total failure in communications: Whereas the
World Bank Mission, the Seers Report, the Anglo-Canadian,
and other surveys perceived the project chiefly in economic terms, Tanzania and Zambia saw the rail link as serving a variety of causes, economic, political, and symbolic.

The lack of response did not signal the rail link's
demise, however. China offered to undertake the project
in 1965, during President Nyerere's state visit to Peking
in February 1965.[4] (President Nyerere paid a second state
visit to China in June 1968.) China's offer was taken a
step further in June 1965, when Premier Chou En-lai visited Tanzania. Chou was reported to have put China's
overture in more precise terms.[5] The stage was now ready
for China's formal commitment.

CHINA'S COMMITMENT

China's offer of assistance was almost immediately
accepted by Tanzania. In August 1965, two months after
Chou's visit to Dar es Salaam, a twelve-man Chinese survey
team arrived in Dar es Salaam to undertake an engineering
survey of the Tanzanian section of the proposed rail project; the team consisted of railway, hydrological, and geological experts and was to survey the Kidatu-Tunduma section (the proposed terminal points of the rail link) in
Tanzania.[6] However, China's offer and the arrival of the
survey team represented only the preliminary acts in an
unfolding drama; China had made no formal commitment to
finance and construct the railway and Zambia had yet to
respond to the offer.

The decision on whether to accept China's offer went
unresolved in 1965. While Tanzania and Zambia were committed to the building of the railway, no consensus had
been reached concerning the question of foreign assistance

---

*In 1966-67, the average transport cost per ton for
copper from the Copperbelt in Zambia by rail through
Rhodesia to the Mozambique ports was around $58.

for the project. The Chinese engineering survey had been made at the sole request of the Tanzanian government.[7] Almost concurrently the Tanzania-Zambia Interministerial Committee, established by the two governments to explore the building of the rail link, had requested Britain and Canada (the Anglo-Canadian Consortium) to contribute to the cost of the preliminary survey. A Tanzanian government spokesman explained the two decisions: "One request is from the Tanzania-Zambia Interministerial Committee, and the other is from the point of view of a survey within its borders. This is separate from the position of the interministerial committee."[8] Meanwhile, Zambia remained unresponsive to China's offer of assistance.*

Zambia's position did not remain in doubt for long. Rhodesia's UDI (Unilateral Declaration of Independence) in November 1965, Britain's refusal to quash the rebellion via force, and the indecision by the Western powers toward the proposed rail link all converged to set the stage for Zambia's acceptance of China's participation in the railway project. Indeed landlocked and surrounded on three sides by hostile forces, Zambia more than ever sought a link with the outside world, fearing that Rhodesia and the Portuguese would sever its traffic to the sea entirely. Meanwhile, the formation of the Tanzania-Zambia Road Services with a fleet of trucks to carry goods between the two countries and the construction of an oil pipeline between Dar es Salaam and Ndola provided only partial answers to Zambia's basic economic and political requisites. Zambia's final conversion to China's offer was symbolized by President Kaunda's announcement that China had agreed to build the railway following his state visit to China in June 1967.[9]

---

*A point should be made on the dates of Tanzania's and Zambia's relations with China. China and Tanzania established diplomatic relations in December 1961. China established a mission in Dar es Salaam in January 1962; Tanzania's mission was established in Peking in October 1964. On the other hand, Chinese-Zambian diplomatic recognition took place during October 1964. A Chinese mission was established in Lusaka in March 1965; Zambia's Peking mission was not established until January 1969. While a variety of factors contributed to Zambia's silence on China's offer, a communication gap was undoubtedly one of them.

Zambia's acceptance of the Chinese offer signaled the
beginning of a new act in the emerging triangular drama;
China, Tanzania, and Zambia became partners in the construction of the Tanzania-Zambia Railway. A succession of
events ensued, including an ever increasing number of visits by officials among the three states and the conclusion
of a series of agreements and protocols. To note these
activities is instructive both for the purpose of following the stages leading to the final construction of the
rail link, and for the pattern of China's commitment. In
the latter context we are presented with an opportunity
to observe in some detail the process of one phase of
Chinese foreign policy and behavior.

On September 5, 1967 the initial railway agreement
among China, Tanzania, and Zambia was signed in Peking;
Fang Yi, Minister of the Commission for Economic Relations
with Foreign Countries, represented China while Tanzania
and Zambia were represented by their respective ministers
of finance. This was the beginning of China's formal
commitment to the rail link.[10] The full terms of the
agreement were not released, though certain provisions
were made public. Returning from the ceremonies in Peking,
Tanzania's Minister of Finance made the following points:
China had formally agreed to finance and construct the
railway; the exact cost of the project and therefore
China's financial contribution would be known only after
the survey and design work were completed; a target of
two years had been set for the completion of the design
work; and the technical and professional manpower for the
various phases of the project would be supplied by China.[11]
Interestingly, the agreement was almost wholly concerned
with the technical aspects of the project; no mention was
made on the specifics of China's financial contribution.
This became the pattern of China's commitment to the project, namely, explicit formal agreements at each stage of
the project regarding "technical" details while continuing
negotiations in the financial sphere.

The next round of negotiations and attendant agreements took place in Dar es Salaam in 1968. The Chinese
delegation arrived in late March and formal negotiations
commenced in April; Chou Po-ping, China's Charge d'Affaires
in Dar es Salaam, served as the head of China's delegation.
A communique issued following the talks stated that "the
discussions centered mainly on the basic technical principles relating to the survey and design of the railway
link."[12] It was further announced that agreement had
been reached on the general route of the rail link (from

Kidatu in Tanzania to Kapiri-Mposhi in Zambia, a distance of about 800 miles). Three protocols were signed: The first pertaining to the "forms of loans," the second relating to "the dispatch of technical personnel" and their treatment and working conditions, and finally a protocol on the survey and design work. Subsequently, a protocol concerning the accounting procedures for the loan was signed.[13]

A third round of negotiations were held in Lusaka in November 1969. The Chinese delegation was led by Kuo Lu, Vice-Minister for Railways. These talks at first were heralded as the "final railway talks" by Tanzania and Zambia; it was reported that "only the last details have to be thrashed out"[14] and that the talks would "give the go ahead for building the railway."[15] China, however, perceived the talks in a different light; the Lusaka meeting would discuss matters relating to "construction problems" of the Tanzania-Zambia railway.[16] The five-day meeting consummated with a technical agreement and a series of protocols. First, a supplementary agreement to the original 1967 agreement was concluded; among others, China agreed to extend the railway from Kidatu, the original terminal point in Tanzania, to Dar es Salaam (a distance of about 200 miles). This was to avoid transshipment of traffic, given the fact that the Tanzania-Zambia Railway was to have a 3.5 foot gauge, different from the existing Tanzanian rail system. Second, a protocol on preparations for the beginning of construction was signed. Finally, a protocol relating to "technical principles" was exchanged.[17] The Lusaka negotiations produced no final agreement; there was no go ahead for the rail link's construction.

It becomes difficult to explain fully the delay in the "final agreement"; our data do not allow us this privilege. This much can be said, however. From Tanzania's and Zambia's viewpoint, their extreme anxiety toward the railway may have led them to premature expectations. This was understandable given the long frustrating history of the rail link and the environmental-situational context. Zambia appeared especially eager in predicting that construction of the rail link would begin early in 1970 and that China had agreed to an interest-free loan of $280 million.[18] Tanzania had also expected the Lusaka meeting to produce the final agreement. Tanzanian sources reported that the negotiations would deal "with the financial aspects of the project" and that "the final loan would be in the region of $400 million."[19] The previous successful negotiations with China may have also led Tanzania and Zambia to expect similar results in 1969. This was partially reflected in an editorial published on the eve of the talks in The Nationalist, the organ of the ruling Tanganyika African National Union. "The outcome of the talks is a foregone conclusion. They will be successful. Similar negotiations in the past ended quickly and with positive results. . . ."[20] Finally, China's position must be considered. As we have mentioned, China perceived the Lusaka meeting as chiefly concerned with "construction problems," implying that technical questions remained to be settled. On the basis of previous Chinese behavior, that each technical detail had to be subject to an explicit formal agreement before proceeding to the next detail or stage in the project, China may have been unprepared for the final agreement because specific technical details remained incomplete. For example the 1969 decision to extend the original terminal point in Tanzania to Dar es Salaam may have delayed completion of the engineering and design survey. Furthermore, the cost factor, China's loan, was tied to the technical question, namely, completion of the survey and design work. A hint of this problem came from Zambia's Minister for Development and Finance following conclusion of the negotiations. The Minister remarked that the design work had not yet been completed and that until the design work was done consideration of the final cost of the rail link was impractical.[21] In short, there was no final agreement in 1969 because China was not prepared to make a formal loan commitment.

The failure to reach a final agreement and begin construction on the railway was accepted by all parties, though with varied response. Zambian sources no longer spoke of a time limit for beginning construction; nor was there any reference to China's loan. The Zambian Minister for Finance stated that he hoped that the design work would be finished by the end of 1969, but, he added, it would be unfair to commit the technicians to a time limit.[22] Zambia still hoped that construction would begin in 1970 and be completed by 1975. The Tanzania-Zambia Railway was not in doubt and "Zambia, Tanzania and China were committed to the project."[23] Tanzania's response was more positive.[24] Returning from the Lusaka talks, Tanzania's Minister of Finance stressed that preparatory work for the construction of the railway was underway, that he was completely satisfied with the progress of the survey and design work, and that Chinese experts and technicians had shown "determination and commitment." Indeed, the rail project was well and truly underway and "there is no turning back." Finally let us consider China's response to the Lusaka negotiations. Chinese sources gave no hint of any conflict at the talks; the Chinese spoke of a prevailing "cooperative attitude" and "unanimity on all problems" at the negotiations.[25] However, the Chinese made no reference either to a time limit for the beginning of construction or to the cost factor. Interestingly, the Chinese referred to the accomplishments of the meeting in far greater detail than either the Tanzanian or Zambian sources. Clearly the meeting had been a success, especially when in the words of the Jen-min Jih-pao, "the conference had proceeded in a highly ardent and cordial atmosphere."

The final agreement to construct the Tanzania-Zambia rail link was concluded in Peking on July 12, 1970 following six days of negotiations. Fang Yi, Minister of the Commission for Economic Relations with Foreign Countries, signed the agreement for China; Tanzania and Zambia were represented by their respective Ministers of Finance, A. H. Jamal and Elijah Mudenda.[26] Earlier in April, it was announced that the survey and design work had been completed. The final agreement for the go-ahead to the construction of the rail link was incorporated into a series of documents, two protocols, and minutes of the talks.[27] One protocol pertained to the financial arrangements, including the amount of the loan extended by China and the method of repayment; another related to the study and approval of the survey and design report by Tanzania and Zambia; and the minutes of the talks covered "construction problems." Subsequently, the Tanzanian Minister of Finance announced that a ceremony would be held in October to mark the official beginning of the construction of the railway. The negotiation phase of the Tanzania-Zambia rail link was thus brought to a close; China had completed the survey and design work and had formally offered a loan to construct the railway line. China's commitment was complete.

The Financial Terms

A basic question of the Tanzania-Zambia Railway was: How much would it cost? The inability to secure financial support was a primary obstacle to the rail link's early realization. This was due, of course, largely to the lack of support stemming from the various surveys which reported that the project was an "uneconomic proposition." In short, the economic benefits of the rail link would not be equal to its costs. The full benefits must await the railway's completion. Our attention will focus upon the cost of the project and China's loan.

China's loan for the rail link was announced at the conclusion of the Peking negotiations in 1970; it consisted of $401 million, divided equally between Tanzania and Zambia. The loan was interest-free, repayable over 30 years, starting in 1983.* Repayments were to be in the form of freely convertible currencies or in the form of goods acceptable to China. The loan covered construction costs and provision of locomotives and rolling stock; no breakdown of the loan in cost terms was provided. It was also revealed in 1970 that China had committed up to $280 million to the rail link in 1967; presumably, the survey and design work costs were drawn from this fund.[28]

China's loan, we can assume, was equal to the estimated primary costs of the proposed rail link; Tanzania and Zambia were also expected to contribute to the total costs. The amount was arrived at after prolonged survey and design work. It was China's insistence that completion of the survey and design was required before a cost estimate could be submitted and the loan extended. It was unfortunate that China provided no breakdown of the estimated costs. However, two earlier surveys have provided us with some cost comparisons which allow us to put the Chinese estimate in wider perspective.

One factor was undeniable: The project required a major outlay of resources and the delay of the rail link had greatly increased the estimated costs. The 1963 World Bank survey estimated the total costs for the railway at around $164 million; the costs had increased to around $354 million at the time of the Anglo-Canadian report in 1966.[29] The estimated costs in the two reports were divided into three general categories: basic construction costs, rolling stock and locomotives, and

---

*At the time the loan was announced, 1973 was given as the date for the beginning of the repayment. (See, for example, Information Services Division, Ministry of Information and Tourism, Press Release [Dar es Salaam], July 12, 1970.) Since then official Tanzanian sources have listed 1983 as the start of the repayment period. We do not know the reason for the change.

interest. The World Bank allocated to rolling stock and
locomotives and interest 5 percent and 12 percent of the
total estimated costs respectively.* On the other hand,
the Anglo-Canadian report allocated 21 percent to rolling
stock and locomotives and 7 percent to interest. The
largest expenditure constituted the basic construction
costs (including contingencies costs and cost of line construction): $136 million or 83 percent of the total esti-
mated costs for the World Bank and $245 million or 70 per-
cent of the total estimated costs in the Anglo-Canadian
report. Basic construction costs included such items as
road clearing, earthwork, bridges, track laying, ballast-
ing, signaling, stations, and work buildings. In the
Anglo-Canadian report the largest single expenditure in
this category was earthwork, constituting about 40 percent of the total basic construction costs. The Anglo-
Canadian report based its construction costs upon an estimated completion date of the rail link within a period of
four years as a minimum and to take a period of up to five
years as a maximum. However, the costs of the rail link
were clearly estimates as a number of factors could pro-
long the construction period, including delivery of materials, the degree of mechanization, and weather. In
the final analysis, what the two reports made clear was
the immensity of the railway project, the important relationship between the estimated basic construction costs
and the total construction period, and the tremendous outlay of resources required for completion of the project.

Let us turn to the Chinese cost estimates ($401 mil-
lion) and attempt a breakdown of the estimated costs utilizing the three general categories provided by the World
Bank and Anglo-Canadian reports.† First, the Chinese loan
for the rail link was interest-free; Tanzania and Zambia
saved in this category. Second, the rolling stock and

---

*Interest on the World Bank loan was not specified;
the Anglo-Canadian report put the interest at 6 percent.

†In our discussion of Chinese cost estimates, the
following cautions should be kept in mind. First, we
have converted the cost estimates (and of course the
loan) into dollar figures; we do not know what monetary
base was used by the Chinese. The Chinese loan was expressed in Tanzanian Schillings and Zambian Kwachas.
Second, we do not know on what sort of prices, world market or their own, the Chinese figure was based.

locomotives were estimated at $70 million or $17\frac{1}{2}$ percent of the total estimated cost; in percentage terms, this was higher than the World Bank figure of 5 percent but lower than the Anglo-Canadian rate of 21 percent. Third, after deducting the cost of rolling stock and locomotives, we are left with the figure of $331 million or $82\frac{1}{2}$ percent of the total estimated costs for basic construction. Again, if we compare this percentage with those of the World Bank and the Anglo-Canadian estimates, the Chinese estimated costs for basic construction, while lower than the latter estimate, were almost identical to the former. On the basis of this analysis, it was evident that China had allocated to the basic construction category the primary costs. Finally, accepting the important relationship between the estimated basic construction costs and the total construction period, the Chinese estimates could only be regarded as tentative; the Chinese, for example, did not formally commit themselves to a completion date for the rail link, although a target date of five to six years was mentioned by the Zambian Minister of Finance following the 1970 Peking talks. Furthermore, in addition to the time factor, the total estimated costs could increase as labor and material costs rose. In the context of our discussion, therefore, a supplementary Chinese loan could not be ruled out. On the other hand, China could always absorb any cost-overrun.

If the total costs to China of the Tanzania-Zambia rail link were an uncertainty, Tanzania and Zambia were also confronted with specific economic questions. One immediate problem was the question of local costs, namely, payments for support of Chinese technicians working on the project in Tanzania and Zambia and the purchase of equipment obtainable in the two states. The problem of local costs was rooted in Chinese foreign aid, which in turn was determined by China's national capabilities. Fundamentally, the problem was that China as a developing society suffered from an overall scarcity of foreign exchange on the one hand and needed to conserve foreign exchange for purchases abroad to meet its own internal requisites on the other. Lacking foreign exchange, other methods were sought to finance China's foreign aid and technical assistance programs. One such technique was the utilization of trade. It worked as follows: Chinese goods would be advanced on credit to the state-owned trading corporation of the aid recipient state and the profits made by selling the goods would then be utilized to defray local incurred costs. In this way, trade became directly tied to aid; however, this raised new economic questions for the aid recipient.

Tanzanian and Zambian government sources announced in 1969 that the railway would be financed by selling Chinese consumer goods through Zambian and Tanzanian state trading organizations; a commodity credit agreement provided for the importation of Chinese goods during the period of construction of the rail link.[30] Sixty percent of the Chinese estimated cost ($401 million) of the rail link would be financed in this manner.[31] Dividing the 60 percent in half, Tanzania and Zambia each were committed to purchase a total of $120.3 million worth of Chinese goods. If we assume that the rail link will require five years to complete, the two states would each need to import $24.06 million worth of Chinese goods annually. Given Zambia's overall annual import bill of $500 million (1969), China's imports should amount to no more than 5 percent. Tanzania's annual imports came to $240 million in 1969; Chinese goods should therefore amount to no more than 10 percent of Tanzania's imports annually.* With minor trade adjustments, Tanzania and Zambia expected to easily absorb the Chinese goods into their respective imports.

A basic question was not whether the required percentage of Chinese imports could be absorbed into the total import bills of Tanzania and Zambia, but rather what commodities did China have to offer to the two states. In part, the question was related to the complementary economic and developmental patterns of the three states. Consider the example of textiles. The place of the textile industry in China's economy and development was well established; in 1949, for example, textiles was second only to food manufacturing in terms of industrial production. Although since the 1950s output declined, textiles continued to be one of China's principal export commodities. Tanzania and Zambia meanwhile have sought to develop industries that could reduce dependency upon foreign sources as part of their economic development plans to achieve self-

---

*In Tanzania's case, Chinese imports had already amounted to $11 million or almost 6 percent of Tanzania's total imports in 1969 before the beginning of the construction of the railway. Tanzanian officials expected no great difficulties in any trade adjustments. Since 1962 imports from traditional sources, such as the United Kingdom, other sterling areas, had been slowly declining; Tanzanian officials expected this pattern to continue. Imports from China would take up a portion of the hiatus.

reliance, conserve foreign exchange, and utilize domestic raw materials. Most of the industries were consumer-oriented; one of the primary industries for development was textiles. The Tanzanian government-supported textile industry had assumed a leading position in the manufacturing sector of the economy. In 1968 there existed a problem of textile overproduction. Zambia also joined the race toward textile self-reliance, opening its first textile mill in 1970. The complementary nature of textile development in China, Tanzania, and Zambia was self-evident; that textiles constituted a primary source of Chinese exports was a question which required study by all three parties.

Tanzania and Zambia were fully conscious of the delicacy of the problem. The Commercial Manager of Tanzania's State Trading Corporation declared that only goods not manufactured in Tanzania would be imported from China.[32] However, given the fact that textiles were already a primary import commodity (over $5.1 million worth in 1968) and given the realities of China's exportable commodities, some duplication of imports from China which Tanzania manufactured could not be avoided. Among the commodities which were already imported or being considered for importation from China were textiles, agricultural equipment and tools, chemicals for use in textiles, foodstuff, buses, hardware goods, medicines, water pumps, and heavy earth moving tractors.[33] Indeed, the range of Chinese goods was almost inexhaustible. Taking consumer goods as an example, Chinese merchandise included everything from canned food (Chinese red cooked pork), to household utensils (from pots to thermos bottles), to soap products (detergent and face soap), to sporting goods (footballs and ping pong sets), to toys (jigsaw puzzles of Canton at night). The price structure of Chinese goods was equally interesting.* Most canned foods sold for around $.40; a small size thermos bottle for $1.10; a football for $7; a ping pong set for $5.60; a four ounce box of detergent for $.40. In many instances, Chinese goods were the only merchandise available; more were expected. As the Tanzanian Minister for Commerce noted in early 1972, "I must tell you frankly that to pay for the local costs of the construction of the Tanzania-Zambia railway line, we will be having plenty of consumer goods from China."[34] The mass importation of Chinese goods could not but have an impact upon Tanzania's

---

*The examples were taken from stores in Dar es Salaam during the summer of 1972.

economy, as Tanzanian elites were fully aware. Tanzania's dilemma was shared by Zambia.

This was vividly reported by the Zambian Industrial and Commercial Association mission led by the permanent secretary to the Trade Ministry which visited China in the fall of 1969. This mission's findings were both instructive and specific.[35] First, the mission was concerned with selecting the types of goods which China could supply for the best value. It found an extensive range of food products, including cereals, fruits, meat, and seafoods; a wide range of textiles was also available, but not the new synthetic fibers, such as warp-knitted nylon and crimplene; building materials were limited in selection and fittings were "generally of utilitarian, rather than decorative, styles"; there was only a limited range of construction equipment which was of "somewhat old-fashioned design" and prices quoted were high in relation to those in other markets; an astonishing range of light industrial products "too diverse to enumerate" were reported; transport equipment was of "robust construction" but the "designs were out of date"; and agricultural tools were of the less sophisticated types (there were no steel-handled shovels). The mission concluded that "There is a limited range of commodities in which Chinese products are competitive, both in price and quality, with those obtainable from other sources." The following commodities were identified as being equal or superior in quality to those from other sources and competitive in price: chinaware, glassware, cheaper-quality clothing, towels and toweling, textile goods, woolen carpets, and bicycles.

Second, the mission considered the problem of delivery. There were two primary facets to this problem. First, Zambian merchants who had brought commodities from China reported that promised delivery dates were often not met; the mission recommended that assurance should be obtained that regular supplies would be forthcoming and that delivery promises would be kept. Second, the mission was also concerned with the experience of other buyers who had tried to place firm orders for large quantities of goods, but had either been told that only smaller orders could be accepted or that the products were not available. The problem was that if Zambia could not obtain what it wanted, it might then be forced to purchase other commodities more expensive or inferior in quality than those obtainable from other sources. The mission recommended that the Zambian government obtain a firm understanding from China that commodities would be delivered regularly and on time.

Third, the report discussed the possible impact of Chinese imports on Zambian industry and commerce. What would be the consequence, asked the mission, if the state trading corporation--committed to buy Chinese commodities--found itself at a disadvantage in terms of price and quality of such goods in relation to the commodities of privately owned stores? There was also the problem of the effect of Chinese goods upon Zambian industry. The report put it thus:

> This possibility appears most likely to
> have serious consequences in relation to
> the clothing and blanket industries, which
> are firmly established in Zambia and are
> already catering for a very substantial
> part of the local market. It should be
> noted, in this connection, that if Chinese
> clothing were to be imported in competi-
> tion with similar locally-manufactured
> garments, the effects on the local cloth-
> ing industry would be disastrous. . . .

Using the argument long raised by the higher wage paying industrial countries against the lower wage paying states, the Zambian mission considered Chinese textile and clothing industries to be at a considerable advantage since the average wage in those Chinese industries was estimated at $24 a month, compared with $70 in Zambia.

Finally given the many uncertainties of trade with China, yet considering the commitment to buy Chinese commodities to finance the rail link, the report concluded "that the commitment might be fulfilled with the least undesirable effects by the creation of an import quota system over a range of goods" and recommended that Zambia should consider meeting its commitment by direct payment.

> Finally, after taking note of all the prob-
> lems and uncertainties involved in any one
> of the means of meeting Zambia's commitment
> to purchase goods which had been discussed,
> the Mission concluded that if, after every
> effort has been made by Government and pri-
> vate enterprise alike, it proves to be im-
> practicable to purchase goods in sufficient
> quantities without endangering the well-
> being of consumers or factory workers, or
> the existence of local industries, the

Government should be advised to consider
meeting its annual commitments by direct
payment, to the extent that they are not
fulfilled by the proceeds of purchases
of goods.

Undoubtedly, the financial agreement to build the rail
link raised economic questions both for the aid donor and
the recipients. The most important consideration was, however, that the project had secured financial support and
that it would now become a reality. The importance of the
realization of this dream to Tanzania and Zambia, with all
the attendant economic, political, and symbolic expectations, and China's grasp of this goal constituted in itself the most significant factor, which for the moment
overrode all other considerations, financial and otherwise. The Tanzania-Zambia Railway would now be built.

The Manpower and Technical Requisites

China had agreed to finance the rail link; its construction was the next act. The decision to build the
railway and supply the rolling stock and locomotives must
be considered a significant departure from previous Chinese foreign policy and behavior. By any standards of
measurement, the construction of the rail link represented
a major undertaking. It required attacking and coordinating the three basic principles of material, labor, and
equipment; in addition, there was the problem of delivery.
We do not mean to suggest that China did not possess the
capabilities. Since 1949 China had manufactured most of
its own locomotives, rolling stock and track materials and
more than 10,000 miles of railway had been constructed.
China had also demonstrated its capabilities in the implementation of foreign aid and technical assistance projects.
The $7 million Chinese financed, designed, constructed,
and equipped Friendship Textile Mill outside Dar es Salaam
stood as a shining monument of Chinese aid. However, the
building and equipping of a textile mill could not be
equated with the construction and the furnishing of a
railway. Namely the magnitude and the requisites of the
rail link outstripped any previous Chinese foreign aid
and technical assistance project; it was one of the few
projects which required extensive support from China's
developing industrial and educational base. In the context of the manpower and technical requisites, the rail

link represented a new departure by China in the commitment of resources to an aid project.

An example of the demands of the rail link's manpower requisites can be partially seen from the known available pool of Chinese resources. Taking two general fields of engineering related to railroad construction and the number of graduates in the two fields from 1953 to 1962, a sense of the demands upon China's manpower can be derived. A study of Chinese scientific and engineering manpower had shown that from 1953 to 1962 only 6,079 (or 2 percent of the total) and 12,703 (or 5 percent of the total) graduated from college in the two fields of surveying, drafting, meteorology and hydrology and transport, post and telecommunications.[36] Even allowing for further growth in the two fields since 1962 but taking into account the impact of the Cultural Revolution upon education, the pool of China's experienced and qualified professional manpower must still be limited. We can assume that China's internal developmental requisites put a heavy demand upon the scarce resources; any additional output must surely add strain to the available manpower.

The total required professional manpower for the rail link's construction was difficult to determine. Zambia's Finance Minister estimated that between 15,000 to 20,000 men would be employed in building the railway. "But it is impossible to say how many of them will be Chinese," continued the Finance Minister, "because this depends on how many skilled men can be found locally."[37] However, the prospects of the availability of "skilled men" in Tanzania and Zambia were unpromising. A survey of manpower resources in Tanzania in 1968/69 provided an idea of the shortages.[38] Though the following category of occupations were not all directly related to railroad construction, the figures provided a picture of the manpower resource deficiency. Tanzania had only 39 general civil engineers, no hydraulic civil engineers, no soil mechanic civil engineers, 3 general electrical engineers, 19 general mechanical engineers, 3 electronic engineers, 7 telecommunication engineers, 23 general surveyors, 2 geologists and no soil scientists. Indeed, most of Tanzania's engineering requisites were already being met by the recruitment of expatriates, "rented skills." Zambia faced a similar situation.[39] The professional manpower for the construction of the Tanzania-Zambia rail link had also to be met by "rented skills," in this case Chinese. A work force of 50,000 plus was engaged in the construction of the rail link in 1972.[40] This included 13,000 plus Chinese engineers, technicians, and supporting staff.

The Tanzania-Zambia Railway could also be expected to place heavy demands upon China's construction, transport, and related industries. Given our limited knowledge of China's industries, it becomes difficult to weigh the effects of the rail link on China, which manufactured most of its own locomotives, rolling stock and track materials, but with a limited production capacity. China's railway requisites continued to exceed the industry's capabilities, necessitating the importation of diesel and electric locomotives. A problem, therefore, was not whether the equipment could be manufactured, but whether China's railway industry possessed the capacity to supply all the requisites of the rail link.

An interesting solution to the problem of limited industrial output was displayed by China in the case of the Japanese bulldozers.[41] Requiring bulldozers for clearing and earthwork in the basic construction phase of the rail link, China turned to a Japanese manufacturing company. The Japanese company (Komatsu Manufacturing) had sold 257 large-size bulldozers to China during the 1969 Canton Trade Fair. The company had expected that the machines would be shipped to China, but the Machine Export Company of China directed that 98 bulldozers (worth about $1.7 million) be shipped to Tanzania. The machines arrived at Dar es Salaam early in 1970 and were put to use in the construction of the rail link. China manufactured bulldozers, but had to turn to Japan because of the limited output in China. The case of the bulldozers, aside from raising hopes in Japanese trade circles for future Japanese-Chinese "cooperation," raised the important question of the extent and impact of China's dependency upon and utilization of non-Chinese equipment in the railway's construction and furnishings. Whatever the extent, the ramifications were certain to have an impact, both in terms of the demands placed upon China's own construction and industrial requisites and upon China's foreign exchange reserves.

THE CONSTRUCTION PHASE

Following the inauguration of the formal construction of the rail link in October 1970, the project proceeded rapidly. A target of 310 miles of completed track for the first year's construction was set. In November 1971 this goal had been achieved with the completion of the Dar es Salaam-Mlimba section of the railway.[42] The most difficult section of the rail link between Mlimba and Makambako

(where the railway climbs up the escarpment from the Kilom-
bero Valley into the Southern Highlands) was completed in
early 1973, bringing the total to nearly 400 miles of completed railway track.[43] To the tam-tam of African drums,
the Tanzania-Zambia Railway crossed into Zambia on August
25, 1973. Given the fast progress of the physical construction of the railway, completion of the Tanzania-
Zambia rail link was now expected for 1974.

Construction of the rail link began in Tanzania; one
advantage to this plan was that equipment and material
could be moved on the railway's own track as the line was
completed. Construction in Tanzania was divided into
three primary sections, work on the railway started from
three points concurrently: Dar es Salaam, Kidatu, and
Makumbako. Each section constituted a semi-independent
working unit, with one main construction base and a given
number of mobile construction camps. The main construction base functioned as the supply and workshop center,
providing equipment and material for its section, including concrete and wooden sleepers for the railway. A main
construction base had a total work force of about 6,000.[44]
The actual construction of the rail link was done by the
mobile construction camps, located along the section's
route, each accommodating a work force of over 1,000. A
similar organization plan was being implemented in Zambia.

The rail link constituted a tripartite project and
the work force was made up of Chinese, Tanzanians, and
Zambians. Through 1972 with the construction of the railway largely in Tanzania, the work force consisted chiefly
of Chinese and Tanzanians: 40,000 plus Tanzanians and a
minimum of 13,000 Chinese. When construction and track
laying reached Zambia beginning in 1973, an additional
work force of 10,000 Zambians were expected to be recruited
to work on the railway.[45] Both the main construction bases
and the mobile construction camps were administered by Chinese, whose experience in dealing with the management and
supervision of large-scale labor-intensive techniques in
public works no doubt proved useful.[46] Whether because of
this or because the construction of the rail link had
reached a stage which required greater coordination (or
both), China agreed in 1971 to dispatch to the projects'
central administration a team of experts to assist "in the
arduous task of coordinating the construction effort."[47]

The progress of the physical construction of the rail
link could be seen from a number of other indicators;
these served also to give a sense of the specific costs of
the project and the economic and other demands upon China.

First, local costs in Tanzania for 1971/72 were reported
at $16 million, to be covered by raising the money through
the sale of Chinese goods under the commodity loan agreement.[48] Most of the local costs were for payment for services for the work force, Chinese and Tanzanian. An annual local costs bill of $16 million constituted undoubt-
edly an indicator of the size of the labor force, and
therefore a sense of the rail link's progress. Second,
Tanzanian trade statistics provided through reports of the
annual value of capital goods imported for the rail link a
measure of the railway's construction. Not all of the
capital goods originated from China; but the value of the
goods counted as part of China's loan. In 1970, the first
year of the rail link's construction, imports of capital
equipment and materials for the project totaled $33.6 mil-
lion; during 1971 the amount had increased to $60.2 mil-
lion.[49] Importation of capital and other goods was expected to remain at a high level until the rail project
had been completed. Finally, as construction of the rail
link progressed, China's dependency upon and utilization
of non-Chinese equipment greatly increased. Most of the
supporting equipment for the project's construction was
of non-Chinese origins. These ranged from British and
Swedish trucks, to British earth moving equipment, to
Finnish rock crushing machinery, to German VW microbuses.
The basic machinery and other capital equipment for the
actual construction of the rail link, however, were of
Chinese origin. These and other indicators gave a sense
of basic requisites and costs of the project; there could
be no doubt that construction of the rail link placed a
heavy resource burden upon China.

Nor were China, Tanzania, and Zambia concerned only
with the actual construction of the railway; plans were
being concurrently formulated for the rail link's future
operation. During 1971/72, the Tanzanian and Zambian governments allocated a total of $4.3 million to run the
railway's administration, the Tanzania-Zambia Railway
Authority (TAZARA), and to start training programs for
the link's future operational staff.[50] A training school
was established at Mangula in Tanzania and another was to
be built in Zambia at Mpika. China also participated in
preparing for the railway's future operation. At the
fifth round of tripartite negotiations held in Dar es
Salaam in December 1971, it was announced that "200 Tanzanian and Zambian trainees" would be sent to China for
technical training.[51] Earlier it was reported that the
Tanzanians and Zambians would undergo a four-year training

program in China for senior technical and managerial positions on the Tanzania-Zambia Railway.[52] China, Tanzania,
and Zambia were looking forward to the rail link's operation in 1974.

THE RAILWAY AND CHINESE FOREIGN POLICY

The full significance of the Tanzania-Zambia Railway
in Chinese foreign policy and behavior must await history;
in the early 1970s China's role in Africa's economic and
political development had yet to fully unfold. Nevertheless, as a case study in Chinese-African interaction specifically and as an instance in the foreign policy and behavior of China generally the rail project did offer interesting suggestions.

First, what were China's objectives in the commitment
to the Tanzania-Zambia Railway? Accepting the factor of
the demands placed upon China's scarce resources, we must
assume that the benefits were perceived as outweighing the
costs. Namely, the decision to commit China's resources
to the rail link was arrived at through a rational process.
We need not repeat the known arguments concerning China's
foreign policy and behavior in relation to the United
States and the Soviet Union; nor do we need to restate
China's own rationale that one of its policy objectives
was to provide leadership to the Third World. Undoubtedly, these and other considerations influenced China. We
should, however, like to suggest a less tangible but no
less significant objective to China's commitment, that is,
it symbolized China's commitment to the forces of change
and it enhanced China's international status.

It has been argued that China's support of the African liberation movements represented an unrealistic policy. The South Africans, the Portuguese, and others were
far too entrenched and could be removed only via force,
which China was thought unwilling to fully support. Yet
China as a self-styled revolutionary force could not deny
support to the forces seeking change in Africa. Tanzania
and Zambia were in the front line against the status quo
forces; by supporting the objectives of the two African
states through the rail link, China was also giving support, real and symbolic, to the larger force of change in
Africa. China's symbolic role can be suggested also in
relation to its drive for international recognition, a
major foreign policy objective. Namely, construction of
the railway constituted a symbol of China's capabilities
and power.

Second, the commitment to the rail link could also be
seen as an indicator of China's increased international
activism. It testified to China's global foreign policy
against a regional one oriented chiefly against the United
States and the Soviet Union in Asia. We should not, of
course, dismiss the "regional" emphasis, namely, China's
greater commitment to and identification with the Third
World.

Finally, the Tanzania-Zambia rail link had to be seen
within the context of Chinese-African interaction. There
were several dimensions to this problem. First, many Africans perceived the rail link as a demonstration of China's
commitment to and identification with Africa's development;
the willingness to build the railway and assist in other
developmental projects lent credibility and enhanced
China's role in Africa. Second, the economic and political
importance of the resource transfer from China to Africa
had also to be considered significant. The short-range and
long-term implications were far reaching, both with respect
to the general retrenchment of the major Western aid donors
and the concurrent decline of Western influence in Africa
and the increased level of economic, political, and technical interaction and attendant ramifications between China
and Africa. Finally, the Tanzania-Zambia rail link represented for both China and Africa a psychological triumph.
The West had long held sway with its technological advantage over much of Asia and Africa. The rail link built
through Chinese-African cooperation symbolized, therefore,
an end to Western technological superiority and dominance
and the economic and technological development and advent
of China and Africa.

NOTES

1. In the words of the World Bank Mission, "Urgent
need for investments in other parts of Northern Rhodesia
(Zambia) and Tanganyika and in other sectors of the economy raises doubts about the feasibility of concentrating
such a large amount of money ($164 million) on one single
project at this time. . . . As far as traffic between
the Copperbelt and the Ocean is concerned, no major addition to existing facilities is likely to be required for
ten or twenty years because existing railway lines to
Beira, Lourenco Marques, and Lobito are operated effi-
ciently and cheaply, have ample spare capacity and will
be able to expand capacity with small investments." Quoted

in R. M. Bostock, "The Transport Sector," <u>Constraints on the Economic Development of Zambia</u>, ed. Charles Elliott (Nairobi, 1971), p. 367. The Mission suggested improved roads as an alternative to the rail link.

2. Richard Hall, <u>The High Price of Principles, Kaunda and the White South</u> (London, 1969), p. 213. Hall was a former newspaperman in Zambia, including editor of the national daily paper, the <u>Times of Zambia</u>.

3. Bostock, op. cit., pp. 366-71.

4. "Comment," <u>The Standard</u> (Dar es Salaam), July 14, 1970.

5. Hall, op. cit., p. 214.

6. <u>Shih-chieh Jih-pao</u> (San Francisco), August 26, 1965.

7. Ibid.

8. Ibid.

9. For an account of Zambia's struggles with the rail project, see Hall, op. cit., pp. 209-23.

10. The 1967 agreement is seen as the beginning of China's role in the construction of the rail link. See "The People of China, Tanzania and Zambia Are Opening the Road of Friendship," <u>Jen-min Jih-pao</u> (Peking), October 27, 1970.

11. <u>The Standard</u> (Dar es Salaam), September 11, 1967.

12. <u>Sunday News</u> (Dar es Salaam), April 28, 1968.

13. New China News Agency, April 27, 1968.

14. <u>The Standard</u> (Dar es Salaam), November 3, 1969.

15. <u>The Standard</u> (Dar es Salaam), November 22, 1969.

16. <u>Jen-min Jih-pao</u> (Peking), November 9, 1969.

17. "The Government Delegations of China, Tanzania and Zambia Sign the Supplementary Agreement on the Construction of the Tanzania-Zambia Railway," <u>Jen-min Jih-pao</u> (Peking), November 18, 1969. <u>The Nationalist</u> (Dar es Salaam), November 17, 1969.

18. <u>The Nationalist</u> (Dar es Salaam), November 11, 1969.

19. <u>The Standard</u> (Dar es Salaam), November 7, 1969.

20. "Tazra Talks," <u>The Nationalist</u> (Dar es Salaam), November 11, 1969.

21. <u>The Standard</u> (Dar es Salaam), November 18, 1969. <u>The Nationalist</u> (Dar es Salaam), November 18, 1969.

22. Ibid.

23. <u>The Nationalist</u> (Dar es Salaam), November 18, 1969.

24. <u>The Nationalist</u> (Dar es Salaam), November 17, 1969.

25. <u>Jen-min Jih-pao</u> (Peking), November 18, 1969.

26. Jen-min Jih-pao (Peking), July 15, 1970. The Standard (Dar es Salaam), July 12, 1970.

27. Data on the documents have been compiled from the following: Jen-min Jih-pao (Peking), July 15, 1970; The Standard (Dar es Salaam), July 12, 1970; and The Nationalist (Dar es Salaam), July 13, 1970.

28. The Standard (Dar es Salaam), July 13, 1970.

29. Data on the World Bank and Anglo-Canadian reports were compiled from Bostock, op. cit., and "How Much Will It Cost," Business Mail, Zambia Mail (Lusaka), February 11, 1970.

30. "Report on the Zambian Trade Mission to the People's Republic of China, 14th-23rd October, 1969," Lusaka, Zambia, 1969. Mimeographed.

31. New York Times, March 4, 1970.

32. The Nationalist (Dar es Salaam), September 26, 1969.

33. Ibid.

34. Sunday News (Dar es Salaam), January 30, 1972. These remarks were made before the Tanzanian General Assembly.

35. "Report on the Zambian Trade Mission to the People's Republic of China, 14th-23rd October, 1969," op. cit.

36. Chu-yuan Cheng, "Scientific and Engineering Manpower in Communist China," in An Economic Profile of Mainland China, 2 (Washington, 1967), 519-47.

37. East African Standard, July 22, 1970.

38. The United Republic of Tanzania, Tanzania Second Five-Year Plan of Economic and Social Development, 1st July, 1968 - 30th June, 1974, 4 (Dar es Salaam, 1969), 12A.

39. Development Division, Office of the Vice-President (Zambia), Zambian Manpower (Lusaka, 1969).

40. The United Republic of Tanzania, The Economic Survey 1971-1972 (Dar es Salaam, 1972), p. 112.

41. Asahi Shimbun (Tokyo), June 23, 1970.

42. The United Republic of Tanzania, The Economic Survey 1971-1972 (Dar es Salaam, 1972), p. 112.

43. Ibid.

44. "One-third of 'Uhuru' Railway Ready this Year," Maelezo Feature Service (Dar es Salaam), October 4, 1972.

45. The Financial Times (London), January 15, 1973.

46. For an informative account of the problems of capital-intensive and labor-intensive techniques in public works in Africa, see J. Muller, "Labor-Intensive Methods in Low-Cost Road Construction: A Case Study," International Labour Review 101, no. 4 (April 1970): 359-74.

47. Information Services Division, Ministry of Information and Broadcasting, Press Release (Dar es Salaam),
December 22, 1971.

48. The United Republic of Tanzania, The Economic
Survey 1970-1971 (Dar es Salaam, 1971), p. 83.

49. The United Republic of Tanzania, The Economic
Survey 1971-1972 (Dar es Salaam, 1972), p. 112.

50. The United Republic of Tanzania, The Economic
Survey 1970-1971 (Dar es Salaam, 1971), p. 83.

51. Information Services Division, Ministry of Information and Broadcasting, Press Release, op. cit; The
Nationalist (Dar es Salaam), December 23, 1971. The group
finally arrived in China in May 1972. Before starting the
technical training, the students were required to take a
year's lesson in Chinese; this was necessary before the
students could take the engineering classes since instructions were to be in Chinese. The Tanzanians accepted the
requirement, but the Zambians reportedly balked. The
Chinese held fast and relations with the Zambians deteriorated. Early in 1973, it was reported that four Zambian
students had been ordered from China for causing a fracas
and assaulting school officials. See The Christian Science
Monitor, January 5, 1973.

52. The Nationalist (Dar es Salaam), March 6, 1971.

CHAPTER

3

CHINESE POLICY IN CENTRAL
AFRICA: 1960-73
Warren Weinstein

The following quotations of Chairman Mao have served
as a source of inspiration and guidance within China; they
indicate the shift in policies in the 1970s followed by
Peking in Central Africa: "If we can take the Congo
[Zaire], we can take all of Africa" (reported in 1964)[1];
"Burundi is the stepping stone for reaching the Congo
[Zaire]" (reported in 1964)[2]; "I lost much money and arms
at attempting to overthrow you [i.e., Mobutu's regime]"
(January 1973).[3]

Prior to 1968-70 the People's Republic of China was
interested in gaining international leverage, to dilute
threats to its own security, and to establish dependency
relationships with African states. This interest in Central Africa stemmed from the desire to establish an ideological client system in the Congo where they believed
the goal was achievable. At the same time, they were prepared to support any oppositionist group of sovereign governments in adjacent states through which they could help
the success of the revolution in Zaire. The Chinese, in
dealing with those states peripheral to the Congo followed
a less lofty policy of "the ends justify the means."

The international leverage sought by the PRC revolved
about its competition with Taiwan to be recognized as the
rightful and legal state of China, with sovereignty over
the mainland and Taiwan. In part the international leverage was important in terms of ideological struggle between
the Maoist and Soviet interpretations of Marxism-Leninism.
Ever since 1960 the Peking leadership felt it had been un-
fairly treated by the Soviets. Peking believed that the
Soviet Communist leaders wished to establish a long lasting hegemony over the much less developed communist countries of Asia and eventually over Africa as well. As a

result the Chinese felt a closer identification between their underdeveloped condition and that of the Third World. Chinese leaders believed that their struggle to avoid an uneven patron-client dependence relationship with the Soviet Union bore strong resemblance to the general Third World struggle to avoid dependence on the developed nations. Perhaps it was for this reason that Chou En-lai, in 1963-64, announced that Africa was ripe for revolution.* The quest for international leverage also involved a desire for prestige courted by a country with big power aspirations. The Chinese, historically, placed great emphasis on prestige in their relations with other states.[4]

ZAIRE (CONGO-LEOPOLDVILLE)

The interest in diluting threats, real or imagined, led Chinese policymakers to support strategies that would tie the enemy up in military activities far removed from the Chinese homeland.[5] It is worthwhile to note this, given that the major Chinese support in Africa during 1964 went to rebellions in what was Congo-Leopoldville then Kinshasa and now Zaire. This state had been a Belgian colony until its independence in June 1960. At that time it fell into a state of chaos and American involvement rose sharply. The Chinese feared that the Americans sought to replace Belgium, and this made it doubly worthwhile to the Chinese to tie the West up in a guerrilla war in Central Africa. By doing so, the Chinese may have hoped to embarrass the United States and thereby lessen its potential influence elsewhere in Africa. The more heavily involved the United States became, so the logic would seem to assume, the less it could be involved in Asian territories close to China, or at the very least, the more China could hope to discredit U.S. actions in both places.

Central Africa was also of interest because the Soviet Union had voted with the Americans in favor of the

---

*We would suggest that the analogy Chinese policymakers drew was, most probably, that of the "sea"--the Third World, and the "cities"--the developed world, and of the struggle between them. The Chinese may have felt Africans were reaching a point of consciousness that made the revolution against the "cities" possible.

original 1960 United Nations decision to intervene in the Congo. The Chinese attacked the Soviets for having done so and accused the United States of using the UN as a cover under which American influence was being spread in that state. This was during the period of increased Sino-Soviet conflict, and Peking may well have sought to deflect its rivalry with the Soviets to Africa and away from Asia.

The Chinese interest in establishing a tight patron-client relationship was never a clearly stated goal. It is more a deduced observation based on actual Chinese actions in Central Africa. It is on this point that the study will dwell, and on the thesis that Chinese policy has shifted gear since 1969-71 away from a hard-line ideological orientation to a more flexible, pragmatic outlook.

Chairman Mao's statement cited above reveals that in the early 1960s the Chinese felt that it was in their interest to "take" Africa in the ideological sense and that they could succeed.[6] The chaos in the Congo during 1960 had given rise to a struggle between left-wing leaders led by Patrice Lumumba and nonradical nationalists led by Kasavubu and others. The Chinese felt that the Congo was located strategically for exporting revolution if the revolution succeeded in this state. They seemed convinced that popular discontent existed in the Congo and only proper guerrilla training and structuring of the revolutionary forces was lacking. The Chinese felt this to be a legitimate reason to intervene. To this end several potential leaders such as Mulele, Soumialot, and others were received in China for guerrilla training and/or political indoctrination.

Within a very short time the Chinese were forced to observe that revolution in the Congo--and in Africa--would not come as quickly or as easily as anticipated. The masses did not rise up and the rebellions in the Congo from 1961 through 1965 suffered from ethnic limitations and struggles over leadership.[7] In 1961 the Chinese waited for some time and then recognized a rebel left-wing government at Stanleyville. Five months later a senior colonel from China was sent as Peking's diplomatic representative only to be withdrawn two months later when the radicals and nonradicals formed a coalition government.*

_____

*Prime Minister Tshombe (Congo) attempted to bring about national reconciliation. Peking denounced this as a "fraud" once it appeared the Congolese central government

58

Owing to the resultant protracted nature of the Congolese conflict, China sought privileged sanctuaries in
neighboring states including Rwanda and Burundi. Hence
Mao's statement: "Burundi is the stepping stone for reaching the Congo."
    The Chinese embassy in Burundi opened officially in
late 1963. Its numbers swelled to between 22 and 24 by
October 1964, although China had no overt projects in
which it was participating on Burundian soil.[8] The Chinese were unable to arrange diplomatic relations with
Rwanda.
    The support or lack of support for Chinese goals was
uppermost in determining policy toward political factions
in Burundi and Rwanda until 1968-70.

RWANDA

    The Rwandan government was based on a philosophy of
Christian socialism set forth by its leader, President
Gregoire Kayibanda. This man gained power by virtue of a
social upheaval during which the poorer and more oppressed
Hutu masses overthrew a monarchy dominated by an ethnic
minority of Tutsi who did not account for more than 15-16
percent of the total population. As Hevi commented based
on China's revolutionary propaganda one would have expected Peking's condemnation of Tutsi "feudalism" and support for the popular Hutu leadership.[9] However, Peking's
primary interest in the early 1960s was to establish a
firm foothold in the neighboring Congo, and it was in
China's interest to supplant the strongly anti-Communist

---

was having some success. In 1965 President Mobutu (Congo)
repeated the attempt at conciliation. There is some reason to believe that various rebel leaders were themselves
becoming disillusioned with Chinese aid during 1965. Some
felt the Chinese were attempting to control the movement
in the Congo. One rebel leader, Soumialot, visited Peking
with some followers after he announced the dissolution of
Gbenye's revolutionary government in which he had been
Minister of Defense. This announcement came on August 5,
1965. It denounced Gbenye and Kanza as unfit to lead the
revolution. Kanza responded with counter-charges that
Soumialot had become the "agent of a foreign country"
(China). (This information was conveyed to the author
in 1965; it was confirmed by Kanza in May 1973.)

government of Kayibanda with a more accommodating group.[10] That group was the Tutsi refugees who had suffered severe status reversal during Rwanda's social violence which lasted from November 1959 until well into 1961.[11]

The Chinese, according to Larkin, withheld support only where the government was willing to deal with them, something President Kayibanda and his government was unwilling to do. Therefore, although chances for success were limited, China decided to support the deposed Tutsi King of Rwanda, Kigeri V, with financial doles while it provided ammunition, funds, and training support for Tutsi refugees in their respective host states.[12]

The Chinese support for Tutsi refugees, known as Inyenzi (cockroaches), incited the more die-hard among them to launch attacks against Rwanda. It also made Burundi an even more strategic post for Peking to provide a privileged sanctuary for Chinese activities against the central government in Zaire and against the Hutu government of Rwanda.

Chinese support for Inyenzi activities contributed to a heightened sense of insecurity on the part of the Rwandan Hutu officialdom. The Chinese were allowed by the Burundian authorities to maintain a guerrilla training camp near a major Tutsi refugee relocation center at Murore in Eastern Burundi. In 1963 the Chinese trained, armed, and financed Tutsi guerrillas launched an attack against Rwanda which has since been known as the Bugesera invasion. The attackers reached within a short distance of Rwanda's capital, Kigali, before they were repulsed by the Belgian advised Rwandan army. The trauma within Rwanda almost equaled that of the 1959-61 ethnic conflict. In the wake of near-victory by the Tutsi, the Hutu rampaged against Tutsi still living in Rwanda and thousands were attacked, killed, or forced to flee into neighboring states: Burundi, Zaire, and Uganda.[13] Despite the Inyenzi defeat and the terrible cost in lives, the Chinese continued to support the exiled Tutsi monarchists.[14] This support began to dwindle when official Chinese representation in Burundi ended abruptly in 1965; it stopped once China and Rwanda normalized their relations in 1972. Once Rwanda was willing to recognize Peking Chinese aid to the Inyenzi appears to have stopped. This fact points to the unideological but very pragmatic nature of the Chinese support to the Inyenzi all along.

BURUNDI

The involvement with Inyenzi helped the Chinese to penetrate into Burundi even before diplomatic relations were established. Ideological reasons played a minor part in influencing the Tutsi refugees toward Peking.[15] Rwanda is a clear example of Chinese intervention in another state's internal affairs, and promoting groups who had very weak ideological credentials.* For the Inyenzi, a desperate group of powerful "has-beens," Chinese material support was the only hope for a successful return to Rwanda on their terms. The Chinese support promoted "tribalism" within Rwanda in diametric contradiction of avowed Chinese ideological condemnation of tribalism as a form of feudalism.

The argument that involvement with the Inyenzi served to promote Chinese penetration into Burundi is supported by the fact that the Bugesera invasion was launched in December 1963 at the same time that the Burundian government established diplomatic relations with Peking. The Chinese made a number of personal contacts among Burundian Tutsi sympathetic to the Inyenzi cause. These individuals were quite active in arranging to have diplomatic relations established with Peking. Chinese involvement in Burundian politics was equally opportunistic; it contributed to a worsening of Burundi's internal problems.

The possibilities for political opportunism by China in Africa have been noted: "there are always some groups or factions ready to deal with the Chinese."[16] Peking sought out these groups in an attempt to use Burundi as a springboard into the richer and more strategic Congo.

---

*This very much goes against the impression given by Larkin that China did not involve itself in internal politics. It also leads one to question an analysis of Chinese policy on the basis of ideological commitment alone. The involvement by Peking in Rwandan politics was based on the logic of pursuing Chinese national interest. Support for the Inyenzi is not an example of supporting the spread of Marxism-Maoism as an ideology but rather one of the end justifies the means. The end pursued here was the victory for Chinese supported rebels in the Congo and the need to have Rwanda as a privileged sanctuary through which to tunnel aid to those rebels.

Chinese activities began in 1962 at independence and continued surreptitiously until December 1963.[17] The Chinese, guided by their experience with Rwanda where the Tutsi were their allies, sought out Tutsi oppositionists in Burundi rather than Hutu.

Burundi in ethnic terms was fairly similar to Rwanda. The Tutsi, a minority of some 15-16 percent, had enjoyed considerable political, economic, and social advantages until a few years before Belgium granted independence in July 1962. The ethnic violence in Rwanda had influenced Burundi, and the more politically active Burundian politicians of each ethnic group viewed their opposites with a great deal of suspicion. Above this ethnic antagonism was the chiefly structure of a somewhat westernized monarchy. Many Hutu and Tutsi politicians were unhappy with their reigning king, Mwambutsa IV, and with his tendency to rule somewhat capriciously while taking extended vacations in Europe whenever the country faced a serious problem. This provided just the "unsettled political milieu" that attracted the Chinese in the early 1960s.[18]

The Chinese wished to establish a dependence relationship with Burundi to promote their interests in the neighboring Congo and Rwanda.* However, the King of Burundi was distrustful of China's ideology since it was anti-aristocratic at the very least (despite the support for King Kigeri V of Rwanda).

According to one account, the decision to establish diplomatic relations with Peking was engineered without the Mwami's agreement, while he was on one of his extended visits abroad. Upon his return, July 29, 1964, he refused to give the Chinese ambassador designate (in Burundi since April 1964) an audience. He is said to have sent this emissary a note which stated somewhat bluntly, "The accreditation of the representative of the People's Republic of China will take place as soon as the policies of the United States and China have become somewhat harmonized."[19] He finally received the ambassador on September 16, while Burundi radio commented rather loudly on a technical and financial cooperation agreement that had just been concluded with the United States.

A Hutu Prime Minister, Pierre Ngendendumwe, under whom relations with China were established, was dismissed by the Mwami in May 1963. A Tutsi Prime Minister, Albin Nyamoya,

---

*The Chinese are said to have concluded an aid agreement with Burundi in 1964 to provide them with $3 million.

was called upon to put together a new government. The
Tutsi opposition had been able to convince Mwambutsa to
dismiss the Hutu Prime Minister because he had established
relations with China. The new Prime Minister was closely
connected with the Tutsi oppositionists whom the Chinese
had been courting for quite some time. Almost immediately
Chinese influence in Burundi soared. The Chinese success
was due to their style: a traditional preoccupation with
personal relationships, their predisposition to think in
terms of status and hierarchy which may have prejudiced
them in favor of the Tutsi, and their policy of seeking
contacts beyond formal diplomatic ones on whom they pressed
lavish gifts and goods.[20] As Lemarchand aptly put it:
"the Chinese quickly discovered the venality of Burundi
politicians."[21] The extent of the Chinese use of gifts to
corrupt Burundian Tutsi is well documented in several
sources.[22] The Chinese also courted certain Tutsi leaders
in the country's political party youth movement, the
Jeunesse Nationale Rwagasore, as well as Tutsi who with
Chinese funds and help, established a local trade union--
The Burundi Federation of Workers.

The Chinese interest in Burundi in no way turned
about an ideological concern for an amelioration of the
internal sociopolitical conditions of that state, but was
a function of logistical support China was providing to
the rebellions led by Gbenye, Soumialot, and Olenga in the
Kivu which bordered Rwanda and Burundi. Owing to this,
Burundi presented a situation replete with contradictions
for China's theoretical position on Africa and on revolution.

The Tutsi whom China supported made radical foreign
policy statements but were interested primarily in sup-
pressing any potential Hutu threat in purely power terms.
The Chinese did not support those Tutsi who were more moderate on ethnic relations and were willing to allow the
majority Hutu to play a greater role in the country's
politics; this amounted to support for the most elitist
faction within Burundi. Even the King and certain of his
close advisors appeared more willing than this faction to
share power with the Hutu majority.

During 1964 Hutu leaders became increasingly alarmed
over rumors that the Chinese-supported Tutsi hard-liners
were preparing to overthrow the monarchy to establish a
minority Tutsi regime of a racist nature, dedicated to
keeping the Hutu masses under Tutsi domination. Chinese
influence within Burundi had become so extensive that
relations with the central government of Zaire reached an

all-time low. On August 10, 1964 Burundi's embassy in the
Zairian capital, Kinshasa, was sacked.[23] The King of
Burundi decided to remove the Tutsi faction that had allowed Chinese influence to grow and asked the same Hutu
whom he had dismissed earlier to form a new government.
The incumbent was assassinated on January 15, 1965, shortly after he was asked to form the new government, and
China was implicated in the murder, although this was
later denied. Several leading Tutsi who were known to
have received funds from the Chinese were arrested in connection with the assassination; caches of arms were discovered. This confirmed suspicions of Burundi's authorities that these Tutsi, with Chinese support, were planning
some action against the monarchy. The King decreed mar-
tial law, had the Chinese embassy cordoned off, and asked
the Chinese to close their embassy and leave. China's official stay in Burundi was just barely a year in length.[24]
The Chinese were expelled in February 1965 and diplomatic
relations were "temporarily" suspended. However, their
influence was not ended and they continued to support the
more intransigent Tutsi radicals.

Ethnic relations continued to deteriorate. In part
it was the availability of Chinese support for the more
hard-line Tutsi that contributed to this by making it
profitable for them to pass themselves off as anti-Hutu
and to associate Hutu in Burundi with Hutu in Rwanda. By
October 1965 Hutu-Tutsi tension reached an intensity that
Burundi had never experienced in its past. Hutu leaders
attempted to launch a popular uprising but it was poorly
organized and failed. The Tutsi were able to capitalize
on this to kill off the leading Hutu intellectuals and
within several months in November 1966, to overthrow the
monarchy and replace it with a Tutsi dominated republic.
During all this time, the Chinese continued to support
more extremist Tutsi ethnics with whom they had cultivated
close personal ties before, and during the year China had
hoped for a diplomatic representation in Burundi.

The new regime in Burundi was headed by a Titsi military officer, Colonel Michel Micombero, and the army's influence was rather prominent. Since most military assistance came from Belgium--and Belgium had not recognized
the Peking regime--Burundi's new authorities were somewhat
hesitant to resume relations with Peking. Owing to this,
the Chinese attempted to use their personal allies to sub-
vert the new government and to force a resumption of relations. When the Chinese were asked to leave in 1965 they
informed Burundi that it was an imperialist plot and that

China would welcome a resumption of relations at any time. In September 1966 the Burundi Foreign Minister, Pie Masumbuko, visited Brazzaville, where Chinese influence was still officially present. Masumbuko was one of those Tutsi whom the Chinese had subsidized with lavish presents and funds. He is rumored to have been an important link in the illicit arms shipments made by the Chinese to Congolese and Rwandan guerrillas.[25]

While in Brazzaville, Masumbuko announced that Burundi was ready to resume relations with Peking. After he returned to Burundi, Masumbuko was relieved of his position for this unauthorized act. In 1967 the Chinese welcomed the Burundian Minister of Education, Francois Gisamare, at Peking. The visit was an unofficial one and not welcomed by Burundi's President, Colonel Micombero. Gisamare was traveling in his capacity as an official of the country's single party youth movement which was dominated by pro-Chinese Tutsi. The Tutsi pro-Chinese faction included the Foreign Prime Minister Niyongabo, once himself the head of the youth movement, and the Cabinet Chief at the Presidency, Gilles Bimazabute, who had been a student activist in France. The Prime Minister arranged the establishment of diplomatic relations with North Korea in March 1967, while the Cabinet chief had announced two months earlier a press conference at which the resumption of relations with Peking would be announced. The conference was not held because President Micombero objected; the North Korean presence was an alternate strategy for reestablishing Chinese influence. It is known that some Chinese came to Burundi traveling on North Korean diplomatic passports.* The two pro-Chinese Tutsi officials were dismissed on March 13 and by mid-April anonymous tracts appeared calling for the overthrow of President Micombero. The move failed and several suspected pro-Chinese Tutsi were imprisoned.[26]

Chinese activity in Burundi had helped to precipitate a Tutsi takeover. However, they had miscalculated: a conservative, pro-Western military leader captured the revolution.[27] Since the Tutsi regime was unwilling to resume relations, the Chinese resorted to a pragmatic "derogation of normal diplomatic activities, to a place behind that of informed connections."[28] One side effect of the

---

*During 1964 two Chinese made daily morning visits to an African township outside the capital. It was presumed these Chinese met with Tutsi clients.

Chinese influence against President Micombero was an attempt by this Tutsi leader to draw closer to the Soviet Bloc. Accusations that Chinese propaganda was directed from Tanzania against the Republic of Burundi were followed by the arrival of a Czechoslovak ambassador. His arrival received unusually friendly commentary on Burundi's official radio.[29]

The Chinese attempt at subversion continued despite setbacks. In September 1971 the new ambassador from North Korea (China's unofficial go-between) was made to wait for an extended period before he was received by President Micombero. This action was in retaliation against subversive documents given to the Burundi single party youth movement by North Korean youth militants in which Micombero was stigmatized in veiled terms as a lackey of American imperialism.[30]

SHIFTS IN CHINESE POLICY

Chinese policy in 1971-72 shifted gear as it became increasingly apparent that Peking would be admitted to the United Nations and feelers were put out to seek a diplomatic modus vivendi with the United States. With the exception of Southern Africa where the governments of independent African states also favored political subversion, Peking slowly abandoned its earlier policy of support for revolutionary parties and subversive activities in opposition to established African governments. Having failed to achieve dependency relations by revolutionary means, and given a changed international context after 1971, the Chinese turned to a more flexible policy and worked to expand influence through more conventional bilateral trade and aid agreements.

In the implementation of Chinese policy in Central Africa during the first period of their attempt to gain influence, 1960-70, they failed to avoid the pitfalls of "unreasonable jeopardy to useful government ties and ill-chosen attachment to half-hearted opportunities."[31] Evidence cited in a number of sources points to a conclusion that the Chinese did contribute to international politics in host states. The Chinese attempted in several states (Burundi is one example) to influence local politics and to exploit internal cleavages to bring groups willing to cooperate with Peking to power. The opportunism in Chinese policy, as in big power politics practiced by other major non-African states, amounted to supporting opposi-

tionists where China judged the existent government to be
an inviting target (as in the Congo [Leopoldville], Rwanda,
and Burundi) but withholding support where the opposition
did not serve Peking's purpose (as in the case of the Hutu
oppositionists in Burundi). Even where a government dealt
with China, as Burundi did in 1963-64, Peking desired unconditional support and worked with Tutsi oppositionists
because the monarchy also maintained close ties with the
West.

The different sets of priorities and goals among varying target groups in central African states, as well as
between these groups and the Chinese actors, made it impossible for China to escape inconsistencies. The nature and
thrust of Chinese influence differed given the very different nature of each state's internal politics. In the Congo
the Chinese supported what they judged to be revolutionary
groups which fought in the name of social change and social
justice.[32] To foster a climate favorable to the revolutionary bands operating in the Congo the Chinese were willing to assist a Tutsi ethnic minority in Burundi, and in
Rwanda subjugating the peasant masses who belonged to a
different ethnic group, the Hutu. This amounted to supporting groups who pushed for a regime based on social injustice, and this support was given because these groups
could be counted upon to exercise control over their respective states and willingly cooperate in making both
states available to the Chinese to serve as privileged
sanctuaries for aid funneled to the rebels in Zaire.

In pursuing its ambition to establish client regimes
in Rwanda and Burundi, the Peking policymakers exploited
a source of weakness in many new African states--ethnic
antagonisms. They also courted potential oppositionists,
many of whom had the most flimsy of revolutionary credentials. Indeed it is difficult to find anywhere a definition of what Peking understood to be radical leaders or
radical movements. Given the inconsistencies that charac-
terize Chinese intervention in Rwanda, Burundi, and the
then Congo, radical meant to Peking someone who supported
the People's Republic of China, much as moderate meant to
American decision-makers someone who supported the West
(and more specifically, the positions of the United
States).[33]

POST-1971 CHINESE INVOLVEMENT IN CENTRAL AFRICA

The aura of legal legitimacy and power conferred by
China's seating at the United Nations in the fall of 1971

made it easier to obtain normal diplomatic relations with
existent independent African governments. Increased bilateral diplomatic recognition from West European states
and relations with the United States further facilitated
this since it removed the fear of reprisals against dealing with Peking. In addition China's economic and technical assistance to Tanzania and Zambia impressed most African leaders. The Chinese committed $400 million on gen-
erous terms: interest-free long-term credit made available
in installments with provision for a long grace period with
a repayment schedule spread over one or two decades.[34]

By 1973, even the once most anti-Chinese governments--
Zaire (Congo), Ethiopia, and Madagascar--had established
diplomatic relations and negotiated aid and trade agreements with Peking. The new international climate and
China's success in gaining recognition for her status as
a big power was reflected in a shift of policy "to extend
and diversify its relations as well as to look for unconditional allies. As the example of Zaire already shows,
Peking deals easily with regimes judged subservient to
capitalism by a section of African intellectuals."[35]

The Chinese still appear to be interested in establishing clientships in Africa--that is, a dependency on
China which will provide political and economic leverage
to Chinese policymakers with regard to the target state(s).
What has shifted is the maturation in Chinese outlook, the
understanding that tightly held clients are not possible,
and a realization of the need for flexible relationships.

In the implementation of Chinese aid, credits extended and their repayments are spread out over a 30- to
40-year period. Agreements are concluded with states that
have strong ties to the West (as Zaire). Much of the
credit, which is bilateral, is promised not as cash but in
the form of supplied equipment and expertise, while repayment is expected to be made in local African primary or
processed items. The distribution of aid is balanced with
significant cultural and military aids. China seems to be
embarked on a policy of extending its influence to create
the markets of tomorrow for its economy, as well as for
political support on international matters. This behavior,
pragmatic and flexible, does not differ from the pattern
of "big and superpower" relations with Africa displayed by
other states: the USSR, the United States, England,
France, etc. It carries with it a stigma since the "Chinese may lose among those who have viewed Peking as an
exception to power politics among the great powers."[36]

TABLE 3.1

African Relations with the People's Republic of China

Country	Diplomatic Relations	Other Agreements	UN Vote 1970	1971*
Burundi	Established Jan. 1964. Broken off Feb. 1965. Renewed Oct. 1971. (Ambassador Chen Feng)	E, T, C	Yes	Yes
Rwanda	Established Nov. 1971. (Ambassador Huang Shih-Hsieh)	E, C	Yes	No
Zaire	Established Nov. 1973 (Announce decision to recognize PRC). (Ambassador Kung Ta Fei)	N.D.	No	No

*Albanian Resolution of 1971 to seat the People's Republic of China as the legitimate and sole government of China.

E = Economic, T = Trade, C = Cooperation, N.D. = No Data.

Burundi

The big power opportunism inherent in actual Chinese policy was pointed up sharply by Peking's reaction to the brutal suppression of a popular revolt in Burundi during 1972. The details of the revolt and its aftermath have been studies elsewhere.[37] Chinese policy was, in 1972, no longer made in terms of goals pursued in the adjacent Congo (now Zaire); it was based on the new flexible approach: to deal with and accept existent African governments provided they had official diplomatic relations with Peking. Diplomatic relations had been resumed with Burundi after China was seated in the UN. A Chinese delegation visited Burundi for the celebration of the African republic's fifth anniversary, November 28, 1971. President Micombero gave a speech in which he played down revolution, a veiled warning to both the Chinese and the Tutsi faction closely identified with Chinese policy in the past.

The Burundian President also gave the Chinese a warm
greeting in the same speech. On January 3 (or 6), 1972,
Burundian officials signed an economic and technical cooperation agreement with China at Peking.[38] The details
of this agreement are as follows:

Commercial Agreement:
    1. Both parties commit themselves to favor commer-
cial exchanges.
    2. Both parties agree to apply the most favored na-
tion treatment.
    3. Payment will be made in convertible currency.
    4. Agreement is renewable and valid for one year.

Cooperation Agreement:
    1. 50 million Yuan (Renmenbi) at 35.545 Burundi
Francs will be loaned.
    2. Installments will be spread over 5 years.
    3. Repayment will be over 10 years, 1/10 per year
from January 1, 1982–December 31, 1991.
    4. Serve to furnish to Burundi equipment and mer-
chandise and converted into local currency for payment of
local projects to be determined by both governments.
(These are a dam and central for electricity on the Mugera
or Ruvubu; extension of macadamized road to Burundi in the
south from Bujumbura; execution of agricultural projects
along the Zaire border in the Ruzizi plain.)

Military Aid:
    1. Construct a base near Rwandan border in the
north, and three others (but none in southern Burundi).
    2. Provide military advisors.

The information contained in this agreement is a com-
posite of data obtained from a variety of sources and subject to caution. The projects are still in the preliminary study phase. In Burundi the Chinese are moving
ahead with a project to build a dam, to take over a bank-
rupt textile plant, and to build military bases. However,
progress is slow. In Burundi, a state trading corporation has been set up to funnel in Chinese products. The
sale of these imports will be counted toward repayment of
Burundi's credits obtained from the PRC.

During the time Chinese relations were being reestab-
lished, ethnic tension and Tutsi factionalism within
Burundi had worsened. Suddenly, on the night of April 29,

the tensions erupted in a naked confrontation. Hutu rebel
bands attacked in at least three areas, killing local
Tutsi and Hutu who refused to join. According to official
Burundian sources, the rebels were joined by or trained by
Mulelists. The Mulelist connection has been questioned
but whatever, the rebels quickly declared a "liberated"
region in southern Burundi to be the People's Republic at
Martyazo. The revolt was suppressed with extreme brutal-
ity by the Tutsis who controled the armed forces. Hutu
soldiers and officers were executed as well as thousands
of Hutu in government service or at schools independent of
any proven connection to the rebels. It is reported that
the Chinese had placed pressure on Tanzania to offer
Chinese-provided ammunition to Burundi's armed forces to
help in the suppression of the revolt.

The revolt raised doctrinal problems for the Chinese
owing to official statements of ideology. The rebels had
used tactics copied from the Mulelist rebels who in turn
had been led by Chinese-trained guerrillas. It had been
a left-wing popular movement and an uprising of the type
Maoism had called for in ideological terms: Hutu guerrillas operating against a repressive minority regime are
more justifiable clients than the Inyenzi who attacked
Rwanda throughout the 1960s. The suppression after the
uprising was aimed at the Hutu peasantry and the liquida-
tion of any potential leadership among its ranks who could
articulate the interests of the peasants. Yet when the
traditional supplier of arms to Burundi refused any further military assistance (this was Belgium), the Chinese
offered it. They agreed to build a military base near the
Rwandan border to prevent any Hutu guerrilla infiltration
as this region has the densest Hutu population in the country. The Chinese sent advisors to replace Belgian military
advisors whom Belgium plans to withdraw.[39] Chinese deliveries of arms have already been made and a team of Chinese
army engineers held secret talks with the Burundian army
high command in January 1973.[40]

By supplying arms to one side in Burundi as a reward
for past action and promise for future support, China contributed to the capacity of a minority oligarchy to exploit, politically and economically, the masses. Chinese
aid is confirming a status quo situation based on wide-
spread social injustice and Caprice. Assistance to the
Tutsi army provides the ruling oligarchy with the requisite potential power to maintain itself by periodic
slaughter of Hutu opposition, thereby assuring continued
Tutsi supremacy. Thus, China contributes to the thesis

that might makes right.[41] This is in direct contradiction
to what China purports to be its philosophy. This contradiction supports an argument, it would seem, that Chinese
policy is not ideologically motivated.

Rwanda

     The conclusion drawn above is supported by recent
(1971-73) Chinese gestures to Zaire and Rwanda. In November 1971, Rwanda established diplomatic relations with
China. The Taiwanese diplomats and technical assistants
were expelled and on May 13, 1972 an aid and trade agreement was signed in Rwanda's capital, Kigali. The Chinese
have promised $20 million (50 million Jenmenbi or Yuan) in
long-term credit. In June 1972 a Rwandan delegation visited Peking. At an official reception, the Chinese announced that Rwanda's government "won the praise of the
Afro-Asian peoples." Furthermore, "At present, the situation in Africa is excellent. The African people have made
new progress in their struggle to oppose imperialism, colonialism, and neo-colonialism, oppose racial discrimination and to win and safeguard national independence
[against neo-colonialism]."[42] The details of the Rwandan
agreement with China are as follows:

     1.   50 million Yuan (Renmenbi) at 1Y = 40.623 Rwandan
Francs will be loaned.
     2.   Installments will be spread over 5 years: July
1, 1972-June 30, 1977.
     3.   Repayment will be over 15 years, 1/15 per year.
July 1, 1987-June 30, 2002.
     4.   Both governments will facilitate commercial ex-
changes and conclude a trade agreement.
     5.   China undertakes to provide a number of engineers
and technicians to help in technical assistance.   (The
Rwandans have been reluctant to allow the Chinese to bring
in large numbers of Chinese laborers.)
     6.   The salaries and conditions of labor for Chinese
assistants is to be agreed upon in consultation with the
two governments.

     The information contained in this agreement is a com-
posite of data obtained from a variety of sources and subject to caution. The projects are still in the preliminary study phase. The Rwandans have acted to prevent a
large number of Chinese workers being brought in for road

construction work (see Map 3.1). There has been some indication that not all Rwandan officials are satisfied with
the Chinese but nothing concrete.

This praise was for a government that condemned President Micombero's repression of the Hutu majority in
Burundi. These Rwandans were also the same Hutu against
whom the Inyenzi had fought for an entire decade with Chinese support. In June 1972 the Chinese embassy opened at
Kigali confirming the shift in policy.* The decision to
shift support away from the Tutsi refugee groups, the Inyenzi, and give it to the Hutu incumbents in Rwanda further
lends credence to viewing Chinese policy as a flexible one.
The Chinese have, in a very realistic way, attempted to discover who has power, or who could take power, and then work
with that group. The flexibility of African foreign policy has perhaps led Chinese decision-makers to conclude
that the once unacceptable cooperation with nationalist
bourgeois regimes is now possible. It may well be that
Chinese decision-makers accept that complete victory in
terms of China's earlier ideologically motivated foreign
policy goals cannot be achieved given the great variation
in African states. Chinese policy, as policy of other
states involved in many parts of Africa, is forced to
glide over these internal contradictions or decide not to
recognize most African governments.

Zaire

China's most recent central African success was its
overture to Zaire. President Mobutu had declared in
April 1972 that the condition for recognition of Peking
was evidence of a "radical and absolute" change in China's
attitude toward Zaire.[43] Mobutu personally has been implicated in the death of two major Zairian rebels admired
by Peking: Pierre Mulele and Patrice Lumumba. Nonetheless Peking seems to have decided that it was costly and
unproductive to keep pushing for a Chinese inspired revolution in Zaire, and was prepared for a pragmatic relationship with the existing nationalist leadership. There
are unconfirmed reports that the Chinese went so far as to

_____

*Relations with North Korea were established on April
22, 1972. The Rwandans also signed a cultural agreement
with the USSR in April and with Czechoslovakia in November.

MAP 3.1

Foreign Assistance for Road Projects: An Example
of Aid Diversification   (Rwanda)

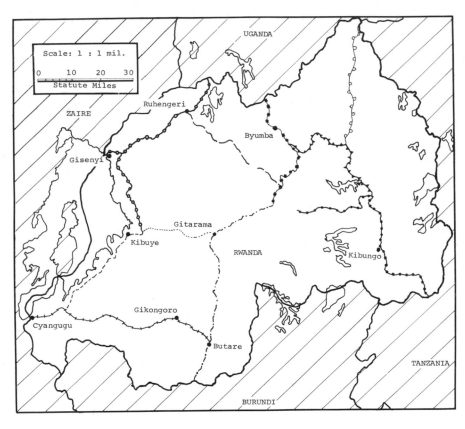

.—.—.—.— European Development Fund
——————— International Bank for Reconstruction and Development
---------- African Development Bank
.... West Germany
●–●–●–●–● People's Republic of China
+–+–+–+–+–+ United States
▲–▲–▲–▲–▲ Belgium
o–o–o–o–o– Soviet Union
■–■–■–■–■ International Development Association
◡–◡–◡–◡– North Korea

recognize Mobutu's own ambitions to achieve political hegemony in eastern central Africa. China signed an agreement
to provide $100 million worth of long-term credit to Zaire
for agricultural projects.

In January 1973 Mobutu made a triumphant trip to
Peking where Mao confided that he had "lost much money and
arms attempting to overthrow" the Zairian leader.[44] This
newest demarche in central Africa is in a state where
China had focused its energies on creating a revolution;
it is evidence of the flexible, straightforward policy now
practiced by Peking.

The details of the Chinese agreement with Zaire are
as follows:

Yuan equivalent of $100 million U.S. will be loaned.
(The details were not available but the author has been
told they resemble closely those given for the Rwandan
and Burundian agreements.)

The projects are still in the preliminary study phase.
Chinese agricultural teams have toured parts of the country. Movement is slow in implementation of Chinese aid,
but it is progressing.

CONCLUSION

The questions remain what potential does China have
to establish dependency relationships in Africa, and does
China have an interest in tight clientships it had desired
in the early 1960s. China is itself a developing country.
Although it has made spectacular promises of aid credits,
these are of a long-term nature. It seems safe to assume
that China will be unable to make more large sums available for the next 10 to 20 years after this first round
is completed.* The Chinese agreements have an emphasis on
long-term repayment in kind which may lead to a Chinese
"neo-colonialism" (in competition with the "neo-colonialism"
of the Soviet Union and various capitalist states).

China's economic productivity is increasing more
quickly and on a larger scale than economies in various
independent African states. As time goes on, China may

---

*The limitations of China's own economy is admitted
openly by the Chinese. They have attempted to capitalize
on this to establish a better rapport with African
statesmen who still remember the more aggressive China
of the 1960s.

be able to tie up larger portions of African foreign trade, thereby shifting trade patterns. This shift will, in all probability, bring with it economic leverage and this will have political implications. Shifts in trade patterns have already begun to occur in east Africa.

There is also strong feeling that states in Africa which had once supported American positions at the UN may now start to follow a more independent line and even support China on certain issues. The implications in a shift of trade and influence patterns with respect to China has not gone unnoticed by the Africans--they have also learned much from the initial ten years of independence and the "ideological scramble" for the continent. Jeune Afrique, an African periodical of note, commented candidly that China is a big power "in gestation" with its own interests to defend and that "African states must be conscious of this."[45]

China has just begun a long-range economic involvement in Africa and it will be some time before anyone will know what the payoffs and costs for Peking are. We suggest that China's policy toward independent Black Africa and North Africa will increasingly reflect the types of interaction big powers tend to have with developing areas. China will probably accept more and more the syndrome of big power competition for clients that has characterized U.S.-USSR-EEC relations in sub-Saharan Africa: an emphasis on trade, cultural relations, and obtaining support for international positions favorable to (Chinese) national interest.

It is of course not easy to predict the future of Chinese foreign policy. The very recent turbulence within China, with its implications for Peking's foreign policy, may portend some zigzags which are unforeseeable as of this writing. Independent of such short-term shifts, we would argue that the long-term direction of China's foreign policy is what we have suggested: movement toward big power behavior.

It is difficult to imagine what major policy changes China will opt for in its dealings with Africa, or reasons for China to do so. A renewed drive for ideological purity at home need not necessarily cause a shift in Sino-African relations since the Chinese have come to view Africa in the aggregate as part of the have-not oppressed world which she desires to lead. If anything, there may be increased pressure placed upon the leadership in African states to be more forceful in criticizing the capitalist West and the USSR. Those in the Chinese policymaking process who oppose harmonizing relations with the United States may push for increased use of international forums as ancillary arenas in which to criticize American policy and its sociopolitical system. But this would amount to an intensification or change in emphasis of existing policy. More probably there might be stepped up assistance to splinter liberation movements in Portuguese and minority dominated southern Africa, possibly, some support to an oppressed majority like the Hutu of Burundi. But this raises the question of how Machiavellian is Chinese foreign policy? Is it not possible that China finds it advantageous to let such problems fester and place blame for them on the United States and the USSR?

A potential but hardly expected turn in policy might be a reemergence of Chinese introspection which characterized the first great cultural revolution. Were this to occur, the Chinese might decide to withdraw from Africa and leave projects unfinished. This would appear irrational but it did happen to some extent in the mid-1960s. The singular indicator that China would not do this is the fact that throughout the cultural revolution Chinese commitment to the TanZam Railway remained present and was acted upon.

Whatever the potential short-range shifts in its policy toward Africa, the political realities of that continent limit the policies that can be pursued other than yanking one's diplomats out. African states are not that well organized and still face many social problems related to modernization as well as the mere passage of time. Most of these states and their political institutions are weak, and there are limits as to what an outside state can expect to achieve. For this reason, China's activity will be limited as is that of all other outside states with a presence in Africa. China's political benefits will be limited because of these factors as well. It is doubtful that the Chinese would again commence support to oppositionists in Black African states because they have learned that this will not work very well. Besides, China is recognized by almost every African state and need not dwell on getting its presence accepted. To the extent that China is interested in a ready supply of minerals and primary products, its foreign policy may dwell on aid projects in Africa that will help to move those commodities in China's direction and to secure their continued flow. Such a policy requires China to capitalize on ways in which she and Africa complement each other and share global concerns.

China's foreign relations are not hammered out in a vacuum. Africa is far removed from the immediate geo-political concerns of China's leaders and it is difficult to see why China would look to shift its policies toward that continent at this time. The present level of China's economy places critical limits on additional outflows to Africa or the provision of additional arms for liberation movements and/or oppositionists. In part the low profile maintained by the superpowers in Africa has permitted the Chinese to obtain major support politically with little in the way of aid outflow on a comparative basis. Why should Chinese policymakers choose to ignore this now? There are the gains China could anticipate in any ideological war of words that may break out once more against the Americans and the Soviets. In any such renewed ideological disputes, to have the African voice on the side of the Chinese would bolster their position, and the Chinese know this.

NOTES

1. Bruce D. Larkin, China and Africa: 1949-70 (California: University of California Press, 1971), p. 72.
2. Rene Lemarchand, Rwanda and Burundi (New York: Praeger Publishers, 1970), p. 390.
3. Le Monde, March 19, 1973.
4. On this point see Rene Servoise, "Les Relations de la Chine avec l'Afrique au XVe siecle," Le Mois en Afrique, no. 6 (June 1966): 30-45, passim.
5. This point is made by Larkin, op. cit., p. 45.
6. Mao said that "if we can take the Congo, we can have all of Africa." This was most probably meant in an ideological and not imperialist sense. A correspondent wrote in the Christian Science Monitor (July 6, 1965), ". . . until early 1964 Chinese diplomacy had been concentrated on Egypt, Algeria, Mali, Guinea and Ghana. . . . But it has shifted its emphasis to East and Central African states where domestic conflicts may give its [China's] revolution easier access."
7. For more details see Larkin, op. cit., pp. 55-57. Peking's recognition of the Stanleyville government was intended as a sign of support. It failed to take into account the complex realities of Congolese politics and the willingness of the "rebels" to compromise with the central authorities. Within a short while, the Stanleyville regime put itself out of existence by entering into a coalition with politicians leading the central government

at Leopoldville (now Kinshasa). In 1964 Peking did not commit the same "blunder" in its support to rebel leaders in the Congo although these rebels headed movements which controlled large sections of the Congo. Peking did not extend diplomatic recognition to any of these groups as the legitimate government of the country.

8. Some sources state there were even more Chinese than this. See Emmanuel John Hevi, African Student in China (New York: Praeger, 1964), p. 108; Lemarchand, op. cit., p. 390. Lemarchand placed the figure at 24.

9. Hevi, op. cit., p. 107.

10. Rwanda, in its constitution, forbade any communist activity on its territory. Rwanda also recognized Taiwan as the official government of China until 1972. For these reasons, Peking refused to accept the government of Kayibanda as a legitimate one. See J. Vanderlinden, La Republique Rwandaise (Paris: Editions Berger-Levrault, 1970), p. 30.

11. See Rachel Yeld, "Implications of Experience with Refugee Settlements," Conference Paper, East African Institute of Social Research, Kampala, 1964, pp. 1-13.

12. The Tutsi refugees were scattered in Tanzania, Uganda, and Zaire. Lemarchand states that the Chinese transferred £17,000 to King Kigeri's personal account in Dar es Salaam, the capital of Tanzania. He further claims that the arms and ammunition were supplied to Tutsi refugees via ports in Kenya and Tanzania. Lemarchand, op. cit., p. 227. Cooley claims Kigeri began to collect a regular pension from China after settling in Kenya (no date given), and that several thousand pounds sterling were provided to organize Tutsi refugees at irregular intervals. J. Cooley, East Wind Over Africa (New York: Walker and Co., 1965). Cooley claimed arms and ammunition were shipped overland to Tutsi refugees in both Burundi and Uganda.

13. Aaron Segal, Massacre in Rwanda, Fabian Research Series, 240 (London Fabian Society, 1964).

14. According to Lemarchand, op. cit., p. 227, the £17,000 transferred to Kigeri occurred after the Bugesera defeat, and China confirmed supplying arms and ammunition to the Inyenzi.

15. Lemarchand, op. cit., p. 389.

16. Larkin, op. cit., pp. 145-46. Although Larkin does not use this in the context we propose, namely, to indicate a certain cynicism in China's policy.

17. This is spelled out in an article by a "radical" Tutsi from Burundi. See Gilles Bimazubute, "Burundi:

Les relations diplomatiques entre le Burundi et la Chine,"
Remarques Africaines 7, no. 236, 14-17.

18. See Larkin, op. cit., pp. 145-46. P. Decraene
also makes this point, "Difficultes communistes chinoises
en Afrique Noire," _Le Mois en Afrique_, no. 6 (July 1966):
85. Decraene claimed Peking's goal was to maintain a zone
of political instability in Burundi.

19. Quoted in _Le Soir_ (Belgium), September 22, 1964.
See Also _Africa 1964_ (England), no. 19 (September 25,
1964): 1-2.

20. A. Doak Barnett stressed the continuities he
found in China when he visited it after relations with the
United States had been somewhat improved. When one thinks
of the myth that surrounds the Tutsi as natural born rulers with a deep sense of status superiority, it would appear that this might attract the Chinese who "still show
deep rooted traditional predispositions to think in terms
of status and hierarchy, stress protocol, submit to authority, conform to orthodoxy and fit into the roles required
of them." (A. Doak Barnett, "There are Warts, Too," New
York _Times Magazine_, April 8, 1973, p. 101. The status
and occupational divisions within Burundi between the
smooth, genteel Tutsi rulers and the much less refined
Hutu peasant or merchant seems to have had its impact on
the Chinese. This is not strange since the Tutsi and Hutu
have had a similar impact on American, Soviet, Belgian,
French, and other officials who have spent time on a tour
in Burundi.

21. Lemarchand, op. cit., p. 391.

22. See Lemarchand, Cooley, Hevi, and Larkin, op. cit.

23. _Africa Research Bulletin (Political)_ 1, no. 8
(August 1-31, 1964): 1296. Relations were suspended between both states on August 19, 1964.

24. Tareq Y. Ismael, "The People's Republic of China
and Africa," _The Journal of Modern African Studies_ 9, no.
4 (December 1971): 517. Tareq wrote "The finishing touch
was the discovery at Kitega of an arms shipment, apparently for Rwandan refugees." It is more probable the arms
were to be delivered to Congolese rebels as well.

25. See Lemarchand, op. cit., p. 221.

26. See ibid., pp. 450-53.

27. On this point see R. Hull, "China in Africa,"
Issue 2, no. 3 (Fall 1972): 49-50.

28. Ismael, op. cit., p. 526. The Chinese were probably unhappy when Burundi, Rwanda, and the Congo signed a
mutual security pact in September 1966. (_Africa Bulletin -
Political_ 3, no. 9 [September 1-30, 1966]: 607b). On the

previous July 26, Burundi and the Congo concluded an agreement for the extradition of Congolese rebels. The Burundi authorities promised to request rebels or refugees who obtained asylum to return to the Congo. This normalization of regional interstate relations made it impossible to support officially Congolese leftist rebels or Rwandan Inyenzi guerrillas. Both of these groups were major Chinese clients. See Africa Bulletin - Political 3, no. 7 (July 1-31, 1966): 596c.

29. "Burundi: China's Hand in Spiel," Internationales Afrika Forum 3, nos. 9/10 (September-October 1967): 439-40.

30. This information was supplied to the author by a second-hand source who was in Burundi at the time. The North Korean Vice-Minister of Foreign Affairs stayed two weeks in the Burundi capital, but his efforts failed to obtain an audience for the new ambassador.

31. Larkin, op. cit., p. 157. Although Larkin suggests the Chinese did try to avoid this, their policies in central Africa indicate they did not succeed.

32. The analysis of the 1964 Kwilu rebellion done in 1965 suggests that the local population saw the rebels as bringing a second independence. This was a more meaningful independence in which the rural peasantry hoped to also benefit, whereas the "first independence" has benefited the officials and more urban populations. Most news reports on the 1964 revolt in the eastern Congo agree that the movement had lightning success among the local populations. See Renee C. Fox, et al., "The Second Independence: A Case Study of the Kwilu Rebellion in the Congo," Comparative Studies in Society and History 8, no. 1 (October 1965): 78-109. The authors emphasized how the Kwilu revolt drew upon general disgruntlement of the rural population "with the material and social consequences of Independence" (p. 91).

33. Larkin, op. cit., p. 160, agrees that Chinese "judgment replaced any objective test of whether or not a person was a Marxist-Leninist." The subjectivity of China's attitude over this was blatant during the maneuvering for a second Bandung conference. China's attitude was inflexible: "Either the conference would follow the Chinese line, or the Chinese would not participate." (Ismael, op. cit., p. 521.)

34. For an analysis of the Chinese effort in Tanzania and Zambia see George T. Yu, Chapter 2, pp. 29-55. The general shift in Chinese policy is discussed in Paul Bertenel, "La Chine et l'Afrique," Jeune Afrique, no. 642 (April 28, 1973)and Jean de la Gueriviere, "La nouvelle realpolitik de la Chine," Le Monde, March 18-19, 1973.

35. Jean de la Gueriviere, op. cit. De la Gueriviere pointed out that Chinese support for the Eritrean Liberation Front dried up when diplomatic relations were established with Ethiopia. It seems safe to assume this happened to the Inyenzi when full diplomatic relations were established with Rwanda's Hutu government in 1972. Paul Bertenel, op. cit., commented that the "Chinese now admit their revolution is not for export, that the Chinese experience is [profoundly Chinese] . . . [with the exception of southern Africa liberation movements, Chinese have little or nothing to do with] pyromaniacs who set fire to African regimes."

36. Ismael, op. cit., p. 528.

37. W. Weinstein, "Conflict and Confrontation in Central Africa: The Revolt in Burundi, 1972," Africa Today 19, no. 4 (Fall 1972): 17-37; W. Weinstein, forthcoming, Pan African Journal.

38. Internationales Afrika Forum 8, no. 2 (February 1972): 106.

39. This information was provided by several primary and secondary sources who asked not to be quoted.

40. Much of this information was provided by several secondary sources close to Burundian politics.

41. Several points attributed to Maoist philosophy seem to suggest the Chinese have made a long-term blunder. Mao has argued that "where [revolutionaries] can outwait [the Foe] . . . time is on their side. . . . The process of struggle itself will force [the enemy] to more desperate acts, which in turn will win men and women to the revolution. In the end the enemy will be overcome." (These points about Maoism are in Larkin, op. cit., pp. 122-23.) Maoist thought seems to imply a Hutu victory is unavoidable. Given the adverse conditions for Hutu peasants and the hostile environment for populist revolutionaries the Chinese model of the "Hutu sea" engulfing the "Tutsi city" may be a source of support to future Hutu revolutionaries.

42. NCNA International Service in English, 17:35 GMT, June 22, 1972. The Rwandans have refused to allow Chinese laborers to work on a proposed road project. Rwanda has diversified road building programs in terms of external support.

43. International Africa Forum 8, no. 4 (April 1972): 249.

44. de la Gueriviere, op. cit.

45. Bertenel, op. cit., p. 66.

4

SOVIET ECONOMIC AID
TO AFRICA: 1959-72
AN OVERVIEW
John D. Esseks

From 1959 through 1973 the Soviet government pledged $1.3 billion in economic assistance to African countries (excluding Egypt) and, by the end of 1973, had delivered to them about $400 million in project aid (see Tables 4.1 and 4.2). Project aid--materials and related technical services supplied, through concessionary credits, for geological surveying and prospecting and for the construction and commissioning of industrial, agricultural, and other facilities--has been the most important category of Soviet assistance, comprising an estimated 80 percent of that state's total economic aid to non-Communist developing countries.[1] Moreover, because the Soviets have published figures for project aid deliveries broken down by recipient country for every year from 1955 to 1972, reasonably accurate estimates of 1973 deliveries can be made.

This chapter evaluates those 15 years of Soviet-African aid relations in terms of (1) the size of the assistance flows relative to both sides' aid ties with other countries; (2) hypotheses as to why some African states had no Soviet economic aid and why a very few others received substantial assistance; (3) some of the apparent benefits realized by the Soviets from their aid efforts in Africa; and (4) speculation about the future

I am very grateful to the Russian Research Center of Harvard University for assistance in preparing this chapter, and, also, for the comments on an earlier draft of the chapter given by Joseph Berliner, Helen Desfosses, and Robert Legvold.

I prefer to classify Egypt as a Middle Eastern rather than African state.

TABLE 4.1

Soviet Economic Aid Commitments to All LDCs and to African Countries, 1954-73
(in millions of U.S. dollars except where indicated otherwise)

	1954-58	1959	1960	1961	1962	1963	1964
Commitments to all LDCs[a]	988	833	395	564	88	160	1,007
Commitments to Africa[b]	--	137	72	192	31	108	217
Africa's share (%)	--	16.4%	18.2%	34.0%	35.2%	67.5%	21.5%
Algeria	--	--	--	--	--	100	127 / 4(g)
Guinea	--	35	17 / 3(g) / 5(t)	--	13	--	--
Ethiopia	--	100 / 2(g)	--	--	--	--	--
Ghana	--	--	40 / 7(t)	42 / 4(t)	--	--	--
Morocco	--	--	--	--	--	--	--
Somalia	--	--	--	44 / 8(t) / 21	3(g)	--	--
Sudan	--	--	--	1(g) / 44	--	--	--
Mali	--	--	--	--	6 / 9(t)	44	--
Kenya	--	--	--	--	--	4(g) / 5(t)	--
Tunisia	--	--	--	28	--	--	--
Sierra Leone	--	--	--	--	--	--	--
Tanzania	--	--	--	--	--	--	--
Uganda	--	--	--	--	--	--	16
Congo-Brazzaville	--	--	--	--	--	--	10
Cameroun	--	--	--	--	--	8	--
Senegal	--	--	--	--	--	--	7
Nigeria	--	--	--	--	--	--	--
Zambia	--	--	--	--	--	--	--
Mauritania	--	--	--	--	--	--	--
Central African Republic	--	--	--	--	--	--	--
Chad	--	--	--	--	--	--	--
Equatorial Guinea	--	--	--	--	--	--	--
Niger	--	--	--	--	--	--	--
Rwanda	--	--	--	--	--	--	--
Upper Volta	--	--	--	--	--	--	--

[a]All dollar figures were converted from roubles at the rate of one rouble equals $1.11. The exchange rate was not altered to take into account the U.S. devaluation of 1971. To do so would have artificially inflated the 1972 and 1973 entries in relation to earlier figures.

[b]Egypt is excluded.

Note: g = grant; t = trade credit. All other commitments listed are lines of credit for projects (factories, power stations, and so on). Information as to which commitment was a grant, trade credit, or line of credit came from a survey of the texts of published aid agreements (see note 5 of the chapter) and of press reports in the Soviet Union and recipient African countries.

1965	1966	1967	1968	1969	1970	1971	1972	1973	Total (1954-73)
193	1,244	269	374	476	194	870	598	622	8,876
28	77	10	--	135	51	197	17	10	1,282
14.5%	6.2%	3.7%	--	28.4%	26.3%	22.6%	2.8%	1.6%	14.4%
--	1(g)	--	--	--	--	189	--	--	421
--	3(t)	--	--	92	--	--	--	--	168
--	--	--	--	--	--	--	--	--	102
--	--	--	--	--	--	--	--	--	93
--	44	--	--	--	36 8(t)	--	--	--	88
--	9(g)	--	--	--	--	3 2(t)	11 6(t)	--	86
--	--	--	--	42	--	--	--	--	64
--	--	--	--	1	--	--	--	--	60
--	--	--	--	--	--	--	--	--	48
--	--	1(t)	--	--	--	--	--	--	34
28(t)	--	--	--	--	--	--	--	--	28
--	20	--	--	--	--	--	--	--	20
--	--	--	--	--	--	--	--	--	16
--	--	--	--	--	--	--	--	4(g)	14
--	--	--	--	--	--	--	--	--	8
--	--	--	--	--	--	--	--	1(g)	8
--	--	--	--	--	7	--	--	--	7
--	--	6	--	--	--	--	--	--	6
--	--	3(t)	--	--	--	--	--	1(g)	4
--	--	--	--	--	--	2	--	--	2
--	--	--	--	--	--	--	--	1(g)	1
--	--	--	--	--	--	1(t)	--	--	1
--	--	--	--	--	--	--	--	1(g)	1
--	--	--	--	--	--	--	--	1(g)	1
--	--	--	--	--	--	--	--	1(g)	1

Sources: U.S. Department of State, Bureau of Intelligence and Research, unclassified research memoranda on trade and aid relations between Communist states and Developing Countries. In recent years they have been entitled Communist States and Developing Countries: Aid and Trade in [the year]. I used also the aid documents listed in note 5 of the chapter.

TABLE 4.2

Soviet Project Aid Deliveries[a] to All LDCs and to African Countries, 1955-73
(in millions of U.S. dollars except where indicated otherwise)

	1955-59	1960	1961	1962	1963	1964	1965	1966
Deliveries to all LDCs[b]	236.5	68.6	138.8	182.5	220.9	297.2	284.1	244.6
Deliveries to Africa[c]	--	.1	9.8	12.9	22.0	25.4	34.3	19.0
Africa's share (%)	--	.1%	7.1%	7.1%	10.0%	8.5%	12.1%	7.8%
Guinea: Soviet aid	--	.1	9.1	7.4	7.4	3.9	1.9	3.5
(Other aid)[d]		na	(2.5)	(10.0)	(23.0)	na	na	na
Algeria: Soviet aid	--	--	--	--	.6	2.0	5.9	1.6
(Other aid)					(276.0)	(252.0)	(140.2)	(116.5)
Mali: Soviet aid	--	--	.6	2.7	3.4	4.1	2.5	3.8
(Other aid)			na	na	na	na	(21.6)	(20.9)
Morocco: Soviet aid	--	--	--	--	--	--	--	--
(Other aid)								
Somalia: Soviet aid	--	--	--	.1	2.7	5.1	5.7	2.3
(Other aid)				(23.5)	(30.4)	na	(29.0)	(29.0)
Ghana: Soviet aid	--	--	.1	2.6	4.6	4.5	8.1	.7
(Other aid)			(2.4)	(5.8)	(27.6)	(40.0)	(60.3)	(80.6)
Sudan: Soviet aid	--	--	--	.1	2.6	3.6	1.0	.4
(Other aid)				(21.0)	(19.7)	na	(30.2)	(17.1)
Ethiopia: Soviet aid	--	--	--	--	--	2.2	6.1	2.9
(Other aid)						na	(26.7)	(40.7)
Uganda: Soviet aid	--	--	--	--	--	--	--	--
(Other aid)								
Tunisia: Soviet aid	--	--	--	--	.7	--	--	2.2
(Other aid)					(95.0)			(92.0)
Congo (B): Soviet aid	--	--	--	--	--	--	.9	.9
(Other aid)							(15.8)	(18.1)
Nigeria: Soviet aid	--	--	--	--	--	--	--	--
(Other aid)								
Tanzania: Soviet aid	--	--	--	--	--	--	--	--
(Other aid)								
Senegal: Soviet aid	--	--	--	--	--	--	--	--
(Other aid)								
Cameroun: Soviet aid	--	--	--	--	--	--	--	--
(Other aid)								

[a]Project aid is defined as materials and related technical services supplied, through concessionary credits, for geological work and the construction of industrial, agricultural, and other facilities.

[b]These dollar figures were converted from roubles at the exchange rate of one rouble equals $1.11. See note a of Table 4.1 for further explanation.

[c]Egypt is excluded.

[d]"Other aid" consisted of net official flows from 16 members of the OECD's Development Assistance Committee and from major multilateral sources.

Note: na = not available.

1967	1968	1969	1970	1971	1972	1973	Total (1955-73)	Average of Annual Ratios of Soviet Aid to "Other" Aid[d]
273.6	293.3	396.9	408.3	366.2	404.7	353.7	4,142.2	
14.0	22.5	39.3	30.4	45.7	69.2	55.2	399.8	
5.1%	7.7%	9.9%	7.4%	12.5%	17.1%	15.6%	9.6%	
1.1	2.2	3.3	2.7	20.1	33.4	29.6	125.7	2.08
na	na	(12.4)	(10.3)	(9.6)	(4.6)	na		
2.9	13.7	26.0	17.2	9.9	20.9	21.1	121.8	.09
(103.3)	(96.1)	(131.3)	(123.4)	(118.1)	(106.8)	na		
5.3	3.7	2.1	.8	.8	.9	.3	31.0	.12
(18.5)	(18.0)	(23.2)	(21.3)	(30.3)	(39.7)	na		
--	--	5.3	4.7	6.2	7.8	1.9	25.9	.06
		(77.4)	(80.4)	(130.3)	(97.3)	na		
2.2	.9	.5	.7	.8	1.2	.4	22.6	.06
na	na	(33.0)	(27.8)	(30.7)	(23.0)	na		
--	--	--	--	--	--	--	20.6	.15
.4	.1	.9	2.0	1.4	.6	.3	13.4	.08
(19.2)	(27.5)	(9.0)	(6.4)	(10.2)	(23.2)	na		
.4	.6	.3	.1	.2	.2	.3	13.3	.04
(28.7)	(46.4)	(38.0)	(39.8)	(47.0)	(47.8)	na		
.2	.3	.5	.4	3.9	3.2	--	8.5	.05
(20.9)	(20.3)	(27.6)	(33.0)	(31.7)	(31.1)			
.9	.7	.2	--	--	--	--	7.6	.03
(104.7)	(75.9)	(116.3)						
.6	.2	--	--	--	.1	1.1	3.8	.03
(20.2)	(33.4)				(22.9)	na		
--	--	--	--	1.1	.3	.1	1.5	.007
				(107.2)	(89.9)	na		
--	.1	.2	.7	.1	.3	.1	1.5	.006
	(33.1)	(37.2)	(51.2)	(61.3)	(58.1)	na		
--	--	--	1.1	.3	--	--	1.4	.02
			(42.7)	(53.2)				
--	--	--	--	.9	.3	--	1.2	.01
				(48.2)	(62.5)			

    Sources: (1) for Soviet project aid deliveries--Vneshnyaya Torgovlya SSSR za . . . god, statisticheskii obzor (Moscow, Vneshtorgizdat), 1956-73; (2) for "Other aid"--OECD, The Flow of Financial Resources to less-developed countries, 1956-63 (Paris, 1963); OECD, Development Assistance Efforts and Policies: 1965 Review (Paris, 1965); OECD, 1969 Review: development assistance (Paris, 1969); and OECD, 1973 Review: development cooperation (Paris, 1973).

direction of Soviet assistance to Africa based on the
record of past benefits and on trends in recent Soviet aid
pledges and project aid deliveries. Before proceeding to
these questions, let me describe the nature and sources of
my data on aid commitments and deliveries.

THE DATA: SOVIET AID COMMITMENTS AND
PROJECT AID DELIVERIES

The Soviet aid commitments listed in Table 4.1 are of
three types: (1) the pledge of grants for educational,
scientific, or health-care facilities and, in 1973, for
food supplies to five famine-stricken countries in the
Sahel region;* (2) the opening of lines of credit for
project aid, that is, geological work and the construction of factories, power stations, and other facilities;
and (3) the extension of trade credits to finance imports
of goods for commercial sales or government use. In at
least five cases, the proceeds of commercial sales were
earmarked to help the recipient government pay its share
of the local currency costs of Soviet-aided construction
projects.[†] Not included in Table 4.1 are the values of
scholarships offered by the Soviet government to African
students; the services of doctors, teachers, and other
personnel serving under cultural exchange agreements; and
the values of occasional small to modest gifts, such as
textbooks and medicines.

In Table 4.1 each known grant commitment is marked
with a "g" in parentheses, while every known trade credit
is labeled with a "t." The promises of grant aid so
listed for 1959 through 1973 aggregate to only $37 million
or about 3 percent of total recorded commitments to African states ($1,282 million--see Table 4.1). The cases of
trade credits aggregate to $90 million or about 7 percent
of total commitments. The remaining entries in Table 4.1,
equaling about $1.1 billion, represent lines of credit for
project aid.

While goods and services offered on a grant basis
normally deserve the label "aid," resources supplied
through credits may not. Since the loans must eventually
be paid back, the "aid" element if any comes from the

---

*Senegal, Mauritania, Chad, Niger, and Upper Volta.
†Those five cases were the trade credits to Guinea
in 1960, to Somalia in 1961, Mali in 1962, Tunisia in
1964, and Somalia in 1971 (see Table 4.1).

"concessionary" nature of the repayment conditions, that is, interest rates, amortization periods, and/or prices (for the aid goods and services or for the exports offered by the aid recipient as repayment) are more liberal than those available at "market terms."[2] According to Soviet sources, trade credits for African countries tended to carry 3 to 3.5 percent interest rates and to be repayable over five years in the recipient state's exports rather than in convertible currency.[3] For Soviet project aid credits, the medium of repayment was reported also to be African exports, in 12 annual and equal installments and at a 2.5 percent interest rate.[4]

The basic terms of project aid credits were usually spelled out for each recipient government in a document entitled "Agreement on Economic and Technical Cooperation between the USSR and [the African country]" and, also, in periodic "protocols" to the initial agreement. I found in published Soviet sources the apparently full texts of ten such agreements and four protocols.[5] They concern nine separate African countries and range in time from 1959 to 1972. Nine of the ten cooperation agreements provided for an interest rate of 2.5 percent. Only one (the 1961 agreement with Tunisia) carried a higher interest rate, 3 percent; and two of the protocols specified that all or part of the credits in question were to be interest-free.[6] All ten cooperation agreements provided for amortizing the loans over 12 years. Of the 12 documents that specified the time when repayments would begin, eight set it at one year after the completion of the delivery of equipment for a project, and two stipulated after the project was commissioned.[7]

The difference was significant. According to these cooperation agreements, the Soviets were fully responsible only for drawing up the project's blueprints and delivering equipment, machinery, and other materials not available locally. The recipient government was responsible for organizing and financing the actual construction, the installation of equipment, and the starting up of the facility, although the Soviets pledged to provide technical assistance for those phases of each project.[8] These were not turn-key projects, with the aid source turning over a fully operational facility. Therefore, if for financial reasons or administrative ineptitude, the host government failed to complete its major contributions within a year after the last component of equipment had been delivered, it would begin paying for a project that was not producing income, saving foreign exchange, or in some other way paying for itself. This problem developed for Ghana and presumably for other African recipients of Soviet aid.[9]

All ten cooperation agreements provided for repayment of the credits in the recipient country's exports, except that for three states (Ghana, Guinea, and Mali) the African government had the option of paying the debt in convertible currency. This option would presumably be taken when the government believed that the exports acceptable to the Soviets as payments would fetch a higher return in hard currency markets.

The levels of Soviet prices--both for the African exports they took in repayment of credits and for their own goods supplied as aid--are critical factors in evaluating the concessionary nature of Soviet credits. The usual 12-year repayment period was no great bargain compared to the 20-year and longer terms offered by other foreign governments and multilateral donors (such as the World Bank), but it was more than commercial sources normally permitted. The nominal interest rates, 2.5 to 3.0 percent, were low enough to qualify as concessionary. However, if the prices of Soviet goods were appreciably higher than those for comparable goods available commercially and/or if Soviet foreign trade organizations offered lower than market prices for African exports supplied in repayment of credits, the effective interest rate could approach or exceed commercial levels.

In their economic cooperation and/or trade agreements with at least nine of the aided African states, the Soviets committed themselves to exchanging goods at market prices or what the agreements specified as "world prices, that is the prices in the principal markets for the corresponding goods."[10] One way to check the faithfulness to such a commitment is by reference to data on the African state's direction of trade by commodity, that is, the values and quantities of particular goods traded, usually in a year, broken down by the countries from which the goods were imported or to which they were exported.[11] These data should yield annual average unit prices both overall and for individual trading partners, so that the average prices paid or charged by the Soviets can be compared to those of other trading partners. Of course, such unit price comparisons are misleading when the goods traded are not of the same quality. This obstacle is found with most of the Soviet aid goods shipped to Africa; they consist of equipment, machinery, and other manufactures whose variations in quality are too great for direction of trade statistics to take account of. Thus, ten "lorries and trucks" from the Soviet Union may very well not be comparable to ten from the United States listed under the same SITC category[12] in the country's commodity directory of trade data.

However, when we turn to goods flowing in the other direction--African exports supplied in repayment of Soviet credits--legitimate comparisons are frequently possible. Most of those exports have been primary commodities-- cocoa, coffee, cotton, groundnuts--whose quality is large- ly similar and for which the published trade data have separate categories, that is, "raw cotton," "cocoa beans," etc. Hence, a thousand tons of "cocoa beans" shipped from Ghana to the Soviet Union is likely to be comparable to the same tonnage sent to Italy.

For Table 4.3 I found suitable though scattered data on six countries to permit comparisons between (1) the an- nual average unit prices received for major commodity ex- ports to the Soviet Union* and (2) the annual average unit prices paid for goods of the same kinds when sold in those years to all other countries taken as a group. In these comparisons, I make the assumption that, in any one year, the Soviets paid largely the same prices for goods received in repayment of credits as for the same kinds of commodi- ties purchased in regular trade. Table 4.3 contains 47 pairs of prices ("Soviet" and "others"). In 35 of the 43 cases, the annual average unit price paid by the Soviets was higher than that paid by all others. The differences averaged $50 per unit (metric tons in all cases). These examples are too few to support a hypothesis that the So- viets tended to pay higher unit prices than did most other purchasers. On the other hand, they seem to be numerous enough to cast doubt on the opposing hypothesis--that the Soviets tended to pay less than the going rates for the exports of aided African states.

In summary, there is some evidence to support the po- sition that Soviet project aid credits to African countries have tended to be concessionary. The repayment periods have been moderately long. The nominal interest rates have been low. And the above comparisons of average annual unit prices for African exports suggest that the effective interest rates were also low.

---

*By "major" commodity exports to the Soviet Union, I mean where the Soviet purchases in the year totaled to at least $250,000. In addition, I was limited to commodities of largely constant quality (not, for example, "sawn timber").

TABLE 4.3

Comparisons of Annual Average Unit Prices Paid by the Soviet Union and Other Trading Partners for Primary Commodity Exports of Selected States, 1961-71
(in millions of U.S. dollars per metric ton)

Country and Commodity	1961	1962	1963	1964	1965	1966	1967	1968	1969	1970	1971
Ethiopia											
Raw cotton	--	--	--	--	--	S-880 / O-848	S-875 / O-754	S-731 / O-762	S-710 / O-787	--	S-829 / O-867
Ghana											
Cocoa beans	S-433[a] / O-463[b]	S-475 / O-436	S-460 / O-473	S-506 / O-492	S-530 / O-433	S-429 / O-352	--	S-388 / O-536	--	S-839 / O-792	--
Nigeria											
Cocoa beans	--	--	--	--	S-558[a] / O-455[b]	--	--	S-722 / O-690	S-894 / O-841	S-1,142 / O-1,059	--
Sudan											
Raw cotton	S-844[a] / O-841[b]	S-776 / O-774	--	--	S-851 / O-842	S-803 / O-701	S-743 / O-680	S-771 / O-757	S-783 / O-824	S-814 / O-806	S-826 / O-830
Groundnuts	--	S-169[a] / O-157[b]	--	--	S-206 / O-179	S-224 / O-191	S-177 / O-171	S-158 / O-147	S-178 / O-212	S-193 / O-231	S-283 / O-220
Tunisia											
Olive oil	--	S-584[a] / O-564[b]	S-978 / O-913	--	S-570 / O-556	S-646 / O-629	--	S-758 / O-668	--	S-765 / O-652	S-771 / O-664
Uganda											
Raw cotton	--	--	--	--	--	--	--	S-828[a] / O-657[b]	S-486 / O-603	S-415 / O-750	--
Raw cotton	--	--	--	--	--	--	S-640[a] / O-590[b]	S-767 / O-682	--	S-671 / O-628	--

[a]Annual average unit price for commodities purchased by the Soviet Union.

[b]Annual average unit price for same commodities (i.e., same SITC classification number) when sales to the Soviet Union have been subtracted.

Note: S = Soviet purchases; O = purchases by all other states.

Sources: United Nations, Economic Commission for Africa, African Trade Statistics, Series B: Trade by Commodity, issues for 1961 through 1971; and Ghana, Central Bureau of Statistics, External Trade Statistics of Ghana, December 1961, December 1963, and December 1965.

SOURCES OF DATA ON AID COMMITMENTS
AND PROJECT AID DELIVERIES

As discussed earlier, important sources for the terms
of Soviet credit commitments are the texts themselves of
at least 14 aid agreements and protocols which the Soviets
have published.[13] The Soviet and African press have given
summaries of some agreements.[14] The most complete source
on the amounts of new Soviet aid commitments by year and
by recipient LDC is a series of unclassified research
memoranda published periodically by the U.S. State Department's Bureau of Intelligence and Research. These publications in recent years have been entitled Communist States
and Developing Countries: Aid and Trade in [the particular
year]. The data for them are reportedly obtained from surveys of the press and radio broadcasts in both donor and
recipient countries and from other unclassified sources.[15]
The most complete source for project aid deliveries
is the series of official Soviet annual trade reviews,
Vneshnyaya Torgovlya SSSR za . . . god (External Trade of
the USSR for the Year . . .). These surveys cover every
year since 1955, and through 1970 they listed total annual
project aid deliveries by country under one of the standard export classification categories used in the foreign
trade statistics of COMECON countries--No. 16, "Machinery
and equipment for complete plants." As explained by an
official of the Soviet Ministry of Foreign Trade, the
"complete plants" were factories, agricultural projects,
and other facilities built abroad with Soviet financial
and technical assistance. And, although published in foreign trade data, the Category 16 entries for each country
included the value of both material goods and the technical services associated with aid goods:[16] the drawing up
of blueprints and the technical assistance in erecting
structures, installing equipment, and commissioning facilities. As just mentioned, COMECON countries use the same
trade classification system. The following is a similar
explanation for Category 16 entries given in a Polish
trade annual (1966):[17]

> Value of complete industrial plants covers
> the value of technical documentation, the
> value of machinery, installations, appli-
> ances, materials and spare parts deliver-
> ies as well as remunerations for such ac-
> tivities as supervision of constructing,
> assembly designer's supervision, training
> of personnel in the country of purchaser
> etc.

This list of goods and services covered under Category 16 is essentially identical to the kinds of aid goods and services listed in the ten economic cooperation agreements which I surveyed.[18] The similarity suggests that the annual Category 16 entries for each LDC represented its drawings of aid that year under those agreements.

Deliveries of goods and services for projects built as gifts were not included in Category 16 entries, one reason being that the export statistics of COMECON countries do not cover goods for which no payment is expected.[19] Curiously, the value of geological surveys and prospecting, a major form of Soviet aid to many LDCs, was included under Category 16,* perhaps on the grounds that such work required equipment which was eventually transferred to the recipient country, but probably also because it was convenient to keep one set of country accounts for all aid extended under the Agreements on Economic and Technical Cooperation.

In 1971 the Soviets revised their "foreign trade nomenclature" (FTN) and, in so doing, abolished Category 16. This was both a loss and a blessing for students of Soviet aid flows. On the one hand, we were denied ready-made country totals for drawings of project aid by year. On the other hand, the new FTN system permits us to estimate, beginning with 1970,† the composition of project aid deliveries. In the Category 16 period, there was no breakdown of the aid--geological work, equipment for textile factories, power stations, and so on. Category 16 entries were simply undifferentiated annual totals, and the goods exported under that heading were not included also under other FTN classifications. With the 1971 FTN system, aid shipments are entered under their various generic categories (e.g., "Equipment for textile industries," "Construction work for agriculture and forestry"--see Table 4.4).

In a forthcoming monograph, Barry Kostinsky of the U.S. Department of Commerce identifies the new FTN categories which are likely to represent "complete plants."[20] If we know--from surveying the published aid protocols and

———————————

*See in Table 4.4 the FTN category 12860 entries for Algeria and Tanzania, and note that the values given "fit" into the Category 16 figures for those two countries in 1970.

†Each of the Soviet trade annuals, Vneshnyaya Torgovlya za . . . god, contains detailed data for two years, the year under review and the one previous. Therefore, the 1971 issue included 1970 data under the new FTN classification system.

other sources--what Soviet aid projects were likely to be in progress in an LDC, we can take Kostinsky's list, with some necessary interpolations,* and scan the Soviet export data for that country, looking for the FTN categories which correspond to those kinds of projects. By adding up the values of the relevant FTN entries, we should come close to the yearly total of project aid deliveries. If there is insufficient information about the nature of projects in progress, we could scan for every category on Kostinsky's list. However, the danger is that an LDC might buy a plant for cash or by means of trade credits. This was the case with a thermal power plant exported to Morocco in the early 1970s.[†]

For Table 4.4 I carried out the above exercise (scanning Soviet export data by country for likely aid shipments) for 13 African countries. I summed the FTN entries so identified and compared these estimates of total annual aid deliveries with the published Category 16 figures for 1970 and comparable data for 1971 and 1972 (see the bottom two lines of Table 4.4). The 1971 and 1972 country totals are published in the 1972 Vneshnyaya Torgovlya under the title "Equipment and materials supplied for projects constructed abroad with the technical cooperation of the USSR."[21] The 1971 and 1972 global totals under this rubric (820.8 million roubles and 895.2 million roubles, respectively) are of the same general magnitude as the Category 16 figures for 1969 and 1970 (865.2 million and

---

*One problem is that, while Kostinsky's list consists almost exclusively of 5- to 7-digit FTN categories (e.g., "12860--Geological prospecting"), two of the relevant export entries encountered for individual African countries were only 3-digit categories. Therefore, I had to assume that part or all of these broader FTN categories represented aid deliveries. In these two cases this assumption was supported by the "fit" between the broader categories' entries and the published annual totals for project aid to the countries. See in Table 4.4 the entries under Guinea, Somalia, and Uganda for FTN categories 140 and 144.

[†]If one uses Kostinsky's list on the Soviet export data for Morocco, 1970-72, one picks up sizable deliveries for a thermal power plant. But the entries under that FTN category (11010) are too large to fit into the published totals for project deliveries to Morocco in those years. The plant was probably supplied through trade credits.

TABLE 4.4

Soviet Project Aid Deliveries to African States by Type of Project, 1970-73
(in millions of roubles)

	Foreign Trade Nomenclature (FTN)*														Total per Country of FTN Entries	Published Totals for Project Aid Deliveries†
	(1)	(2)	(3)	(4)	(5)	(6)	(7)	(8)	(9)	(10)	(11)	(12)	(13)	(14)		
Guinea																
1970	—	—	—	—	—	—	—	.9	—	—	—	—	—	—	.9	2.4
1971	—	—	15.5	—	—	—	—	.9	—	—	—	—	—	—	16.4	18.1
1972	—	—	27.1	—	—	—	—	.3	—	—	—	—	—	—	27.4	30.1
1973	—	—	26.4	—	—	—	—	.3	—	—	—	—	—	—	26.7	na
Algeria																
1970	—	3.4	—	3.7	—	—	7.5	—	—	—	—	—	—	—	14.9	15.4
1971	—	.7	—	3.1	—	—	3.1	—	—	—	—	—	1.3	.3	9.0	8.9
1972	—	—	—	1.3	—	—	11.4	—	—	—	—	—	3.9	1.5	18.1	18.8
1973	—	—	—	10.7	—	—	4.4	—	—	—	—	—	2.7	1.2	19.0	na
Morocco																
1970	4.1	—	—	—	—	—	—	—	—	—	—	—	—	—	4.1	4.2
1971	5.4	—	—	—	—	—	—	—	—	—	—	—	—	—	5.4	5.6
1972	7.0	—	—	—	—	—	—	—	—	—	—	—	—	—	7.0	7.0
1973	1.7	—	—	—	—	—	—	—	—	—	—	—	—	—	1.7	na
Mali																
1970	—	—	—	—	—	—	—	—	—	—	.4	—	—	—	.4	.7
1971	—	—	—	—	—	—	.2	—	—	.2	.3	—	—	—	.7	.7
1972	—	—	—	—	—	—	.2	—	—	.1	.5	—	—	—	.8	.8
1973	—	—	—	—	—	—	.2	—	—	.1	—	—	—	—	.3	na
Congo-Brazzaville																
1970	—	—	—	—	—	—	—	—	—	—	—	—	—	—	—	—
1971	—	—	—	—	—	—	—	—	—	—	—	—	—	—	—	—
1972	—	—	—	—	—	—	.1	—	—	—	—	—	—	—	.1	—
1973	—	—	—	—	—	—	.4	—	—	—	—	—	—	—	.4	na
Nigeria																
1970	—	—	—	—	—	—	—	—	—	—	—	—	—	—	—	—
1971	—	—	—	—	—	—	1.0	—	—	—	—	—	—	—	1.0	1.0
1972	—	—	—	—	—	—	.3	—	—	—	—	—	—	—	.3	.3
1973	—	—	—	—	—	—	.1	—	—	—	—	—	—	—	.1	na
Tanzania																
1970	—	—	—	—	—	—	.6	—	—	—	—	—	—	—	.6	.6
1971	—	—	—	—	—	—	.1	—	—	—	—	—	—	—	.1	—
1972	—	—	—	—	—	—	.3	—	—	—	—	—	—	—	.3	—
1973	—	—	—	—	—	—	.1	—	—	—	—	—	—	—	.1	—

Country / Year	(1)	(2)	(3)	(4)	(5)	(6)	(7)	(8)	(9)	(10)	(11)	(12)	(13)	(14)	16†
Somalia															
1970	--	--	--	--	--	--	--	.6	--	--	--	--	.6	--	.6
1971	--	--	--	--	--	--	--	.7	--	--	--	--	.7	--	.7
1972	--	--	--	.2	--	--	--	.9	--	--	--	--	1.1	--	1.1
1973	--	--	--	--	--	--	--	.4	--	--	--	--	.4	--	na
Ethiopia															
1970	--	--	--	.1	.1	--	--	--	--	--	--	--	--	--	.1
1971	--	--	--	.2	.2	--	--	--	--	--	--	--	--	--	.2
1972	--	--	--	.2	.2	--	--	--	--	--	--	--	--	--	.2
1973	--	--	--	.3	.3	--	--	--	--	--	--	--	--	--	na
Sudan															
1970	--	--	--	--	--	--	.3	.8	--	--	.3	.5	--	--	1.8
1971	--	--	--	--	--	--	.8	1.0	--	--	.8	.2	--	--	1.3
1972	--	--	--	--	--	--	.1	.3	--	--	.1	.2	--	--	.5
1973	--	--	--	--	--	--	.3	.3	--	--	.3	--	--	--	na
Uganda															
1970	--	--	--	--	--	--	--	--	.3	--	--	--	.3	--	.3
1971	--	--	--	--	--	--	--	--	3.5	--	--	--	3.5	--	3.5
1972	--	--	--	--	--	--	--	--	2.9	--	--	--	2.9	--	2.9
1973	--	--	--	--	--	--	--	--	--	--	--	--	--	--	na
Senegal															
1970	--	--	--	--	--	--	--	--	--	--	--	--	--	--	--
1971	--	--	--	--	--	.3	--	--	--	--	--	--	.3	--	.3
1972	--	--	--	--	--	--	--	--	--	--	--	--	--	--	--
1973	--	--	--	--	--	--	--	--	--	--	--	--	--	--	--
FTN totals for 1970-73	18.2	4.1	69.0	18.8	.8	.2	31.9	5.0	6.7	.4	1.2	.9	7.9	3.8	

(1) 11014--Hydroelectric station
(2) 11043--Thermal power station
(3) 12062--Equipment for extraction of nonferrous ores (e.g., bauxite)
(4) 12390--Pig iron, steel and rolled ferrous metal factories
(5) 12730--Oil refineries
(6) 12801--Tools for geological work
(7) 12860--Equipment for geological work
(8) 140--Equipment for food industries
(9) 144--Equipment for textile industries
(10) 15301--Equipment for cement industries
(11) 162--Construction work in agriculture and forestry
(12) 16201--Construction work in animal husbandry
(13) 16402--Educational buildings
(14) 166--Water resources construction

*FTN, "foreign trade nomenclature," is a system for classifying goods traded. The categories given here were introduced in 1971.

†Category 16 figures for 1970, and for 1971 and 1972 I used the country and totals published in the 1972 Vneshnyaya Torgovlya SSSR, p. 316.

Note: na = not available.

Sources: Vneshnyaya Torgovlya SSSR za . . . god (Moscow, Vneshtorgizdat), issues of 1970-73.

859.6 million roubles), and 27 of the 32 countries (including Communist states) listed as recipients in 1969-70 are found also in the 1971-72 data (out of a total also of 32 countries).[22] Moreover, the time series data for individual recipient states look compatible when the 1969-70 entries are compared to those for 1971-72.[23]

The 1973 Vneshnyaya Torgovlya did not include such a listing of total annual aid deliveries by country, so in Table 4.2 that year's delivery figures are estimates derived by the method explained in the paragraph immediately above. But as Table 4.4 indicates, this method works rather well. In that table there are 29 cases in which the sums of the FTN entries believed to represent complete plants can be compared to the published totals of project aid deliveries for the same year (1970, 1971, or 1972). The two figures are identical or within a tenth of a million dollars of each other in 19 of the cases. In the other ten, the differences between published and estimated totals averaged only .9 million U.S. dollars.

Having discussed the nature of the data on commitments and project aid deliveries, and having argued that the terms of Soviet project aid credits to Africa can be considered concessionary, I now turn to evaluating the significance of the aid relations to both donor and recipient states.

THE RELATIVE MAGNITUDE OF SOVIET AID TO AFRICA

In terms of either aid commitments or project aid deliveries, Africa collectively (minus Egypt) has not been a major arena for Soviet economic assistance activities. And for most of the 15 African states which have received project aid, Soviet deliveries have been small, both absolutely and relatively: less than 25 million U.S. dollars cumulative and/or less than 10 percent of the aid receipts in the same years from other major sources of foreign assistance (see Table 4.2). However, for four states--Algeria, Guinea, Mali, and Ghana--Soviet aid was significant during the years under review; and for two of them, Algeria and Guinea, it should continue to be important.

From 1954 through 1973, the cumulative total of Soviet aid commitments (the opening of lines of credit and other pledges of assistance) to non-Communist LDCs is estimated to have been $8.9 billion (see Table 4.1). Africa's share, $1.3 billion, was only 14 percent and spread among 25 separate states (Table 4.1). In contrast, seven

Middle Eastern countries with about half the combined population of the 25 African states received commitments totaling $3.5 billion or close to three times more.[24]

For seven years, however, Africa was much nearer to
center stage. From 1959 to 1965 new aid commitments to
African countries averaged 30 percent of the annual totals.
Those years were a time of optimism among some Soviet leaders that the new African states--with their grievances
against the Western exmetropoles, their typically weak indigenous business classes, their traditions of communal
land tenure, and related characteristics--would tend toward socialism and collaboration with Communist countries.[25]
As will be discussed later in the chapter, the LDCs with
the greatest promise for a transition to "socialism" in the
Moscow sense were called "national democratic states"; and
three of the four countries so labeled in the early 1960s
were African (Ghana, Guinea, and Mali). However, in the
second half of the decade, the optimism greatly dwindled,
in part because aided Marxist regimes in both Ghana (1966)
and Mali (1968) fell easy prey to military coups. An apparent consequence of these defeats and other causes of
Soviet pessimism about securing useful allies in Africa
was that new aid commitments declined, both absolutely
and relatively. They averaged less in annual totals, $62
million for 1966-73 as opposed to $112 million for 1959-65;
and they were smaller relative to total Soviet aid extensions to LDCs--an average of 11 percent per year in 1966-73
rather than 30 percent in the earlier period (see Table 4.1).

In respect to project aid deliveries, Africa's role
was modest for the entire 15-year period. Its share of
total reported disbursements to LDCs fluctuated below 10
percent every year except five, with the high point being
1972, when thanks to large shipments to Guinea and Algeria
it rose to 17 percent (see Table 4.2). Africa's share of
aggregate project aid since 1955 (the beginning of Soviet
aid deliveries to LDCs) was only about 10 percent, that
is, $400 million out of an estimated $4.1 billion (see
Table 4.2). In contrast, deliveries to Middle Eastern
states totaled $2.1 billion or 51 percent (see Table 4.5).
Table 4.5 ranks the 31 recorded LDC recipients of Soviet
project aid according to the cumulative values of their
aid deliveries. Although African countries account for
almost half (15) of the total number of recipient states,
only two of them rank in the top ten (Guinea is eighth;
Algeria, ninth). Nine of the 15 are found in the range
of 19th through 29th positions.

TABLE 4.5

Non-Communist Recipients of Soviet Project Aid
Ranked by Cumulative Deliveries, 1955-73
(in millions of U.S. dollars)*

India	1,182.0	Ceylon	17.7
Egypt	832.0	Greece	14.0
Iran	486.0	Sudan	13.4
Afghanistan	346.0	Ethiopia	13.3
Turkey	316.0	Uganda	8.5
Iraq	196.0	Tunisia	7.6
Syria	195.0	Burma	4.9
Guinea	125.7	Congo-Brazzaville	3.8
Algeria	121.8	Yemen People's	
Indonesia	66.3	Republic	3.8
Pakistan	65.6	Nigeria	1.5
Yemen Arab		Tanzania	1.5
Republic	34.6	Senegal	1.4
Mali	31.0	Cameroun	1.2
Morocco	25.9	Cambodia	1.0
Somalia	22.6	Bangladesh	.9
Ghana	20.6		

*Converted from roubles at the rate of one rouble
equals $1.11. See note a for Table 4.1.

Sources: Vneshnyaya Torgovlya SSSR za . . . god,
statisticheskii obzor (Moscow, Vnestorgizdat), issues for
1956-73.

The average cumulative deliveries for all 15 African
recipients was $80 million, but the mean is a misleading
measure of central tendency in these cases. Guinea and
Algeria have relatively high totals, $126 million and
$122 million respectively. The other 13 countries re-
ceived $31 million or less, with their subgroup average
being only $12 million. Therefore, from the point of
view of Soviet disbursers of project aid, probably only
the two countries, Guinea and Algeria, have been finan-
cially significant.
   Whether $126 million or $12 million was significant
for an individual recipient government depended on its
needs versus the total resources available to it in those
particular years, including aid flows from other external

sources. Table 4.2 includes a breakdown, for the same years (except 1973) as when the 15 African states received Soviet project aid, of their net inflows of official assistance from 16 OECD countries and major multilateral agencies.* For convenience I label this "Western" aid. The same table's extreme right-hand column measures the significance of Soviet project aid in terms of the average of the yearly ratios of (a) the value of this form of Soviet assistance to (b) the value of Western aid.[†] By this measure, Soviet project aid deliveries appear very important to Guinea, averaging about twice the value of net Western aid in the same years. For Algeria, almost the same amount of Soviet assistance was comparatively much less significant, because unlike Guinea that country was not estranged from the exmetropole, but received substantial French aid as well as important assistance from other Western sources. Nevertheless, the absolute value of Soviet project aid, $122 million over 11 years, doubtless made it significant to Algerian policymakers. Since Soviet aid to Ghana and Mali averaged above 10 percent of Western receipts, it seems permissible to label it significant to those countries also. However, for the other 11 states, the averages were from less than 1 percent to 8 percent (Table 4.2).

Soviet aid to Ghana ended abruptly in 1966 when the military junta which overthrew Nkrumah's government expelled all Soviet aid personnel. The new leaders apparently feared that Soviets within Ghana would attempt to support Nkrumah's efforts to return to power. That military government later tried to interest the Soviets in resuming aid, at least to the extent of completing projects begun under Nkrumah; but as Table 4.2 indicates, no new aid deliveries were made through 1973. The army

---

*The 16 countries are the members of the OECD's Development Assistance Committee: Australia, Austria, Belgium, Canada, Denmark, France, West Germany, Italy, Japan, Netherlands, Norway, Portugal, Sweden, Switzerland, United Kingdom, and United States. The multilateral agencies in question are the United Nations, its specialized agencies, the International Development Association, and the European Development Fund.

[†]The "a" and "b" aid flows are not completely comparable, since grant aid is excluded from the Soviet totals and, also, since the "b" values represent net flows.

officers in Mali who toppled another Soviet-aided regime
(in 1968) felt secure enough in their relations with the
Soviets to ask that aid continue without interruption.   It
did in the sense that projects already underway were apparently completed, but only one small new aid commitment
was made ($800,000 in 1969), and unused credits from ear-
lier extensions were not activated to any significant extent.   Therefore, as projects were completed and no new
ones begun, aid deliveries to Mali dwindled to only about
$300,000 in 1973 (see Table 4.2).

     Soviet project aid deliveries to Guinea and Algeria
were relatively high in 1971-73, they probably continued
at substantial levels in 1974, and for at least Algeria
they promise to be sizable for some years after 1974.   According to Table 4.4, deliveries for the Kindia bauxite
mining project in Guinea began in 1971; and through 1973
the total rouble value of materials and services supplied
was $69 million or $76.5 million out of the $92 million
committed to the project in 1969.*   Therefore, only about
another $15 million remained to be delivered, perhaps all
or most in 1974.   Entries in Table 4.4 for Guinea indicate
that in 1973 there was no other sizable project in progress besides Kindia.   Therefore, after it is completed,
Soviet aid to Guinea may drop off sharply.   A quick completion of the Annabah metallurgical complex in Algeria is
unlikely.   According to Table 4.4, only 15 million roubles
or about $17 million worth of aid was delivered to the
project from 1971 (when the $189 million commitment was
made to expand the complex) through the end of 1973.

                HYPOTHESES ON THE COUNTRY DISTRIBUTION
                         OF SOVIET AID

     This section offers three hypotheses to explain seg-
ments of the country distribution of Soviet aid to Africa,
and particularly why some states received no economic aid
at all while a few others--Guinea, Algeria, Mali, Morocco,
Somalia, and Ghana--were relatively very favored.   The
hypotheses are: (1) that many African governments deliberately did not solicit Soviet aid or declined offers of
assistance; (2) that Soviet policymakers in the first half
to two-thirds of the 1960s tended to favor African regimes

_____

     *The rouble/dollar exchange rate at the time of the
commitment was one rouble equaled $1.11.

which were perceived to be socialist or noncapitalist in orientation; and (3) that the Soviets based aid decisions for several countries on the hope of significant strategic payoffs. Additional hypotheses deserve to be examined, such as that the Soviets dispensed aid in part to secure diplomatic support against the West and/or China; however, the data available to me permitted exploration of only the first three.

THE NONAIDED

For economic assistance to flow from one government to another, responsible decision-makers on both sides must desire and work for the transaction. Since the receipt of aid carries economic and probably political costs as well as benefits, LDCs do not agree to every offer of assistance; nor do they indiscriminately solicit aid. There is evidence to suggest that, during the years under review, as many as 8 of the 14 African states which received no Soviet aid commitments had governments that did not want such aid.* For various reasons they opposed it, and an indicator of that opposition in seven cases was the African government's unwillingness to maintain diplomatic relations with the Soviets despite the latter's extension of recognition.[26]

Botswana, Lesotho, and Swaziland have been economic satellites of South Africa, which supplies large shares of their imports, some capital, and major employment opportunities for their large migrant labor forces.[27] The white-minority government of South Africa, with its fear of Communist support of black nationalism, would probably have used its strong leverage over those three neighboring states to block a significant Soviet aid presence on their soils, as presumably it has opposed the establishment of diplomatic ties between those states and the Soviets.

Malawi is another economic client of South Africa which has neither received Soviet aid nor exchanged ambassadors with the USSR. In its case, however, as with Madagascar, Gabon, and the Ivory Coast, which also did not maintain diplomatic relations with the Soviets (except

---

*The 14 nonaided states as of the end of 1973 were Botswana, Burundi, Dahomey, Gabon, Gambia, Ivory Coast, Lesotho, Liberia, Libya, Malagasy Republic, Malawi, Swaziland, Togo, and Zaire.

briefly, 1967-69, in the Ivory Coast's case), outside pressure against accepting Soviet aid was probably not needed. The leaders of conservative governments were themselves suspicious of Soviet intentions. For example, Houphouet-Boigny, the President of the Ivory Coast, stated in a 1962 press conference that he would consider Soviet economic aid when he was "persuaded of the possibility of cooperation without interference in internal affairs."[28]

In the case of Zaire, the Soviets aided the losing side in a civil war; the winners were understandably not well disposed toward cooperation with the friends of their enemies.

FAVORING NONCAPITALIST REGIMES

By being favored, I mean governments which received higher aid commitments than did most of the others in Africa. And by being noncapitalist or socialist in orientation, I mean regimes which Soviet leaders perceived to be committed to minimizing the role of Western private capital in their economies, to maximizing economic cooperation with the East, to gathering under state control the major means of production and distribution, and, perhaps, to propagating an ideology not too far distant from Soviet Marxism. For reasons discussed below, I limit this hypothesis tying aid commitments to perceptions of a regime's orientation to the years 1959 to 1968.

Governments labeled "socialist in orientation" might eventually evolve into full-fledged, Marxist-Leninist party regimes. But if they did not "progress" or change from their left-leaning, nationalistic character, they could nevertheless be useful allies in restricting Western influence in Africa and, perhaps, in achieving other Soviet purposes. While nonsocialist regimes could of course be valued allies, an ideological underpinning for cooperation might make it more lasting and extend it into more fields.

As discussed above, many Soviet commentators in the early 1960s were optimistic that new African states would tend toward socialism. Various factors, including the weakness of the domestic business classes, the traditions of communal land tenure, the eagerness of nationalist leaders to modernize their economies, and the assumed attractiveness of the Soviet model for rapid economic development, were expected to push many states onto a "noncapitalist path of development." Countries which had

progressed a fair distance along that path were labeled by
Soviet commentators as "national democratic states" or
"revolutionary democracies." In both models, the governments were supposed to be striving to minimize the economic
influence of Western capital, developing close ties with
the East, and carrying out the other "tasks" mentioned in
the above paragraph.[29] Both kinds of "democracies" were
presented as transitional stages between capitalism and
"true" socialism; and the transition need not be effected
through armed revolution, but through winning over established nationalist leaders to "positions of the working
class."[30] This scenario may have been inspired by the apparent conversion of Fidel Castro.

What indicators do we have that Soviet policymakers
perceived certain African governments to have ideological
orientations which gave promise of close and perhaps long-
term collaboration? One is that they instructed or permitted their publicists to classify Algeria, Congo-
Brazzaville, Ghana, Guinea, and Mali as "national democratic states" and/or "revolutionary democracies."[31] Another indicator is that the CPSU (Communist Party of the
Soviet Union) leadership cultivated relations with those
same states on the party level. Delegations from Algeria's
ruling party were guests of the CPSU Central Committee
and/or the latter's representatives were on official party
visits to Algeria every year from 1963 to 1968.[32] The
same every-year pattern (1963-68) is found for Mali. The
ruling parties of Guinea and Mali had CPSU delegations to
at least one each of their party congresses in the 1960s,
and they were invited to attend both the 1961 and 1966
Congresses of the CPSU. Nkrumah's party in Ghana was also
represented at the 1961 Congress, and Algeria's FLN (National Liberation Front) and the Congo's MNR (National
Revolutionary Movement) were invited to the Congress in
1966. Mali's Union Soudanaise received substantial gifts
in kind and one in cash directly from the CPSU's Central
Committee to its Politburo.[33] The CPSU also undertook to
build a party school in Mali. And Ghana's ruling party
was invited in 1963 to send a study team to a CPSU school
for ideological workers in Moscow.

One might dismiss these party ties as just so many
more channels by which the Soviets cultivated influence.
They clearly had that function, but also they were indicators of a special relationship. Not every aided LDC
was cultivated in this fashion. In Africa only the above-
mentioned five countries were, out of the 18 countries
aided in the years 1959-68. Inviting an African ruling

party to attend a CPSU Congress or to study at a party school, and despatching a Central Committee delegation to that African party's National Conference or other public occasion implied a legitimacy for that party: a right to govern, which was stronger than that extended by diplomatic recognition or state-to-state economic aid. The implication was that the CPSU·leadership considered the party to be "right and proper" for that LDC at that time. In the case of Algeria, where a Communist Party existed, its members were instructed to join the ruling FLN.[34] In the Leninist expectation that largely agricultural, underdeveloped states can evolve directly to socialism, without waiting for the capitalist stage to be completed, a grant of legitimacy to a ruling party seems best explained in terms of the regime's potential for guiding its country on a socialist path of development. And, as indicated above, this was the evaluation of those five regimes published in Soviet commentaries of the period.

If these five African states were perceived in the 1960s to be socialist-oriented, were they also favored in terms of Soviet aid commitments? They were for the period 1959-68. It makes sense to limit the hypothesis to those years, since by 1968 Soviet optimism about securing ideological allies among leftist African regimes had largely disappeared and been replaced by a pessimism or "new realism," to use Robert Legvold's phrase.[35] I assume that this change in perceptions affected aid policy for Africa and probably weakened, if not ended, any policy of extending aid to a large extent because of a regime's promising ideological orientation.

The Soviets' turn from optimism had begun at least by 1966, spurred by the collapse in that year of a Soviet-aided Marxist regime in Ghana. According to Legvold's extensive analysis of Soviet commentary on Africa in that period, the reappraisal generated by the defeat in Ghana was so destructive of the earlier sanguine expectations that, when a second African ally was overthrown (the Keita regime in Mali in 1968), Soviet commentators seemed neither to be surprised nor to grieve much.[36] They had come to appreciate the gap between socialist slogans and achievement and, also, the severe restraints on political and economic reform posed by tribalism, a scarcity of organizational talent, and other conditions characteristic of new African states.

In a breakdown of Soviet aid commitments to African countries for the years 1959-68 (see Table 4.6), Algeria ranks first, Ghana third, Guinea fourth, and Mali sixth

out of 18. The only one of the national democracies far
down in the list was the Congo at fourteenth. The differences in absolute values are significant. If seventh-
ranked Kenya's $48 million in cumulative commitments is
taken as a point of comparison with aid extended to
socialist-oriented states, Mali's commitment is $11 mil-
lion higher; Guinea's, $28 million higher; Ghana's, $45
million; and Algeria's, $184 million. The Congo's com-
mitment, however, was $38 million lower. Its failure to
secure more generous aid pledges may have been functions
of the change in its government in 1965 and also the country's small size (with a population of less than one million).*

TABLE 4.6

African Countries Ranked by Cumulative
Soviet Aid Commitments, 1959-68
(in millions of U.S. dollars)

Algeria	232*	Sierra Leone	28
Ethiopia	102	Sudan	22
Ghana	93*	Tanzania	20
Guinea	76*	Uganda	16
Somalia	64	Congo-Brazzaville	10*
Mali	59*	Cameroun	8
Kenya	48	Senegal	7
Morocco	44	Zambia	6
Tunisia	34	Mauritania	3

*Countries classified by Soviet commentators in the
years 1960-68 as "national democratic states."

Sources: Same as those for Table 4.1.

---

*The same four "socialist-oriented" states ranked
above all others in the values of their cumulative project aid deliveries, 1960-68. However, it is very difficult to draw inferences about favored treatment from
these deliveries. The latter were functions of the size
of the aid commitments, the time elapsed since the credits
were extended, the complexity of the pre-construction
planning, and other technical variables, as well as political factors.

While these comparisons of aid commitments do not of course prove the existence of favored treatment for socialist-oriented states from 1959 to 1968, they indicate the possibility of such favoritism. That is, four out of the five leftist regimes ranked in the top six out of 18. Another factor supporting the hypothesis is that the cultivation of party ties with the same four states by the CPSU, and the public classification of them as national democracies, occurred in time before major aid commitments. In other words, the sequence of events was appropriate. I assume, however, that the ideological factor was one among others (such as expectations of strategic or diplomatic payoffs) which in combination led to the decisions to commit aid resources.

THE QUEST FOR STRATEGIC BENEFITS

In this section I explore the extent to which Soviet aid decisions were shaped by a quest for strategic benefits: bases, landing and resupply rights, and access to strategic raw materials for oneself and/or denial of such benefits to one's military rivals.

I assume that with virtually every aided African country, the Soviets were fishing for some strategic benefit. However, in at least six cases (Ethiopia, Algeria, Tunisia, Senegal, Guinea, and Somalia), important strategic stakes were clearly visible at the time of the first or subsequent Soviet aid commitment. In 1959, the year of the first Soviet aid pledge to Ethiopia, the United States had a large radio communications center in that country which served its military forces in the Middle East. Similarly, in 1963, the year of the first commitment to Algeria, France occupied important bases in that country. The $100 million lines of credit extended to both states in those years probably had, as one purpose, to increase the Soviets' leverage to persuade the host governments to terminate the Western bases. In Algeria's case, the economic aid was accompanied by substantial military assistance. One source estimated the total value of Soviet arms deliveries of 1962 through 1966 as $150 million.[37] The modest economic credits offered to Tunisia in 1961 and to Senegal in 1964 might also have been in part designed to improve Soviet diplomats' standing when arguing for military nonalignment and the closing of the substantial French bases in both countries.

The United States retained its Ethiopian facility throughout the period under review, as did France its

bases in Senegal. However the French withdrew completely
from Tunisia by 1964, and from almost all installations in
Algeria by 1968 and from the last in 1970.[38] No cause-and-
effect relationship between Soviet aid and French withdrawal is likely in Tunisia's case. But Soviet economic
and military aid to Algeria was considerable, and it may
have been a significant factor in persuading Algerian
leaders that they could afford to press the French to
evacuate bases before the date (1972) provided by the
Evian accords.

The Soviets probably coveted the use of naval and air
installations in Tunisia, Algeria, or Morocco, as during
the 1960s they expanded their Mediterranean naval force.[39]
A reconnaissance base in the Western Mediterranean, near
the U.S. facilities in Spain (including the Polaris submarine base at Rota) was likely a high-priority goal.
Perhaps in pursuit of base rights, the Soviets aided Algeria to expand and modernize military airfields and naval
installations left by the French; supplied all of the war-
ships (39 as of 1973) for its new navy;[40] and provided
virtually all of the planes for its airforce (including
132 fighters and bombers as of 1971).[41] However, they
have apparently failed so far (mid-1974) to secure a base.
Their military ships and planes can probably use Algerian
facilities on an ad hoc basis, but there seems to be no
provision for constant access or guarantee of usage in
time of crisis.

The Soviets' heavy investment in Algeria may yet bear
fruit. They have the example of their patience finally
being rewarded with strategic benefits in Guinea. Before
the second Soviet aid commitment to Guinea, $22 million in
1960, the two sides agreed on Soviet assistance for expanding and modernizing the country's major airport at
Conakry.[42] Guinea was then virtually without important
international friends besides the Soviet Union and its
allies, so that the Soviets could expect that its leverage over the recipient government might be strong enough
to secure access to the field for its military aircraft,
if not on a regular basis at least in time of crisis.
The airport project was completed in 1962; and during the
Cuban missile crisis of that year, the Soviets asked permission to land planes en route to Cuba. It was denied.[43]
However in 1973 (after another 11 years of uninterrupted
economic aid deliveries and Soviet assistance since 1971
in guarding Guinea's coast against Portuguese incursions
from neighboring Guinea-Bissau),[44] the Soviets were
granted permission to fly naval reconnaissance missions
out of Conakry airport.[45] Such missions may monitor U.S.

naval ships sailing into the South Atlantic on their way to the Far East (around the southern tip of Africa and into the Indian Ocean).

In Somalia the Soviets have been allowed to build for joint use with the armed forces of the host country, or for their exclusive control, several military installations. They include refueling and other naval support facilities at the new deep-water port of Berbera and apparently a military airport and a radio communications center.[46] The port, strategically located near both the Red Sea and Indian Ocean, can help to support the growing Soviet naval presence in the region. The number of Soviet ships in the Indian Ocean area during the first half of 1974 was estimated at between 20 and 30.[47] The port itself was built with Soviet economic aid; and since it was one of the projects listed in the first cooperation agreement with Somalia (July 2, 1961),[48] it is likely that the Soviets' initial extension of credits and subsequent commitments were partly based on the hope of using the port for military purposes.

In Ghana, the Soviets were helping the Nkrumah government to build a military airfield with runways much too long for any aircraft the Ghanaians expected to own. Western intelligence sources speculated that the runways were designed for use, perhaps only episodically, by long-range Soviet military jets. However, Nkrumah's regime collapsed before the facility was completed.

Another category of strategic benefits which may derive in part from giving economic aid is the securing of access to raw materials needed for the production of arms. Africa has extensive deposits of bauxite, industrial diamonds, copper, manganese, and other strategic materials. However, through 1973 Soviet strategic imports from aided African countries were limited to relatively small quantities of diamonds, bauxite, sisal, and rubber. Except for diamonds, the aggregate annual imports (from all aided states) were less than $1.5 million per commodity per year. The biggest year for diamonds was 1973, when the Congo and the Cameroun supplied $4 million worth.[49] But for these modest purchases, there were ample other sources of supply open to the Soviets.

A truly privileged supply source for the Soviets in the near future may be the Kindia bauxite-mining complex, built in Guinea with Soviet aid. The largest single Soviet aid project in sub-Saharan Africa, the Kindia mines are supposed to yield for sales to the Soviet Union a reported 2.5 million tons of high-grade bauxite per year

over 30 years.[50] For 12 or more years after the completion of the aid deliveries for the project, part or all
of the bauxite sales to the Soviets will represent repayment of the $92 million line of credit extended for the
mine in 1969 (or whatever portion of the total credit is
used). Therefore, through their aid efforts the Soviets
have largely assured themselves of a substantial source
of good-quality bauxite. Will it be a significant benefit to the Soviet economy? According to a 1972 survey of
Soviet writings on that country's aliminum industry, there
have been shortages of high-grade ores for aluminum.[51]

In summary, I have suggested two factors to explain
Soviet aid decisions affecting Africa: a desire to cultivate close relationships with socialist-oriented regimes,
and a quest for strategic benefits. A combination of both
factors helps to account for the relatively favored positions on aid commitments and project aid deliveries of
Guinea, Algeria, and Ghana. The ideological factor applies to Mali, which was also comparatively favored, while
the strategic motive seems to have been influential in
shaping the relatively generous allocations to Somalia and,
perhaps, also those to Morocco. The Soviets may also have
been interested in cultivating Morocco for its importance
as a trading partner. From 1967 to 1973, it was the second largest customer (after Algeria) in Africa for Soviet
exports (see Table 4.7).

TRADE BENEFITS TO THE DONOR COUNTRY

Africa has much more than strategic materials to offer to the expanding Soviet economy. Long-staple cotton,
raw hides, cocoa, coffee, fruits, and edible oils are
among the continent's exports for which the Soviets have
had a continuing demand and which aided African states
have been supplying to them in substantial quantities.[52]
Of course these same goods could have been obtained without the existence of an aid program; they were available
to any buyer with the requisite amount of convertible currency. The Soviets, however, prefer bilateral barter
trade, which requires the trading partner to import balancing values of Soviet goods. But the latter have not
been easy to market in Africa because of brand loyalty to
Western goods built up during the colonial era; obstruc-
tion by European-owned importing firms that are tied to
suppliers in their home countries; and the reputation of
the inadequate quality of Soviet goods and/or the technical services supporting them.[53]

TABLE 4.7

Soviet Exports to Aided African Countries, Net of Known Project Aid Deliveries, 1959-73
(in millions of U.S. dollars)[a]

Aided Country	1959	1960	1961	1962	1963	1964	1965	1966	1967	1968	1969	1970	1971	1972	1973
Algeria	1.3	2.2	1.4	.8	4.5[b]	13.7	9.5	17.2	28.7	18.1	31.5	52.3	48.5	41.2	50.8
Guinea	.9[b]	5.7	18.1	12.6	6.7	5.3	7.8	7.3	6.1	11.6	5.5	9.7	14.5	16.5	16.8
Morocco	1.7	5.8	3.3	5.6	9.8	8.1	8.4	10.8[b]	20.0	19.2	31.8	31.4	25.1	27.1	29.5
Ghana	--	5.5[b]	15.3	7.3	12.0	15.5	26.4	13.3	7.3	9.2	9.4	11.0	14.1	10.2	10.8
Mali	--	--	7.9[b]	5.8	8.8	9.1	7.3	4.8	4.3	5.7	3.0	4.8	1.8	.3	2.7
Somalia	--	--	--[b]	.8	4.1	3.5	1.2	6.4	3.5	2.7	1.6	2.4	5.3	11.8	12.4
Sudan	3.9	5.4	9.3[b]	10.2	10.9	3.0	6.2	7.0	4.3	15.9	15.1	34.1	20.9	18.4	2.5
Ethiopia	.6[b]	.9	.9	.9	1.1	1.1	1.7	2.3	3.5	1.5	2.1	1.3	1.2	1.6	1.5
Uganda	--	--	--	--	--	--[b]	.1	.1	.7	.5	.9	.8	.4	.6	1.0
Tunisia	.8	3.2	2.3[b]	1.9	3.4	3.1	4.3	5.8	5.2	2.6	4.0	3.4	4.0	3.0	6.5
Congo-Brazzaville	--	--	--	--	--	--[b]	1.8	.4	1.1	.5	.1	.9	4.7	.2	.9
Nigeria	--	--	--	.1	.6	1.2	3.2	4.6	10.8	11.9	16.6	12.1[b]	16.3	9.7	12.1
Tanzania	--	--	--	--	--	.2	.4	1.0[b]	.7	.8	.2	.5	.6	.4	.6
Senegal	--	--	--	--	--	1.1[b]	.1	.2	.2	.2	.2	.2	.7	1.6	5.4
Cameroun	--	--	--	--	--[b]	--	.1	.1	.2	.6	1.1	.7	.7	.7	.8
Kenya	--	--	--	--	--	--	1.0[b]	1.7	.6	.8	1.0	1.6	1.3	.8	.2
Sierra Leone	--	--	--	--	--	--	.1[b]	.7	1.1	.9	.3	1.8	2.5	.9	1.3
Zambia	28.5	26.4	13.2	13.5	16.0	4.2	--	--	7.1[b]	--	--	--	--	--	--
Mauritania	--	--	--	--	--	--	--	--	--[b]	--	1.8	.4	--	--	--
Central African Republic	--	--	--	--	--	--	--	--	--	--	--	--	1.5[b]	.1	.4
Equatorial Guinea	--	--	--	--	--	--	--	--	--	--	--	--	1.1[b]	.1	--

[a]Converted from roubles at the exchange rate of one rouble equals $1.11. See note a in Table 4.1.

[b]Year of first known Soviet aid commitment.

A well-designed aid program could help overcome such obstacles by introducing African producers and consumers to an array of useful, reasonably priced Soviet goods. In addition, to the extent that aid consists of machinery and equipment, it creates a future demand for replacement parts and units. A third force for expanding barter trade may be pressures, actual or anticipated, on the recipient government to reciprocate for the provision of aid by arranging to import larger quantities of Soviet goods (outside the aid program).

While it is beyond the scope of this chapter to test adequately these aid-trade hypotheses, we can at least note in how many cases the provision of aid was followed by a sizable increase in imports from the Soviet Union net of aid deliveries. There were only a few such cases. Table 4.7 lists recorded Soviet exports, 1959-73 (net of known project aid deliveries), to the 21 aided African countries for which the Soviets have published separate export data. If we use, as a baseline for comparisons, the level of net exports in the year that the first Soviet aid commitment was made (marked in the table for each country with a raised b), we find that 11 of the 21 countries absorbed higher levels of Soviet exports, net of aid, in all years following the initial aid commitment. Two of the remaining ten states had higher levels in at least five (but not all) of the following years. However, most of the net increases were very modest. Only five countries--Algeria, Ghana, Guinea, Morocco and Sudan-- raised their imports of Soviet goods by a net of $5 million or more (for at least five years). And just three-- Algeria, Guinea, and Morocco--did so by $10 million or more. Yet these five are among the most important recipients of Soviet aid in Africa. They rank first, second, fourth, sixth, and seventh among the 15 countries which had project aid deliveries (see Table 4.2). Their cases suggest a connection between aid and increases in trade. But the relationship may be parallel rather than causal, and to determine which it is deserves a separate study.

THE FUTURE OF SOVIET AID TO AFRICA

Recent trends in Soviet aid to Africa suggest a future of less assistance or that, if aggregate deliveries increase, they will be concentrated in just a few recipient states. Although 17 new commitments were extended in the four calendar years 1970 to 1973, all except three

were in the range of only $1 million to $8 million; and
they were scattered among 14 separate states (Table 4.1).
From 1969 to 1973 project aid deliveries to four countries--
Tunisia, Uganda, Senegal, and Cameroun--ceased completely
(Table 4.2). If deliveries of at least $2 million to $3
million per year are taken to be substantial, the number
of African countries receiving project aid at that level
peaked at seven in 1964, was four in 1972, but only two in
1973. And of those two, Algeria and Guinea, only one (Algeria) was assured of sizable aid deliveries for several
years in the future (see the discussion of this question
above).

What accounts for this apparent contracting of Soviet
aid efforts in Africa? There is probably the general bud-
getary factor of domestic demands for resources taking
precedence over aid officials' requests for funds. However, in 1973 those officials still had over $600 million
to dispense in commitments (Table 4.1). But Africa received only 1.6 percent of it. Africa has apparently become less interesting to the Soviets as an area to cultivate allies, base rights, increased trade, and so on
through aid. They suffered political defeats in Ghana
and Mali. The basing rights they now enjoy in Guinea and
Somalia may satisfy their strategic interests in sub-
Saharan Africa, especially as the United States' involvement in that region has dwindled. Their past experience
with aided African states has been that economic assistance did not greatly stimulate trade. However, where
significant benefits have already been obtained--the reconnaissance facility and high-grade ore supplies in
Guinea, and the military facilities in Somalia--I suspect
that the Soviets will provide additional substantial aid
so as to secure the continuation of those benefits. The
heavy investment in Algeria may also be added to (beyond
the completion of the Annabah steelworks project), because of that country's strategic position in the Mediterranean and its government's importance in the Arab
world.

Can other African states expect to receive substantial Soviet aid? Claiming aid on the basis that one's
government is socialist in orientation seems unlikely to
succeed. The leaders of Congo-Brazzaville have insisted
for some years that they are scientific socialists, and
the CPSU has maintained party ties with them.* But

---

*For example, the ruling party (renamed the Congolese
Labour Party) was invited to the 24th CPSU Congress in
1971.

between 1964 and 1973 they apparently received only one new Soviet aid commitment: $4 million for a veterinary research laboratory.

A more successful lever for extracting aid may be the possession of raw materials required by the expanding Soviet economy. The decision to support the Kindia project in Guinea was based in part (perhaps mostly) on the Soviet aluminum industry's need for high-grade bauxite. And the Soviets have shown considerable interest in Morocco's deposits of phosphates for fertilizer use. In early 1974 the two governments signed a 30-year agreement involving Soviet aid in prospecting for phosphates, and have apparently agreed that the Soviets will purchase a sizable part of whatever is found and mined.[54]

NOTES

1. See U.S. Congress, Joint Economic Committee, Soviet Economic Performance, 1966-67 (Washington, D.C.: U.S. Government Printing Office, 1968), p. 128.

2. O.E.C.D., Development Cooperation, 1973 (Paris, 1973), pp. 39-40.

3. Institute of Africa, Academy of Science, Ekonomicheskoe Sotrudnichestvo SSSR so Stranami Afriki (Economic Collaboration of the USSR with Countries of Africa) (Moscow: Nauka, 1968), p. 145.

4. Ibid., p. 20.

5. See USSR, Ministry of Foreign Affairs, SSSR i Strani Afriki, 1946-62: Dokumenti i Materiali (The USSR and Countries of Africa, 1946-62: Documents and Materials) (Moscow, 1962), 2 vols., for: "Exchange of Letters on Economic and Technical Cooperation between the USSR and Ethiopia," July 15, 1959, vol. 1, pp. 450-56; "Agreement on Economic and Technical Cooperation between the USSR and Ghana," August 4, 1960, vol. 1, pp. 580-84; "Agreement on the Broadening of Economic and Technical Cooperation between the USSR and Ghana," November 4, 1961, vol. 2, pp. 441-43; "Agreement between the USSR and Guinea on Economic and Technical Cooperation," August 24, 1959, vol. 1, pp. 460-62; "Protocol to the Agreement between the USSR and Guinea on Economic and Technical Cooperation from 24 August 1959," September 8, 1960, vol. 1, pp. 627-29; "Agreement on Economic and Technical Cooperation between the USSR and Mali," March 18, 1961, vol. 2, pp. 227-32; the same for Somalia, June 2, 1961, vol. 2, pp. 303-08; the same for the Sudan, November 2, 1961, vol. 2, pp.

469-74; and the same for Tunisia, August 30, 1961, vol. 2, pp. 395-401.

See _Vedomost' Verkhovnogo Soveta_ (Register of the Supreme Soviet), No. 35, 1965 for: "Agreement between the Government of the Union of Soviet Socialist Republics and the Government of Uganda on Economic and Technical Cooperation," November 30, 1964, pp. 823-27; ibid., No. 8, 1968, the same for Zambia, May 26, 1967, pp. 78-81; ibid., No. 40, 1968, "Protocol between the Government of the Union of Soviet Socialist Republics and the Government of Mali," June 22, 1967, pp. 683-85; ibid., No. 17, 1972, "Protocol to the Soviet-Somali Agreement on Economic and Technical Cooperation from 2 June 1961," February 5, 1971, pp. 219-22; and ibid., No. 50, 1973, "Protocol to the Soviet-Somali Agreement on Economic and Technical Cooperation from 2 June 1961," May 6, 1972, pp. 811-14.

6. The protocol of June 22, 1967 with Mali and the protocol of February 5, 1971 with Somali. See the sources listed in note 5 above.

7. Two others (those two listed in note 6 above) specified a particular year for the beginning of repayments. The two which stipulated after the project was completed were the agreement with Sudan of 1961 and the 1972 protocol with Somalia (see note 5 above).

8. This same division of responsibilities between donor and recipient governments is described in Institute of Africa, op. cit., p. 19.

9. Ghana, Committee on Economic Cooperation with Eastern Countries, "Review of Contracts, Progress Report" (memorandum, no date), p. 1.

10. This provision about pricing is found either in the aid agreement itself, or in the Soviet trade agreement with the same country which was in operation during the period of the aid program. See USSR, _SSSR i Strani Afriki_, vols. 1 and 2, for the following trade agreements: with Ethiopia, signed July 11, 1959; with Ghana, August 4, 1960; Guinea, February 13, 1959; Mali, March 18, 1961; Morocco, April 19, 1958; Sudan, November 1, 1961; and Tunisia, March 14, 1962.

11. The United Nations' Economic Commission for Africa publishes a series of such data, drawn from member country reports, entitled _African Trade Statistics, Series B: Trade By Commodity_.

12. Standard International Trade Classification.

13. See note 5 above.

14. The most extensive survey of the press, journals, and radio broadcasts in both the Soviet Union and LDCs

which bear on relations between the USSR and developing
countries is provided by USSR and Third World (London).
Its predecessor, 1966-70, was Mizan Supplement A; and
prior to 1966, new surveys appeared in the main journal,
Mizan, itself.

15. Interview with an officer of the Bureau of Intelligence and Research, Washington, D.C., June 1974.

16. In an interview with Marshall I. Goldman. See
the latter's book, Soviet Foreign Aid (New York: Frederick
A. Praeger, 1967), p. 27.

17. Poland, Central Statistical Office, Yearbook of
Foreign Trade Statistics, 1966 (Warsaw, 1967), p. 8. I am
grateful to Barry Kostinsky for suggesting this source.

18. See note 5 above.

19. Statisticheskii Yezhegodnik: Stran-Chlenov
Sovieta Ekonomicheskoi Vzaimopomoshchi, 1972 (Statistical
Yearbook of the Country-Members of the Council of Mutual
Economic Assistance) (Moscow, 1972), p. 464.

20. Barry L. Kostinsky, Description and Analysis of
Soviet Foreign Trade Statistics (forthcoming, Department
of Commerce), ch. III.

21. USSR, Vneshnyaya Torgovlya SSSR za 1970 god,
p. 316.

22. Compare ibid., p. 316 with Vneshnyaya Torgovlya
SSSR za 1970 god, passim for Category 16 entries.

23. Compare the data for 15 African aid recipients
in Table 4.2 of this chapter.

24. Egypt, Iran, Iraq, Syria, Turkey, and the two
Yemens. See U.S. Department of State, Bureau of Intelligence and Research, Communist States and Developing Countries: Aid and Trade in 1973 (forthcoming).

25. See Alexander Dallin, "The Soviet Union: Politi-
cal Activity," in Africa and the Communist World, ed.
Zbigniew Brzezinski (Stanford, California: Stanford Uni-
versity Press, 1963), pp. 18-19; and Robert Legvold,
Soviet Policy in West Africa (Cambridge, Mass.: Harvard
University Press, 1970), pp. 68-76, 174-80.

26. Until at least mid-1969, the following nonaided
states had no diplomatic relations with the Soviet Union
despite the latter's extension of recognition: Botswana,
Gabon, Lesotho, Liberia, Malagasy, Malawi, and Swaziland.
U.S. Department of State, Director of Intelligence and
Research, Research Memorandum: Soviet Diplomatic Relations and Representation (Washington, D.C., 1969).

27. For material on the many economic ties between
these three states and South Africa, see International
Monetary Fund, Surveys of African Economies (Washington,
D.C., 1973), vol. 5, chapters 2-5.

28. Cited in _Mizan_, 7, 1962, p. 24. The former
President of the Malagasy Republic defended the presence
of French bases in his country as necessary protection
against Soviet and Chinese "aggression." He is cited in
Africa Research Bulletin (Political, Social and Cultural
Series) 2, 1964, p. 30.

29. See William T. Shinn, "The National Democratic
State," World Politics 15 (April 1963): 382-84; Milton
Kovner, "Soviet Trade and Aid," Current History, October
1965, p. 228; and also L. M. Entin and S. A. Sosna,
Natsional'no-Demokraticheskoe Gosudarstvo i Ekonomicheskii
Progress (The National Democratic State and Economic Prog-
ress) (Moscow: Mezhdunarodniye Otnosheniye, 1968), pp.
17-38.

30. Cited from a 1962 article by V. Tyaguenko. See
Mizan, 7, 1962: 16-17.

31. See the three sources cited in note 29 above,
the same pages. Early in the 1960s, Ghana, Guinea, Mali,
and Indonesia were the only LDCs which "qualified" for the
label "national democratic state." Later in the decade
they were joined by Algeria, Burma, Congo-Brazzaville,
Egypt, and Syria. However, as military regimes took control in Indonesia (in 1965) and Ghana (1966), those two
countries were dropped from the list.

32. My main sources for these party ties are the
surveys of the press and radio broadcasts in the Soviet
Union and African countries provided by Mizan, 1960-65;
Mizan Supplement A (Soviet and Chinese Reports on the
Middle East and Africa), 1966-70; and USSR and Third World,
1970-72.

33. In 1965, 2 trucks and a reported £20,000; in
1967, 4 river launches and 6 mobile "bus-clubs"; and in
1968, 10 Soviet vehicles. Sources: see note 32 above.

34. Yearbook of International Communist Affairs,
1973 (Stanford, California: Hoover Institution Press,
1973), p. 235.

35. Legvold, op. cit., chapter 8.

36. Ibid., pp. 275-302.

37. Africa Research Bulletin (Political, Social and
Cultural Series) 4, 1967, p. 768.

38. Ibid., 2, 1969, p. 1336; and 1, 1971, p. 2002.

39. Michael MacGwire, "The Mediterranean and Soviet
Naval Interests," International Journal 27 (August 1972):
516, 525-27.

40. Jane's Fighting Ships, 1973 (London: Sampson
Low, 1973), p. 19.

41. Robert C. Sellers, Armed Forces of the World
(3rd ed., New York: Praeger, 1971), p. 8.

42.   Ministry of Foreign Affairs, SSSR i Strani
Afriki, vol. 1, p. 532.
43.   Goldman, op. cit., p. 172.
44.   In apparent retaliation against Guinea's support
of African nationalists in neighboring Guinea-Bissau, the
Portuguese military landed a commando force near Conakry
in November 1970, which briefly occupied parts of the
Guinean capital. To prevent further incursions by sea,
Guinea asked the Soviets for a protective naval force to
stand off the coast. Such a force was reportedly on station by October 1971. Africa Research Bulletin (Political,
Social and Cultural Series) 10, 1971, p. 2268.
45.   New York Times, December 1973, based on a Pentagon report.
46.   J. Bowyer Bell, The Horn of Africa, Strategic
Magnet in the Seventies (New York: Crane, Russak and
Company, 1973), p. 42.
47.   Economist, February 9, 1974; and New York Times,
June 2, 1974.
48.   Ministry of Foreign Affairs, SSSR i Strani
Afriki, vol. 2, p. 304.
49.   Vneshnyaya Torgovlya SSSR za . . . god, 1960-73
issues.
50.   USSR and Third World 4, 1972, p. 230.
51.   V. V. Strishkin, "The Minerals Industry of the
USSR," in Minerals Yearbook, 1971 (Washington, D.C.,
1973), vol. 3, p. 822.
52.   See Carole A. Sawyer, Communist Trade with Developing Countries, 1955-65 (New York: Frederick A.
Praeger, 1966), pp. 72-75; and David Morison, "USSR and
the Third World: Questions of Economic Development,"
Mizan 12 (December 1970): 141-42. For the mix of aided
countries' exports to the Soviet Union, see Vneshnyaya
Torgovlya za . . . god, 1960-73 issues.
53.   The Soviets have been aware of the dissatisfac-
tion of African trading partners with the quality of their
goods, the supply of spare parts, the availability of repair services, and other aspects of buying from Soviet
sources. See Institute of Africa, Ekonomicheskoe
Sotrudnichestvo, pp. 152-53.
54.   Africa Research Bulletin (Economic, Financial
and Technical Series) 3, 1974, p. 3086.

5

SOVIET BLOC-GHANAIAN RELATIONS SINCE THE DOWNFALL OF NKRUMAH

Valerie Plave Bennett

Most case studies of relations between great and small powers dwell upon the efforts of the great power to gain influence within or resources from the small power. If these efforts prove ultimately unsuccessful, academic interest in the relationship wanes, as scholars avidly search for new cases to examine. Diplomats cannot, however, as easily turn their attention elsewhere. Involvement between the two unequal combatants invariably leaves a residue of treaties, protocols, trade agreements, debts, contracts, legations, and personnel exchanges. Particularly in cases in which diplomatic relations between the two powers are not severed, a new modus vivendi must, often painfully, be reached. Soviet-Ghanaian relations since the ouster of Kwame Nkrumah in the 1966 coup d'etat provide an opportunity to examine this dilemma.

Post-1966 Soviet-Ghanaian relations also present the scholar concerned with Soviet ideology with the chance to discover Soviet reaction to the disappearance of so many of the "revolutionary democracies" that held so much promise for Soviet ideologists in the early sixties.

In 1963 Nikita Khrushchev lauded "revolutionary democratic statesmen," who "sincerely advocate noncapitalist methods for the solution of national problems and declare their determination to build socialism."[1] This optimistic assessment encompassed Mali's Keita, Algeria's Ben Bella, Ghana's Nkrumah, and Egypt's Nasser. The possibility was for the first time considered that nations might be able to build socialism without communist parties. Instead socialism would arrive under the aegis of the independence based single mass parties. Nkrumah and the CPP were the leader and the party perceived as the most devoted to the task of constructing a new socialist state.

The 1964 ouster of Khrushchev led to an ideological downgrading of the efforts of the revolutionary democracies. Ghana, Mali, Algeria, and Egypt were once again described as states "on the noncapitalist path," a stage considerably less exalted than the road to socialism.[2]

Between 1965 and 1968 Ben Bella, Nkrumah, and Keita were all removed from power by military coups. The demise of so many revolutionary democracies led to a reevaluation of the nature of the revolutionary democracies and a reassessment of the prospects for African states to build socialism.

THE BACKGROUND TO DISENGAGEMENT

The story of Soviet involvement in Ghana during the Nkrumah era is too well-known to need much elaboration. Only a brief description of Soviet-Ghanaian relations before 1966 is needed to understand Soviet efforts to arrive at an accommodation with post-Nkrumah Ghana.

Both the Soviets and Nkrumah found their close relations between 1961 and 1965 rewarding. For the Soviets, Ghanaian support on international issues was perceived as important in an era of Soviet-U.S. rivalry. Ghana was on the verge of providing the Soviet Union with an airbase that could be used as a transshipping area for Cuba, and Ghana was a ready seller of cocoa to the Soviet Union. Nkrumah, for his part, saw the Soviet connection as a means of increasing his foreign policy options, limiting British influence (both economic and political), and amplifying the Ghanaian voice on the international stage. But this satisfying relationship was almost exclusively one between the Soviet Union and Kwame Nkrumah, rather than between the Soviet Union and Ghana.[3] The Soviets did little (being in a position to do little) to create a climate which would have permitted long-term close relations between Ghana and the Soviet Union after Osagyefo passed from the scene.

Declining cocoa prices and the exhaustion of Ghana's foreign currency reserves led to economic stagnation; Nkrumah's popularity plummeted until the conservative, pro-Western, British-trained Ghanaian army intervened to remove the Convention Peoples Party and Kwame Nkrumah from power in February 1966. Consequently within a week of the February coup d'etat Ghana's new military leaders began dismantling Nkrumah's political establishment and reorienting his foreign policy. The ideological orientation

of the National Liberation Council was immediately apparent. Major-General Ankrah, the NLC's Chairman, announced
four days after the coup that the new government was going
to "re-think the economic set-up."[4] Socialism, along with
close relations with the Soviet Union, was to be a thing
of the past.

The NLC expelled Soviet advisors "spread across Ghana
from the Tamale airfield to the University of Ghana, from
Shai Hills to the Kwame Nkrumah Ideological Institute, and
from Flagstaff House to the Tema seaport."[5]

The ouster of Nkrumah and the Soviets meant the exo-
dus of the staff of Ghana's medical school, one-third of
the secondary school teachers of mathematics and science,
advisors to the Ministry of Defense, geologists, the
staffs of the state farms, technicians at the atomic-
research facility, and the top Soviet embassy officials
(expelled for alleged espionage activity).[6] All of the
Soviet and Chinese sponsored projects were shut down, including the atomic research center which was under the
directorship of Dr. Alan Nunn May, the British scientist
who had been convicted of espionage in the United Kingdom,
a fish-processing complex, a concrete panel factory, a
gold refinery in Tarkwa, a pencil complex in Kumasi, and
the giant Tamale airbase (Job 650). In addition, all
Aeroflot flights to Ghana were cancelled, and the Soviet
embassy was ordered to reduce its staff from 67 to 18.
Four newly acquired Iluyshin aircraft were returned to
their seller.

After the extent of the debacle became clear, the
Soviets faced two interrelated problems: What were to be
their relationship to Nkrumah on the one hand, and to
post-Nkrumah Ghana on the other?

The prospect of any positive payoff from diplomatic
relations with the NLC seemed dismal. The NLC was not
ideologically disposed to provide either support for the
Soviets in the international arena, or to provide facilities to the Soviets. Further the NLC was also opposed to
trade relations with the USSR. One scholar described NLC
foreign policy in these terms: "Instead of maneuvering
between the great powers, as Nkrumah did, the junta tried
to extract the utmost from the West alone by going as far
to the right as possible."[7] Consequently the Soviets had
small incentive to normalize relations with Ghana after
1966, and rather strong incentive to support Nkrumah.
However the Soviets ignored Nkrumah while recognizing
the new Ghanaian government.

Instead of attacking the new regime in the media,
refusing it recognition, aiding Nkrumahist sympathizers,

or refusing to trade with the NLC, the Soviets chose to
ignore Nkrumah, while maintaining correct relations with
the NLC. Attempting to restore Nkrumah was unappealing
for both practical and ideological reasons. The Soviets
had, in a sense, given up on Nkrumah by late 1965; Ambassador Rodionov had tried and failed to convince Nkrumah to
mend his extravagant and unpopular ways. In ideological
terms, the downfall of Khrushchev marked, as we have noted,
the end of Soviet enthusiasm for the possibility of revolutionary democratic regimes building "scientific socialism." After Khrushchev's departure Soviet policy in Black
Africa was based on the creation of businesslike relations
with a wide variety of African states (regardless of ideological proclivities), attempts to build long-term influence based on educational and cultural ties, and a desire
for economic links that would stress trade over aid.

Given this disenchantment with Nkrumah and desire for
long-term, stable relations with Africa, it is not surprising that the Soviets quickly jettisoned Nkrumah. The coup
occurred while Nkrumah was in Peking on a self-appointed
mission to end the war. His Chinese hosts declined to intervene on his behalf; Nkrumah then headed for Moscow.
The Soviets sent Foreign Minister Gromyko to the airport,
". . . after a day of presumably evading any form of response to Nkrumah's pleas, placed him on a secret flight
to Guinea. Toure awaited Nkrumah with military honors
and a presidential appointment."[8]

In view of the new Soviet interest in "stable, businesslike relations with a broad segment of African states,
there remained few alternatives other than stoic acceptance" of Nkrumah's ouster.[9] As a result of the new con-
servatism, the Soviet media "deleted from their coverage
of Nkrumah's speeches and radio broadcasts to Ghana his
exhortations to the Ghanaian people to rise up against
the 'military clique' and overthrow their 'illegal' regime."[10]

Although in the final analysis Nkrumah could be ignored, Ghana could not. The Soviets quickly made known
their desire to maintain cordial relations with the new
military government. The Soviet press was reported as
saying that:

> The Soviet Government used to maintain
> friendly relations with the Government
> of Ghana, and it strives to do so now.
> The Soviet people have sincere friendly
> feelings for the Ghanaians.[11]

SOVIET BLOC-GHANAIAN RELATIONS
DURING THE NLC-BUSIA ERA

The Soviets recognized the new military government three weeks after the coup. The Chinese on the other hand, "refused to extend recognition and, after Chinese officials had been sent home, addressed a violent note of protest to the Ghanaian government."[12] Finally, the Chinese closed their embassy in Ghana in November 1966 at the request of the NLC.

Although the Russians were anxious to maintain relations with the NLC, the diplomatic waters were turbulent. Early in March 1967 the Soviets were accused by the NLC of trying to smuggle arms and explosives into Ghana via a freighter. The Soviets denied the allegation. Three months later the NLC expelled <u>Pravda</u>'s West African correspondent for dissemination of anti-NLC propaganda. After their correspondent's expulsion, <u>Pravda</u> accused the Ghanaian leaders of serving the Western powers more and more openly, "hoping to maintain [themselves] in power with their help." [13] Finally an anti-Soviet article in the <u>Ghanaian Times</u>, describing the Russians as the political assassins of history, provoked the Soviet ambassador to threaten to close the Soviet embassy if a retraction was not printed.

These irritations led to the Soviet refusal to upgrade their embassy to the ambassadorial level. Finally in October 1967 the Chairman of the NLC "curtly informed the Soviet charge d'affaires: 'If by the time I come back from Canada, you have no ambassador here, I'll recall our man in Moscow.' Within a few weeks the Soviet government had posted Vasily Safronchuk to Ghana as its new ambassador."[14]

If diplomatic problems could be solved by threats, economic problems could not. After the coup, three kinds of Soviet-Ghanaian economic relations remained to be ironed out: debt repayment, unfinished aid projects, and the ramifications of the 1961 trade agreement.

Ghana and the Soviet Union, like a couple on the brink of divorce, found themselves in a situation in which sentiment was long dead but legal entanglements lingered on. The Soviet position during negotiations with the NLC seems to have been rather consistent. In light of the NLC's ideological convictions, there were few advantages to be gained by a flexible negotiating posture, so the Russians had no reason to offer concessions. The NLC's first reaction after seizing power was

to try to undo all of Nkrumah's efforts to build economic
bridges to the East. But "economic and political realities outside and inside Ghana forced the junta . . . to
effect a gradual evolution of its own thinking from rabid
anti-communism to a more realistic reappraisal of conditions."[15]

In June 1961, after two years of negotiations, a
Soviet-Ghanaian trade agreement was ratified by both nations. Trade between the two countries had begun in 1959
when the Soviets purchased $18.9 million in cocoa beans.
Observers took this agreement to be a "rather energetic
attempt to ingratiate the Soviet Union with the new
Ghanaian leadership."[16] These sizable imports were also
probably indicative of a decision to take advantage of
low world market prices to build up Soviet cocoa stocks.
In July 1961, in his famous tour of the Soviet Union,
Nkrumah made known his desire to expand trade relations
with the Soviets. A new trade agreement was therefore
negotiated in November 1961. The new five-year agreement,
unlike the previous one, provided for a sizable swing
credit of $11 million. A set of protocols (not legally
binding) "reflected the Soviet Union's intention to purchase annually a specified quantity of cocoa beans, increasing to 60,000 tons in five years, and to pay for
these purchases partially in a freely convertible currency, decreasing annually from 55% of the first year's
purchases."[17] The Soviets also offered Nkrumah credits
totaling $42 million to finance the reinforced concrete
panel plant, paper mill, textile mill, machine-tool plant,
and several other projects.

The importance of Soviet credits increased in 1963
when President Kennedy "instructed AID [the Agency for
International Development] to extend no more long-term
credits to Ghana."[18] Kennedy had exhausted his patience
with Nkrumah's anti-Western propaganda and economic mis-
management. [Even with the ending of American aid, however, by the end of 1964, less than 27 percent of Soviet
credits extended to Ghana had actually been drawn upon.][19]
Soviet trade with Ghana grew by 56 percent between 1961
and 1964, but still accounted for only 7 percent of Ghana's
total foreign commerce. Ghana's total trade with all the
centrally planned economies by 1965 totaled almost 32 percent (see Table 5.1).

There is considerable controversy among Western
economists as to whether trade with the Soviet Union and
East Europe was beneficial to Ghana. The attitude of the
NLC was clearly that trade with the East was not beneficial.

After the coup the Ghanaian Ministry of Trade "prepared a memorandum recommending that a review of all trade agreements with the socialist countries be undertaken 'with a view to removing their harmful effects on the economy.'"[20]

TABLE 5.1

Ghanaian Imports and Exports Between 1965 and 1970

Ghanaian Exports as a Percentage of Total					
1965	1966	1967	1968	1969	1970
To USSR					
10.0	9.4	8.4			
			9.2	6.8	10.0
To other socialist nations					
21.3	22.0	15.5			
Totals 31.3	31.4	23.9	9.2	6.8	10.0

Ghanaian Imports as a Percentage of Total					
1965	1966	1967	1968	1969	1970
From USSR					
6.7	5.8				
		7.6	7.6	8.5	5.0
From other socialist nations					
26.3	15.2				
Totals 33.0	21.0	7.6	7.6	8.5	5.0

Advocates of trade with socialist nations have on the one hand argued that trade with socialist countries can exercise a stabilizing influence on the national economy of noncommunist developing countries. Additionally it has sometimes been argued that the socialist countries do not drive as hard bargains as the capitalist traders, leading to better price performance in trade with socialist nations.

There is very little evidence to support either of these suppositions. One student of Ghanaian economic conditions has argued that "it should be stated 'for the record' . . . that there is little evidence that [the reorientation of trade with the Soviet Bloc] was against Ghana's interests. It appears that the prices Ghana received and paid in her trade with the East were comparable with the terms of trade with Western countries," but not any better than Western terms of trade.[21] In the 1961-64 period Russia and East Germany paid above-average prices for imports from Ghana, while Bulgaria, China, and Czecho-slovakia were paying below the average.[22] Stevens has shown that when cocoa prices are declining the Russians tend to pay prices higher than the world average, and that the opposite is the case when the world price is rising.

If it cannot be said that terms of trade with the Soviet Bloc were any worse than world market prices, can it be said that the terms were any better? The answer to that question is an unequivocal no: the price performance of the Western Bloc as a whole is consistently better than the price performance of the Eastern Bloc.[23] The negative aspects of trade with the Soviet Union often center on the shoddy nature of some of their consumer goods. Consumer goods, however, composed a minute part of Soviet-Ghanaian trade, although this aspect of Soviet-Ghanaian trade may have been most visible to the Ghanaian consumers.

In the NLC's haste to become a client of the Western powers, they indicated that they wished to renegotiate the trade and payments agreement of 1961.

> As it had been written, however, the
> agreement would automatically be renewed
> unless one of the parties notified the
> other of its desire to change matters six
> months before the agreement's expiration
> date. (December 1966) In the confusion
> after the coup, officials had neglected
> to act swiftly enough (some said they
> confused the notification period on the
> Soviet agreement with the much shorter
> period provided for by the agreements
> with East European countries), and now
> the Soviet Union insisted that the
> agreement was in force for another five
> years.[24]

The Soviets refused to discuss the trade agreement; according to Ghanaian sources, the Soviets would talk only about the annual protocol by which the agreement would be implemented.[25] Indications that Ghana's civil servants, unlike the NLC, did not believe the Soviet Bloc agreements to be detrimental to Ghanaian interests are abundant after 1967. According to W. Scott Thompson, the professional diplomats and economic advisors "succeeded, by and large, in persuading the NLC that Ghana had a vital interest in stabilizing its political relations with the socialist states and in rationalizing, rather than jettisoning, the economic exchanges undertaken during the Nkrumah period."[26] The Western powers were not willing to expand trade with Ghana merely to freeze the Soviet Bloc out of the Ghanaian market.

After protracted negotiations, the Soviet Union and Ghana signed a new trade protocol in June 1968 under which the Ghanaians sold cocoa and timber to the USSR, and imported machinery, crude oil, sugar, and drugs. The total amount of the trade was between 34 and 40 million cedis. (In 1968 95¢ = 1 cedi.) Between 1966 and 1970 trade between the Soviet Bloc nations and Ghana declined precipitously, as shown in Table 5.1.

The problem of the uncompleted projects was never to be resolved during the NLC era, or during the period of the succeeding pro-Western civilian government of Dr. Kofi Busia (1969-72). In 1967 E. N. Omaboe, chairman of the NLC's Economic Committee, traveled to Moscow; during the discussions the Ghanaians requested the return of the Soviet fishery experts and the Soviets complied with the request. In May 1968 the two sides reached an agreement enabling Soviet experts to tour Ghana with an eye to renewing work on the abandoned projects. A 12-man Soviet delegation arrived early in June, spending approximately a month examining the abandoned projects. Omaboe returned to Moscow to negotiate the final arrangements for the resumption of project construction; agreement, however, foundered on the sensitive question of the unresolved Soviet-Ghanaian debts. There is in retrospect no economic reason that work on these projects should have been halted after the coup. There is no reason to believe that the Soviet-sponsored projects were less in Ghana's interest than similar Western-sponsored aid projects. In fact, "there were cases in which the Eastern countries were more particular about the viability of proposed aid projects than the Ghana government."[27] The terms upon which the aid was received from the Eastern Bloc were less favorable than for Western aid in the late sixties, because Soviet aid was repayable over a somewhat short ten-year period. However, these terms were considerably more favorable than the Western-backed suppliers' credits which became a mainstay of Ghanaian borrowing in the last years of the Nkrumah government.[28] The Soviets were not willing to complete the unfinished projects until some settlement was reached on the outstanding debts.

DEBTS TO THE SOVIET BLOC, YUGOSLAVIA, AND CHINA

In the final months before the 1966 coup d'etat, as Ghana's international financial position worsened, a moratorium on the debts to several East European countries was granted to Ghana. Between December 1964 and October 1965 the USSR was forced to grant debt relief moratoriums to Guinea, Ghana, and Mali as the economic condition of the once hopeful "revolutionary democracies" turned sour. The two-year moratorium on the Ghanaian debt was not announced until December 1965, although it had undoubtedly been negotiated earlier. After the 1966 coup it was calculated that Ghana's debts to Communist countries totaled approximately $112 million in long-term obligations, while another $91.2 million was due on medium-term suppliers' credits. To put this figure in perspective, it should be noted that Ghana owed her Western creditors approximately $550 million. A breakdown of the Eastern debts is presented in Table 5.2.

TABLE 5.2

Ghana's Debts to the Centrally Planned
Economies in 1966
(in millions of U.S. dollars)

Country	Long-Term Debt	Suppliers' Credits
USSR	$56.0	$48.0
Yugoslavia	28.0	--
Poland	12.5	10.6
China	7.0	5.5
Hungary	3.5	3.6
East Germany	2.0	2.0
Rumania	2.0	2.0
Czechoslovakia	1.0	19.9
Total	$112.0	$91.6

The long-term debts due to the Communist nations had been contracted for a 10-to-12-year period, mostly at a $2\frac{1}{2}$-3 percent rate of interest (except for two credits for fishing trawlers which carried higher interest rates). Although a substantial portion of the expenditure for these loans was made in cedis, repayment was due in foreign currency, particularly in Sterling. The Ghanians did not drive very hard bargains when negotiating these loans.

The Soviet Bloc nations refused to join the Western sponsored debt renegotiations. A year after the NLC came to power, E. N. Omaboe journeyed to Moscow and East Europe in search of debt relief. The Czechs and Poles agreed in 1967 to renegotiate their debts, but the Soviets could not come to terms with the Ghanaians. During the following summer Omaboe returned to Moscow and several East European capitals to discuss the rescheduling of the debts once again. This time only the Rumanians agreed to new rescheduling.

SOVIET BLOC-GHANAIAN RELATIONS IN THE BUSIA ERA

The NLC viewed its rulership as but a temporary state of affairs. One of the military's stated goals was to restore constitutional government to Ghana. Consequently, in late August 1969 a national election was held, propelling Dr. Kofi Busia and his Progress Party into office. One of the leading members of Ghana's pro-Western intelligentsia, Busia had been one of the many opponents of Nkrumah who had chosen exile. Busia, a firm proponent of laissez-faire economic policy, was eager for Western aid and foreign investment. The new Ghanaian Prime Minister was also an advocate of Ivory Coast President Houphouet-Boigny's call for "dialogue" with, rather than isolation of, South Africa.

Busia's assumption of office in October 1969 coincided with a new decline in international cocoa prices. By 1970 as a result of the cocoa slump, Ghana's foreign trade position was little improved. Finance Minister Mensah complained in a lecture at the University of Ghana that the debt rescheduling with the Communist countries had meant extra payments of well over $5 million, or an increase of 16 percent on the socialist debts. (Western moratorium interest had added more than $85 million to those debts.) The Ghanaians and the Soviets had been unable to agree on terms for rescheduling for several reasons: The expulsion of the Soviet technicians complicated negotiations; the Soviets were accused by the NLC of trying to aid Nkrumah, particularly at the time of the arrest of Air Marshal Otu who purportedly had had contacts with Soviet officials; and the previously mentioned seizure of a Russian fishing trawler added up to a background of strained relations between the two nations.

Even without all these small annoyances making debt settlement difficult, the Soviet Union would still have been unwilling to compromise on the debt question. The Russians entertained the same fears that Ghana's Western creditors suffered, namely, that renegotiations with the Ghanaians would open an uncloseable Pandora's Box. If the Soviets agreed to renegotiations with the Ghanaians, could they refuse the Malians or Guineans? The inviability of debt was a particularly real problem to the Soviets because the Egyptians were asking for forgiveness and renegotiation on more than a billion dollars worth of debts.

The Ghanaians put at least a partial end to the Soviets' dilemma by unilaterally rescheduling their Soviet debts on the terms previously agreed upon with the Western creditors when the two-year moratorium expired. The repercussions of this unilateral action were minimal. The USSR lacks the two weapons that give the Western creditors leverage: they could neither threaten to half aid, nor cease to provide insurance to their nationals doing business in Ghana. Moreover, the Russians had little to gain by a display of complete intransigence.

The message of Ghana's Western creditors in the post-Nkrumah era seems to have been that if Ghana followed a laissez-faire economic policy at home; a convertible money policy; paid her debts; and followed a pro-Western diplomatic course, substantial Western aid and investment would be forthcoming, resulting in improved economic conditions in Ghana. In reality some aid and little investment resulted. The more immediate results of the NLC-Busia policies were increased unemployment, a widened gap between the rich and the poor, and an increased flow of luxury goods into Ghana for consumption by the bourgeoisie, coupled with rising inflation.

THE COUP OF JANUARY 13, 1972

It was not surprising that Busia soon found himself removed from office by Ghana's ever-watchful military. It could have also been predicted that the military leaders who ousted Busia would call for the by now familiar reorientation of both domestic and foreign policy.

A month after the latest coup, Colonel I. G. Acheampong, the new head of the National Redemption Council (NRC) signaled the direction Ghana's economic policy would take:

> The political frame of reference which
> has guided . . . actions and . . . advise

in the past two years must be cast into
the rubbish heap of history. This means
a departure from the laissez-faire so-
called free market economy and the institution of effective planning in the
allocation and utilization of resources.[29]

The Progress Party government of Busia, in Acheampong's words, "preferred a doctrinaire attachment to a
free market economy which meant that we had to leave our
fate in the hands of market forces whose operations are
beyond our control."[30]
The NRC announced that they intended to send trade
delegations to the USSR and other socialist countries.
The NRC also took steps toward reactivating five development projects undertaken by the Russians, Chinese, and
Yugoslavs during the Nkrumah period.
Under NRC leadership, Ghana has reopened diplomatic
relations with some socialist nations, reactivated relations with the radical African states, and ended the
dialogue approach to the Southern African question.
Shortly after the coup, Colonel Acheampong announced
that the NRC's foreign policy would be based on nonalignment and positive neutralism. Following this decision,
Ghana made known her desire to resume diplomatic relations
with the Peoples' Republic of China and welcomed a six-man
North Korean mission. But Acheampong argued that these
measures did not augur an attempt to substitute one set of
alliances for another. The Colonel insisted that the NRC
was only "expanding the range of our friendship and giving
effect to our policy of non-alignment."[31]
The NRC hoped to reorient both Ghana's trade and aid
toward the socialist countries. The NRC was destined to
be disappointed on both counts.

THE FAILURE TO WIN AID

It is plausible that the NRC expected that the new
policy of nonalignment would again make Ghana the sought
after aid recipient that she was in the early years of
the Nkrumah era. But as W. Scott Thompson has noted,
neither the Soviets nor the Western nations are any longer
engaged in that type of composition. "The attenuation of
interest in Africa," by the mid-1960s, "had devalued nonalignment as a bargaining device for small states."[32]
Since 1965 the Soviets have cut back their foreign aid

programs; sending much of their aid to Cuba and North
Vietnam. The ouster of Keita, Nkrumah, Ben Bella, and
Sukarno in Indonesia has made the Soviets increasingly
disillusioned with the possibility of the Less Developed
Countries (LDCs) building socialism.[33] Soviet ideologists
now emphasize the political, social, and economic weaknesses of African nations, which on the whole, disquali-
fies the area from building socialism.

The revolutionary democracies turned out to be inadequate for the construction of socialism. The African
masses were too traditional, tribalistic, and backward to
enable revolution to succeed. Africa's progressive post-
independence leaders in general, and Nkrumah specifically,
had monopolized power, failing to improve the conditions
of the masses and failing to engage the masses in political activity. The mass parties contained too many petit-
bourgeois bureaucrats but not enough socialists. The
revolutionary democracies were easy prey for military
leaders who desired political power.

Less attention is paid in the 1970s by the USSR to
the political return from aid to Africa. Concern now centers on adequate economic return; hence the close economic
ties the Soviets have constructed with Nigeria and the
military aid the Russians supplied to the Federal Military
Government during the civil war.[34] There was neither sufficient economic nor political return to be garnered from
Soviet aid in the 1970s. Poor planning, project choice,
and management meant that there was little economic development generated by Soviet aid to Ghana. Lack of political payoff after 1966 needs no elaboration. If Ghana
lacked the natural resources to encourage renewed Soviet
interest, the international climate made it even more unlikely that the Soviet Union would once again be interested in Ghana's future. In the era of detente with the
West, the Russians are less concerned with support for
their international positions from small countries. Detente has led to a significant devaluation of the value
of a United Nations vote, for example. Ghana, and most
of Africa, is now perceived as lacking economic, political, or strategic importance. Ghana has neither the strategic importance of Somalia, the economic importance of
Nigeria, nor the ideological importance of the Southern
African liberation movements. There are simply no potential short-term benefits for the Soviets that would encourage renewed close cooperation between Ghana and the
Soviet Union.

One indication of the lack of Soviet interest in Africa has been a decline in ceremonial meetings between African leaders and top Soviet officials. Upper Volta reduced the status of its embassy in Moscow due to the poor treatment received by an Upper Voltan parliamentary delegation. Three African heads of state (the Presidents of Senegal, Mauritania, and Congo) reportedly cancelled their visit to the Soviet Union "because of the low level of meetings which would have been available."[35] The Upper Voltan Ambassador to Paris acknowledged that the aims of the Soviet Union and the LDCs were quite different:

> Developing countries expect a great deal
> from the economic co-operation established
> between them and rich countries like the
> Soviet Union. But, it seems that the
> Great Powers are more concerned about ex-
> tending their influence in developing
> countries, than effectively contributing
> to their economic growth.[36]

As economic issues such as international monetary arrangements, fuel supplies, and tariff preferences come to the fore, there is a tendency for small states such as Ghana to perceive both the United States and the Soviet Union as wealthy countries whose interests are fundamentally different from the poorer nonaligned states.

Decline in Soviet interest in Africa has not, however, mirrored a concomitant decline in East European interest in the continent. The Hungarians have been particularly anxious to resume closer ties with Ghana. After the visit of President Losonczi to Ghana in November 1973 two agreements for technical cooperation were signed in agriculture, oil, and aluminum. The Hungarians were also going to provide technical assistance for a brick and tile industry and for the expansion of the pharmaceutical division of the Ghana Industrial Holding Corp.[37] In 1974-75, 20 Ghanaian students will study agriculture, mineral and oil industries, pharmaceuticals, building engineering and aluminum; eight Hungarian experts will assist Ghana in such enterprises as the Aluminum Commission, Geological Survey and State Gold Mines Corporation. Small-scale technical assistance from East Europe does not seem to suffer from the same drawbacks as Soviet assistance.

The Chinese are faring considerably better under the second Ghanaian military government than under the first. A team of Chinese agricultural experts recently conducted

feasibility studies on irrigation canals and dams at
Dawhenya, near Accra, in connection with possible Chinese
assistance in rice cultivation.[38]
   The Soviets, cognizant of the belief that they are
against economic development, have tried to improve their
image. The International Investment Bank (SIIB) established in 1971 to extend credit to Comecon countries, will
now have a special credit fund to assist developing countries. The bank will grant credits for up to 15 years for
construction of new enterprises and modernization of existing ones, out of a fund totaling a billion transferable
roubles.[39] It is yet to be seen how useful an instrument
the SIIB will be in fostering economic development in
Africa.
   Soviet-Ghanaian talks are still continuing on the
question of the uncompleted Soviet projects. Carl Gorev,
the chief specialist of the State Committee of Soviet Foreign Economic Relations, came to Accra in the summer of
1973 to discuss the reactivation of the pre-fab housing
scheme, the fish complex, and gold refinery. Gorev departed, promising only to submit a report to the Soviet
government.

                SOVIET-GHANAIAN TRADE

   The signals emanating from the Soviet Union regarding future trade relations between the USSR and Ghana
have been somewhat contradictory. In September 1972
Major Kwame Baah traveled to Moscow to sign a protocol
calling for increased trade between Ghana and Russia.[40]
Less than four months later the Soviet trading organization announced that the USSR would be buying less cocoa
in 1973 than in the previous year. The statement issued
said "it had been decided to reduce purchases of cocoa
beans [and] cocoa butter . . . in 1973 in view of unfavor-
able market conditions and the fact that Soviet industry
is enjoying considerable stocks of these commodities."[41]
Translated into capitalist jargon, the Russians were saying that they had bought enough cocoa when prices were
depressed to have no need to buy when prices were at
their peak. (In May 1973 cocoa prices on the London market reached an historic high of $1,250 a long ton.)
Present Soviet trade needs are in the areas of consumer
durables, agricultural staples, and advanced technology.
The developed Western powers, not the Third World, are
the potential sources of these items. The Ghanaians,

for their part, are suffering from a long-standing inability to diversify and expand their exports. The Ghanaians cannot count on greatly increased exports of cocoa to the Soviets even if there is a decline in the world price. The Soviets prefer to buy from all the major cocoa producers rather than becoming dependent on a single source.

DEBT NEGOTIATIONS AND THE EAST

The Soviets have not been as successful at maintaining a united front for the Soviet Bloc, as the British have been in the Western-sponsored debt negotiations. British success is due to the fact that Ghana's major Western creditors (the United Kingdom, the United States, West Germany, and Japan), are also substantial creditors for most of the LDCs. They are, therefore, individually interested in maintaining the principle of nonrepudiation and debt obligation regardless of circumstances. In addition, the leverage of the United States and the United Kingdom on the World Bank and the IMF makes it difficult for Ghana to borrow from these sources after her 5th of February debt repudiation.* The Soviets, by contrast, have found it impossible to keep those East European countries who have a substantial export trade with Ghana in line. The Rumanians, Czechs, and Poles have all agreed to new reschedulings and further trade agreements. Only the Russians and Bulgarians have been intransigent on the question of debts.

CULTURAL INFLUENCE AND EDUCATIONAL EXCHANGE

Long-term Soviet influence in Ghana, or any other country for that matter, might be more dependent on the creation of a series of interconnecting ties of trade, aid, investment, cultural exchange, technical assistance, and educational opportunities than on any single policy position the Soviets might take. It is, after all, precisely these types of influences that compose much of the "special relationship" that exists between a metropole

---

*On the 5th of February 1972, the NRC repudiated $94 million of the Nkrumah debts owed to four British construction companies, on the grounds that these contracts were "tainted by corruption."

136

and a former colony. Generations of Ghanaians have been
taught by British teachers, read British literature, attended school in the United Kingdom, and adopted British
customs as their own. It is not even necessary for these
experiences to be completely pleasurable for them to have
a long-lasting effect. Even Ghanaians who were abysmally
poor or who suffered racial discrimination while pursuing
their overseas education still remember some aspects of
their time in Britain fondly. Cultural and educational
influences are not necessarily translatable into political influence on any single issue, but these myriad influences do make for a positive climate of understanding.
For these reasons, the Soviets and East Europeans have
been anxious and willing to educate young Ghanaians at
their universities, technical institutes, professional
schools, and military institutions. Although Nkrumah encouraged these exchanges, they were not particularly popular with Ghana's British trained elite. Ghana's elite,
which had always looked somewhat askance at American acquired credentials, put very little stock in Soviet Bloc
expertise. Ghana's attitude toward the qualifications
acquired by her students in the Soviet Union and other
East European countries has consequently been another
irritant standing in the path of improved Soviet-Ghanaian
relations. For example, aspiring Ghanaian physicians who
had studied in the United Kingdom were not required to
pass an examination upon their return to Ghana, while
Ghanaians who had studied in the Soviet Union were. The
peak of Soviet exasperation with this slight to the Soviet educational system was reached in 1967-68, when
"sixteen young Ghanaian doctors trained in the Soviet
Union received instructions to return to medical school,
after tests revealed their preparation to be inadequate."[42]
One mark of the fact that this problem did not so much represent Ghana's involvement in the Cold War as it symbolized
Ghanaian respect for, and emulation of, the British educational system, was that students returning from West German
schools also needed to be examined upon their return to
Ghana.

The NRC issued a White Paper on Educational Structures in Eastern Europe and West Germany. The White Paper
squarely came down on both sides of the issue. On the one
hand, the White Paper absolved the Soviet Bloc of responsibility for graduates with substandard knowledge. The
government was satisfied that certain deficiencies observed in some Soviet trained Ghanaians were due "to their
weak educational background rather than their training."

There was some truth in this position: often the best
students going abroad opted for the Commonwealth and the
United States; the Soviet Bloc often received the West's
rejects. The need to learn a new language was another
problem facing Ghanaian students in East Europe and West
Germany. The White Paper also mollified the East Europeans by regarding Ghanaians who had attained professional
qualifications in medicine, dentistry, and veterinary science in East Europe as having attained the standard required for practice in Ghana. On the other hand, the
White Paper admitted that "reasonable deficiencies should
be expected from professional men trained in environments
outside Ghana." In view of this problem, professional
bodies should take steps to organize remedial courses for
Ghanaians trained in the Soviet Union, Rumania, Yugoslavia,
Hungary, East Germany, Poland, and West Germany. The hu-
miliation of a separate exam was ended, but the alleged
deficiencies still had to be corrected. The NRC was
clearly committed to continuing educational exchange with
Soviet Bloc nations. But it does not necessarily follow
that students educated by the Soviets will be "in the
pocket" of the USSR. Nkrumah had been educated in the
United States, Colonel Qaddafi of Libya, at Sandhurst,
Zaire's General Mobutu in Israel, and Ghana's Colonel
Acheampong in England. The overseas educational experience may be unhappy or pleasurable, of substantial emotional impact, or merely ephemeral.

Additionally, the largest portion of Ghanaians going
to the Soviet Union and Eastern Europe are studying technical and medical subjects. Very few of these students
are potential political leaders. Ghana's future governments are likely to be composed of law graduates from the
University of Ghana and the Ghanaian Military Academy,
not graduates of Rumanian petrochemical institutes.

PROSPECTS FOR GHANAIAN FOREIGN POLICY:
THE NEW REALITIES

If the NLC and Busia found the West unwilling to
make investment and donate aid sufficient to develop
Ghana, and the NRC finds (as I argue they already have)
the Eastern countries similarly disinclined, what policy
can then be pursued? The only option open is to turn the
lack of aid into a virtue. This is, in fact, the tactic
adopted by Acheampong. He has called for a policy of
self-reliance and made known his refusal to accept aid

not given without strings. Through programs such as "Operation Feed Yourself" (a program designed to decrease food
imports while increasing food production for domestic consumption and export), the NRC is attempting to teach
Ghanaians to live within their means.[43]

How much the military's attitude toward foreign assistance has changed in three years can best be seen in the
statement of Lt. General A. K. Ocran. Ocran, a former member of the National Liberation Council that had placed such
high hopes on the possibility of attaining substantial foreign aid from the West, praised Acheampong's policy of
self-reliance: "Our salvation lies in our own hands and I
will therefore, support any effort the Government and
people of Ghana would make to minimize the dependence on
outside help."[44]

Little differentiation exists in the minds of Ghana's
present leaders between capitalist and socialist aid.
Both the United States and the Soviet Union, as already
noted, are perceived as superpowers interested in their
own welfare, not the development of the poor countries.
Ghana's future, according to this mode of thinking, lies
in accepting aid and assistance from whatever source will
provide useful goods and services. (The last meeting of
the Non-Aligned Powers in Algiers in 1973 found only Fidel
Castro willing to stand up and argue that there was a substantial difference between American and Soviet policy toward the Third World. For this statement, Castro was dismissed as a client of the Soviet Union, rather than a
truly nonaligned leader.)

In the face of the disillusionment of the seventies,
the NRC seems to be pursuing what Franklin B. Weinstein
has referred to as a strategy of independence rather than
a strategy of development. According to Weinstein, Third
World critics often feel that their nation is in danger
of sacrificing its independence in the search for economic
aid.[45] According to the logic of this position, the
avoidance of foreign aid ensures independence.

The nature of nonalignment has changed over the last
decade. In the early 1960s nonalignment was an ideological stance designed to lessen the influence of the imperialist European powers, increase economic aid and raise
the collective voice of the nonnuclear powers in protest
against nuclear testing. In the 1970s nonalignment is
perceived as a means of avoiding excessive dependence on
both East and West. The salient ideological issues of the
nonaligned nations in the 1970s are peripheral to the concerns of independent Black Africa. Today's important

issues are, on the whole, Middle Eastern questions and the problem of the white minority regimes of Southern Africa. There is no advantage to be gained by the Ghanaians from either of these issues.

Both the nonaligned nations and the superpowers seem to favor multilateral rather than bilateral aid. From the point of view of the major powers, bilateral aid can commit their countries to support a weak leader such as South Vietnam's Diem or Ghana's Nkrumah. From the vantage point of aid receivers, multilateral aid removes the onus of gratitude toward the donor. Consequently, Ghana and many other LDCs are turning toward the United Nations, the Scandinavians, West and East Europeans for aid and technical assistance. The ultimate result of this trend might be the depoliticization of aid and assistance.

NOTES

1. Robert Legvold, Soviet Policy in West Africa (Cambridge, Mass.: Harvard University Press, 1970), p. 187. Much of the discussion in the first seven pages follows Legvold.
2. Ibid., p. 228.
3. W. Scott Thompson makes this point in "Parameters on Soviet Policy in Africa: Personal Diplomacy and Economic Interests," in Soviet Policy in Developing Countries, ed. W. Raymond Duncan.
4. Anton Bebler, Military Rule in Africa (New York: Praeger Publishers, 1973), p. 39.
5. Legvold, op. cit., p. 263.
6. Ibid.
7. Bebler, op. cit., p. 41.
8. Legvold, op. cit., p. 264.
9. Ibid., p. 267.
10. Ibid., p. 269.
11. Ibid., p. 268.
12. Ibid.
13. Ibid., p. 308.
14. Ibid., p. 311.
15. Bebler, op. cit., p. 41.
16. Legvold, op. cit., p. 47.
17. Ibid., p. 139.
18. Arthur Schlesinger, Jr., A Thousand Days (Boston: Houghton Mifflin, 1965), p. 574.
19. Legvold, op. cit., p. 212.
20. Ibid., p. 309.

21. Tony Killick, "Development Economics in Action: A Study of Economic Policies in Ghana," Ch. 5, pp. 48-49, Mimeo, 1973.

22. Stephen H. Goodman, "Eastern and Western Markets for the Primary Products of Ghana," Economic Bulletin of Ghana 4 (1966): 28.

23. Ibid., p. 26.

24. Legvold, op. cit., p. 309.

25. Ibid., p. 310.

26. W. Scott Thompson, "Foreign Policy under the National Liberation Council," Africa Report (May-June 1969): 10.

27. Chris Stevens, "In Search of the Economic Kingdom: The Development of Economic Relations Between Ghana and the U.S.S.R.," Institute of Commonwealth Studies Seminar Paper, 1972.

28. Killick, op. cit., p. 50.

29. The Speeches of Colonel I. G. Acheampong 1 (Accra, 1973).

30. Ibid.

31. Ibid.

32. Thompson, "Foreign Policy under the NLC," op. cit., p. 8.

33. David Morrison, "Tropical Africa: The New Soviet Outlook," Mizan 14 (August 1971): 50.

34. Ibid., p. 53.

35. West Africa (September 17, 1973): 1305.

36. Ibid.

37. Ibid. (June 25, 1973): 866.

38. Ibid. (August 6, 1973): 1093.

39. Ibid. (July 2, 1973): 890.

40. Ibid. (September 15, 1972): 1233.

41. Ibid. (January 1, 1973): 18.

42. Legvold, op. cit., p. 308.

43. On NRC economic policy see Valerie Plave Bennett, "Ghana's Search for a New Economic Policy," West Africa (March 1973): 346.

44. Ibid (September 3, 1973): 1246.

45. Franklin B. Weinstein, "The Uses of Foreign Policy in Indonesia: An Approach to the Analysis of Foreign Policy in the LDCs," World Politics 24, no. 3 (April 1972): 369.

CHAPTER

6

**SOVIET AID TO
GUINEA AND NIGERIA:
FROM POLITICS TO PROFIT**
Angela Stent

     The Soviet Union began its foreign aid program to
Africa during the iciest days of the Cold War, at a time
when both protagonists regarded the continent as one of
the decisive areas in which the struggle between communism
and capitalism would be resolved. The prime motivation
for Soviet foreign aid in the late 1950s, therefore, was
political; thus one can only understand the evolution of
Moscow's aid program in the context of the USSR's changing
global strategy and shifting international priorities. In
the early years, Soviet leaders hoped that foreign aid to
Africa would, at a minimum, win a promise of neutrality in
the Cold War from the recipient country. By the end of
the 1960s, however, the thaw in the Cold War and disappointment with the lack of political payoffs from aid programs in Africa altered the character of Soviet foreign
aid. There was a greater emphasis on economic feasibility
and a more realistic appraisal of the relationship between
economic assistance and political dividends. The USSR has
apparently learned some salutary lessons from its initially troubled forays into the field of foreign aid, and the
era of detente with the United States has altered the
place of economic aid in the general framework of Soviet
foreign policy.[1]
     This study will analyze the evolution of Soviet eco-
nomic assistance to Africa, examining Guinea and Nigeria
as case studies that demonstrate how both the theory and
practice of Soviet foreign aid has changed since the late
1950s.[2] The case studies will deal with four main areas:
the initial motivation for aid; the type of projects constructed and experiences on both sides during the building
of projects; the impact of these experiences on Soviet aid
policies; and the relationship of these experiences to

overall Soviet foreign policy. However, before embarking
on a detailed study of Soviet foreign aid in Guinea and
Nigeria, we must briefly survey the genesis of the Soviet
foreign aid program.

Prior to 1954 the USSR had virtually no economic or
political contacts with Africa.[3] The main reason for the
paucity of Soviet-African economic contacts was that such
relations were considered economically unfeasible before
the Second World War. The USSR itself was isolated and in
the throes of industrialization and was clearly in no position to extend credits to other nations. If the USSR
was in no position to render economic aid to the colonial
territories, foreign aid was also politically unfeasible.
There were no opportunities to expand contacts because the
colonies were controlled by the metropolitan countries,
and their economies were geared toward the needs of Britain or France. Foreign aid, before the war, was not part
of Soviet or American policies, since neither of these
countries was a traditional colonial power and each, in
its own way, remained isolated from world affairs.

In the new postwar balance of international forces,
both the USSR and the United States became involved in
foreign aid. Decolonization and the rise of the two
superpowers meant that both the USSR and the United States
were in a position to fill the vacuum in the Third World
created by the departure of Britain and France from their
colonies. However until Stalin's death, the USSR showed
little interest in the Third World.[4]

The nature of Soviet politics demands that any major
shift in policy be rationalized in ideological terms. In
the case of economic affairs, ideology has served more as
an ex post facto rationalizing device than an interpretive
tool. Prior to the mid-1950s Soviet ideas on the Third
World were dogmatic and unrealistic. Stalin had substi-
tuted "socialism in one block" in place of "socialism in
one country," and Zhdanov's rigid "two-camp" analysis left
no room for a third political path. Nasser and Nehru were
dismissed as "imperialist lackeys" and independent India
termed a "British colony." When Khrushchev came to power,
decolonization was imminent, and, discarding Stalin's conservative attitude toward overseas entanglements, he realized that the Soviet Union now had the power to extend her
influence to areas formerly under the aegis of the West.
In terms of the current political climate, the Cold War,
now stabilized in the West, could move to the periphery.

In 1948 the USSR regained its prewar levels of production and by 1954 was in a position to expend some of

its resources on economic aid. Moscow therefore had the capacity to instigate the global policies to which Khrushchev later on became increasingly attached. He realized that many nationalist leaders in the developing nations were determined not to be drawn into the Cold War alignments. When China, and not Russia was invited to the Bandung Conference of neutralist countries, Khrushchev acknowledged that neutralism was a force with which to be reckoned. If the USSR were to make inroads into these countries, it had to revise its ideas about international relations. At the Twentieth Party Congress, Khrushchev introduced a new, innovative concept into Soviet political language: a "zone of peace" replaced the two-camp analysis. Poised between East and West, nationalist leaders were now "progressive" and economic categories were softened. "Peaceful coexistence" was "the strategy of world revolution in the atomic age under the leadership of the USSR."[5] Finally, in 1960, the announcement of the "noncapitalist road" enabled the USSR to single out African countries which were patently not socialist for specially favorable treatment.[6]

In the mid-1950s the main reason for extending Soviet aid to the Third World was political, the USSR hoped to deny the West a monopoly of influence in the developing countries, at a minimum. At a maximum, she hoped for the establishment of communist regimes there. Real expectations probably lay somewhere between these two extremes. The USSR consolidating its rise to great power status envisaged the creation of a global Soviet policy with aid being given in return for friendly neutralism. This analysis was implicit in the writings of a Soviet commentator who wrote:

> In its relations with the capitalist countries, the Soviet Union utilizes economic contacts principally as an important lever for strengthening peaceful relations and establishing the desired confidence between states of different social systems. [7]

Concerns for economic returns on aid took second place to a desire for political dividends.

Although foreign aid was not primarily intended to reap economic benefits under Khrushchev, it was nevertheless explained by Soviet commentators in terms of its economic value, and both policy statements and theoretical discussions about aid began to increase. However there were two contradictory explanations for aid. On the one hand Soviet writers were anxious to stress that their aid, unlike capitalist aid, was "disinterested" with no strings attached:

> In giving economic and technical aid to underdeveloped countries and in providing them with credits on favorable terms and developing trade with them on a mutually profitable basis, the Soviet Union is guided by the sole desire of accelerating the revival of these countries, hastening the development of their productive forces and by these means promoting the rapid improvement of the well-being and culture of the peoples of these countries.[8]

Soviet aid, it was claimed, promoted the creation of an independent national economy in formerly dependent countries, whereas capitalist aid created dependence.

On the other hand, lest he be accused of political motivation since aid was allegedly unconcerned with economic returns, Khrushchev at the same time emphasized the commercial nature of Soviet aid: "We are not a charitable institution. The Soviet Union gives aid on fair commercial principles."[9]

Thus, according to Soviet sources, in the late 1950s Soviet aid was prompted by noncommercial motives, although concern was also shown to maintain relations with underdeveloped countries on a proper commercial basis.[10]

The initial economic rationale behind the first Soviet aid agreements with sub-Saharan Africa was the desire to woo African countries away from their traditional purchases of Western goods by extending credits for the financing of Soviet goods, which would not otherwise have been bought. There is little evidence that the pursuit of comparative advantage was a significant motivation in early Soviet trade and aid agreements.[11] The USSR's comparative advantage had shifted away from primary goods to manufactured products in the process of industrialization. Like other developed nations the USSR was faced with a scarcity of raw materials and a surplus of some capital goods for which there was no secure market in the West.[12] However if the USSR had been pursuing a policy of comparative advantage, its trading policies would have been different than they actually were. In some cases raw materials from Africa were resold on the world market at a higher price and were not used in the Soviet economy.* Thus the USSR has not altered the structure of its economy in such a way that would enable it to reap the full bene- fits of its trade and aid agreements with African coun- tries. Autarkic practices remain predominant and led an early Western analyst of Soviet aid to conclude, in 1956, "The pursuit of economic advantage does not appear to be an important motive behind the Soviet aid program."[13]

THE MECHANICS OF SOVIET FOREIGN AID

Although the projects for which Soviet assistance is now given are different from those in the early years of foreign aid, the institutional arrangements under which aid is dispensed have remained largely the same. Most Soviet assistance is bilateral and comes in the form of project aid, although commercial-type credits for the pur- chase of equipment and machinery are not unknown. Project aid usually comes in the form of long- and short-term cred- its to be drawn over a period of about five years, and they carry a low interest rate of 2.5-3 percent.[14] Commercial- type credits carry 3-3.5 percent interest.[15]

Loans are made for specific projects and are "tied" in the sense that they are not made in convertible cur- rency and are repayable in local currencies or the export of local goods. The amortization period on project cred- its is 12 years, payable in local currency for Soviet pur- chases of the recipient country's goods, and 8-10 years on commercial credits.[16] Repayments were initially supposed to begin one year after the project was completed so that the recipient could start to repay at a time when the ini- tial investment had begun to produce income. The interest rate is calculated exclusively on the outstanding balance of utilized credits.

The Soviets stress that their aid program is insepar- able from their trade agreements[17] and usually aid and trade are integrated. Agreements for financial and tech- nical assistance are signed in connection with the conclu- sion of trade agreements, and the deliveries of materials and equipment for the completion of technical assistance projects are often included in the commodity list attached to the current trade protocol. Notwithstanding the above it is often difficult to calculate the volume of Soviet

---

*Egyptian cotton is an example of this.

aid, because the Soviets themselves have no hard and fast definition of aid.* The USSR rarely gives outright grants and claims that these are a demeaning form of charity which must, by implication, have strings attached.[18]

Soviet credits are typically used for the construction of industrial installations within the public sector. They are used in much the same way as under Western "turn-key" arrangements.[19] Credits cover geological surveys, deliveries of machinery and equipment not available within the recipient country; and the cost of travel for experts from the donor country with the exception of preliminary visits. Soviet technicians and workers are paid Soviet wages out of these funds, while the Chinese insist that their workers accept the wage-rate of the local population. The Aswan Dam in Egypt and the Bhilai steel mill in India are both examples of early Soviet aid which rescued projects rejected by the West for political reasons.[20]

In the early years the USSR displayed a lack of stringent criteria in evaluating the merits of a project. Often agreements were signed in advance, and evaluations came later. The donor country normally undertook the evaluation of the overall effectiveness of the project, the availability of raw materials, and the level of contribution to the recipient's economy. In the mid-1960s about 40 percent of Soviet aid to Africa had been utilized to build irrigation and hydroelectric power plants.[21]

One of the most complicated aspects of discussing Soviet foreign aid is the problem of statistics. Although Soviet figures may appear straightforward, we must bear certain major caveats in mind. First there is the problem of definition. In Soviet terminology, "aid" means the grant of credits plus the exchange of goods used for repayment. Thus it is a fairly broad definition. Soviet aid consists of credits and loans in nonconvertible roubles which can be utilized to purchase only specific goods. Of aid that is actually drawn, about 55 percent takes the form of commodities imported and sold locally to help defray

---

*Normally Soviet aid consists of goods and equipment supplied on a credit basis with repayment to be in the form of bartered goods or cash over a fixed period. In some cases, the USSR supplied exports for what it expected would be immediate repayment, but the recipient was unable to pay. The Soviet Union in such cases has converted this export surplus into foreign aid credit, even though this was not formally announced.

local costs associated with Soviet projects; about 15 percent is used to cover the foreign exchange costs associated with hiring the services of technicians; and the rest is used for imported Soviet machinery and equipment. The 2.5 percent interest rate on Soviet loans is not a capital charge in the Western sense because it does not bear any relation to productivity of capital. There is also the problem of the Soviet pricing system. One economist has calculated that, because of the Soviet practice of bilateral trading agreements, the prices of goods differ from those on the world market to the advantage of the USSR. Exports from the Soviet Union tend to be overpriced and imports underpriced.[22]

The other main source of error in calculating figures on Soviet aid is the failure to distinguish between aid promised and aid disbursed. There have been considerable lags in the utilization of credits. The Soviets themselves give no figures for disbursements and all their information on aid is based on promised assistance. These figures for aid drawings are therefore only estimates. There does appear to be a wide discrepancy between aid extensions and disbursements, which suggest that Soviet assistance may amount to less than official figures indicate.[23]

The institutional framework under which credits are given is not uniform. Under Khrushchev unilateral decisions were not unknown, for instance his spontaneous announcement of a $280 million loan to Nasser in 1964. The more important the decision, the higher the level at which it is taken. However, as in all branches of Soviet economic life, there are the appropriate central organs with their bureaucratically delegated power.[24] GKES (State Committee of the Council of Ministers of the USSR for Foreign Relations) was created in 1957 to cope with the increase in foreign aid both to satellite and neutralist countries. In addition to a network of offices, GKES relies on various outside organizations for advice, particularly Tekhnopromeksport (Technical and Industrial Exports) which handles engineering and irrigation projects, such as the Aswan Dam, and Tekhnoeksport, which undertakes geological surveys and builds industrial installations. Many other state corporations are involved in the network of aid operations, and the system has not always run smoothly. The failure on the part of manufacturers to deliver materials and other such bottlenecks often cause concern. When the USSR dispenses large amounts of aid, negotiations are handled by special branches of the GKES in that particular

country. When aid activities are more limited, arrangements are handled by the economic counselor of the Soviet
embassy. Requests for aid usually come from the recipient,
although on occasion the USSR has initiated offers. Thus
an administrative complex of organizations has evolved to
deal with the dispensing of aid.

GUINEA: KHRUSHCHEV'S UNSUCCESSFUL GAMBIT

Soviet economic involvement in Guinea is an extreme
example of the Khrushchev regime's misguided foreign aid
policies which the current leadership has managed to sal-
vage and improve upon. In a microcosm it shows how initial, hasty commitments, which neglected to consider adequately questions of economic viability, not only failed
to produce the anticipated political payoffs but had de-
cidedly negative effects. However subsequent assistance,
in which project feasibility was a serious criterion,
yielded more concrete economic and political results. At
the beginning of the Soviet-Guinean relationship, there
was a sense of euphoria on both sides which led to exaggerated expectations about the role of Soviet foreign aid
both as a catalyst to Guinea's economic development and
as the lynchpin of Soviet influence in Guinea.[25] A period
of intense disillusion followed, but this hostility has
now been replaced by a growing sense of realism on both
sides and a mutual appreciation of the correct role of
foreign aid both economically and politically. Soviet-
Guinean relations are now more cordial than at any time
since 1961, but this has only been achieved at the cost
of much frustration and economic failure.
     The dramatic circumstance under which Guinea suddenly
achieved independence was the main factor which influenced
the Soviets to seize on the former French colony as their
first client in sub-Saharan Africa.[26] As in all the other
French colonies, Guinea's economy was entirely in French
hands, with few trained indigenous personnel, and was
largely oriented toward the requirements of the metropolitan economy. When de Gaulle asked all the African colonies to vote in a referendum in 1958 affirming their acceptance of remaining in the French community, Guinea surprised the General by voting "non." Literally overnight,
the French officials threw their machinery into the ocean
in disgust, ripped out the telephones and withdrew all
military, medical, and technical advisors, leaving Guinea

destitute.* Clearly de Gaulle wanted the collapse of
Guinea's economy to be an example to any other state which
was contemplating defying him. Until that time 75 percent
of Guinea's exports had gone to France. France had given
Guinea preferential treatment, since Guinea's exports were
sold to France at about 15 percent higher than they would
have been sold on the world market. When the French abolished their subsidized prices for Guinean exports, the
Guinean banana crop was especially hard hit since it could
not compete effectively in an unprotected world market.[27]
The Guinean economy was at a low level of development.
Most of the population lived by subsistence agriculture in
1958, and there was a dire shortage of indigenous adminis-
trators and technicians. Guinea's trade balance was in
deficit, and although she exported bananas, coffee, and
diamonds, her major assets--deposits of bauxite and iron
ore--were only just beginning to be exploited. Thus in
1958 the abrupt withdrawal of French aid and France's insistence that the rest of the Western world boycott Guinea
made that country an ideal target for Soviet aid.

Two days after Guinea proclaimed its independence in
October 1958, the USSR recognized President Sekou Toure's
state. When the Soviets entered Guinea, they were ignor-
ant of the problems of African society having had virtually no prior contact with it. Clearly, the overriding aim
for the USSR was to appear as the savior of an African
country, asserting its independence from the "imperial-
ists," with a President who had known leftist leanings.[†]
Guinea gave the USSR one of its first opportunities to extend its influence in sub-Saharan Africa. At this early
stage it is doubtful that the USSR was particularly concerned with the economic dividends to be gained from aid
to Guinea, although its mineral potential was known to be

----

*In 1957 there were 7,000 French in Guinea. By 1960
the number had dwindled to fewer than 2,000. Also Guinea's
trained bureaucracy was reduced by 75 percent when the
French left.

†Sekou Toure, grandson of the famous Samori Toure who
led the resistance to the French in the 1880s, received
his political education as a post office official when he
became a member of the communist controlled Confederation
General du Travail. However, Toure has repeatedly denied
that he is a communist and indeed his eclectic political
philosophy bears this denial out.

considerable. Aid was a major weapon in what was initially a preemptive political strike, whose ultimate political
payoff would be the industrialization of Guinea.

The first formal economic link between the USSR and
Guinea was a trade agreement signed on February 13, 1959.
Guinea was to import Soviet machinery and cars and to export bananas, coffee, and oilseeds,[28] all traditional exports which formerly went to France. For a short time the
USSR replaced France as Guinea's main trading partner.
This agreement was followed in August 1959 by a $35 million
(140 million roubles) agreement for financial and technical
aid.[29] The specific projects under the Soviet loan were
spelled out in a detailed protocol of March 1960. It was
intended to finance geological prospecting as well as the
construction of a polytechnical institute, factory installations, and a stadium in Conakry.[30] The first loan was
supplemented in 1960 with a further $40 million to finance
a fruit and vegetable cannery at Mamou, a refrigeration
plant, a railway sleeper works, and a sawmill factory at
N'Zekoure. In addition there was a gift of $7-8 million
for a radio station and a hospital at Conakry, and a $3
million military loan.[31] At first the USSR was willing
to supply most of what Guinea requested, including a
7,000 hectare state rice farm at La Fie, and a 120 room
hotel at Conakry. The Soviets shipped cattle to a dairy
farm at Dittnn and supplied aircraft. Thus, Soviet aid
covered a motley mixture of agricultural, industrial, geological, and "prestige" projects, such as the radio station, hotel, and stadium. None of the projects were properly appraised before they were started, and credits were
subsequently increased without much deliberation. It
seems strange in retrospect that there was so little apparent concern for the feasibility of projects. Perhaps,
in Khrushchev's heyday, political dividends were thought
to accrue inevitably from economic assistance and were
considered more important than the intricacies of economic
calculation.

The connection between aid and politics becomes clear
when one examines Soviet attitudes toward Guinea's internal development. The Soviets had paid little attention to
Toure before Guinean independence, but after 1960 they
elevated hin, together with Nkrumah of Ghana and Keita of
Mali, to a new ideological rank. Toure was considered the
leader of a "progressive" one-party state, already embarked on the "noncapitalist" path of development.[32]
Whereas other African statesmen were praised for their
neutralism, Toure was awarded the Lenin prize in 1961 and

was described as a socialist. Khrushchev clearly thought
that there was a possibility that Guinea might become a
second Cuba. Guinea officials reinforced this hope by
saying that "Guinea will not take the road of capitalism
or of bourgeois development."[33]

In December 1961 the Soviet ambassador was expelled
and the Soviets became the object of considerable hostility in Guinea. In order to understand how, in the short
space of two years mutual attraction soured into mutual
vituperation, we must examine the fate of Soviet aid to
Guinea. Western literature abounds with anecdotes, possibly apocryphal, of the inappropriateness of Soviet aid.
The sending of snow-ploughs to tropical Guinea may indeed
be a myth, but certainly one of the main reasons for the
failure of Soviet aid was the speed with which it was
given and the lack of forethought and prior investigation
on the part of the Soviets, who rushed in unprepared for
the sub-Saharan environment. Soviet tractors, equipped
with sealed cabs through which an exhaust pipe was passed
to provide extra heat were hardly suitable for subtropical
climates.[34] The remoteness of Guinea and the difficulties
of supplying equipment with the Soviet Union's inadequate
merchant marine fleet were severe handicaps, and as a result the docks in Conakry were crammed with equipment
waiting for installation.

A more serious defect of Soviet aid was its tendency
toward excessive scale. The USSR, with a population of
200 million, was not equipped to build projects for a
country with 3 million people. The Soviet-built factories
were generally too large both in size and productive capacity for Guinea. The excess capacity in Guinea could
theoretically be used for export sales, but it was not
necessarily prudent to produce for foreign markets before
the plant had proved efficient in terms of the domestic
market. There was also the question of how much trade
Guinea could sustain, since her neighbors often produced
the same kinds of food and clothing. A large but under-
utilized plant usually costs more money than a small, but
fully utilized factory. Soviet ignorance of economic
realities in Guinea can be related to the structure and
problems of the Soviet economy in general. The somewhat
inflexible centralist planning system within the USSR,
where prices do not necessarily reflect scarcity values,
have often led to distortions of production and to considerable waste.* Early Soviet aid to Guinea, therefore,

_____

*These defects were recognized in the mid-1960s and
since the "Liberman reforms" some of this waste has been
eliminated.

152

which was not always appropriate for Guinea's economy, was
to some degree a reflection of the Soviet Union's own economic experience.

Another difficulty with the Soviet aid program under
Khrushchev was Soviet willingness to build prestige projects which the Guineans wanted for their own political
reasons, but which could contribute little to earning foreign exchange or, more importantly, to building the necessary infrastructure for industrialization. The 100-kilowatt
radio transmitter at Conakry was built on Mount Kakoulima
which turned out to be very rich in iron ore, and therefore
poor in radio transmission, with the result that it was
useless to the airport. Conakry airport was subsequently
refurnished with American equipment.[35] The stadium built
at Conakry, with 25,000 seats for a town with a population
of 120,000 brought in no foreign exchange or goods that
could be used for repayment. The motel, which could have
generated foreign exchange from tourists, was a burden for
a long time because the Guineans could find no one to operate it. The Soviets would not take over the running of
the hotel and in 1964 it was empty for most of the year.
Possibly the greatest failure was in the agricultural
field, where the rice farm at La Fie yielded no results,
despite large expenditures on it, and was subsequently
abandoned.[36] Thus Soviet aid, paying scant attention to
cost factors, location, or climate conditions, was largely
inappropriate and wasted the resources invested in it.

Apart from Soviet mistakes, the environment in which
Soviet aid programs were operating did little to promote
the success of the enterprises. The first $156 million
Guinean Three-Year Plan, inaugurated in 1960, was designed
to increase GNP by approximately 8 percent per annum. It
provided for an extension of the state and cooperative
sectors of the economy at the expense of the private ones,
and envisaged the establishment of 500 collective farms.
Of the $156 million, $131 million was promised in aid from
the Soviet bloc (including China).[37] In 1963 the nexus of
state corporations was suppressed and private enterprise
encouraged. Later on this was reversed.[38] In addition
the highly volatile political atmosphere and prevalence of
corruption and smuggling* made it difficult to establish a

---

*After Guinea left the franc zone, the Guinean franc
had no value outside Guinea and its free rate of exchange
was far below its formal rate of par with the franc.
Guinean traders avoided this exchange rate by illicitly
carrying goods over the border, and purchasing with the

viable base for industrialization. Thus although early
Soviet aid did little to help Guinea's economic development, the viability of any aid at that time was question-
able because of Guinea's internal difficulties.

The Guinean experiment had other drawbacks for the
USSR. The Soviets found the Guineans unskilled and incom-
petent. As Ambassador Solod told William Attwood, the
Guineans "did not want to work, were ruining Soviet equipment, and were not to be taken seriously."[39] He rationalized Russia's initial involvement by saying, "Guinea was
in such a state of economic and psychological shock, we
felt we could not refuse her requests."[40] The dissatis-
faction, however, was not one-sided. In September 1961
Guinea announced that 18 Soviet technicians had been arrested for smuggling diamonds, and in December, Ambassador
Solod was expelled for alleged "subversion."[41] Whatever
the truth about the allegations, the Soviets had certainly
made themselves unpopular in Guinea, largely because of
their aid, and relations deteriorated in 1961.[42]

After the Solod incident Soviet-Guinean relations remained strained, and in May 1963 Toure signed his first
aid agreement with the United States. The Soviet fiasco
temporarily left the field wide open for the West, and
Toure supported Kennedy during the Cuban missile crisis.
During the crisis Toure refused Soviet requests to land
aircraft bound for the Caribbean on an airstrip that the
USSR had just lengthened there to accommodate traffic.
Toure continued to seek rapprochement with the West since
he needed outlets for agricultural products at remunera-
tive prices. It is much easier for Guinea to sell bauxite,
aluminum, and iron ore than coffee and bananas. The rapprochement with France came in November 1962, together
with the switch away from the state-run economy. At the
same time, the USSR reduced the price on Guinean bananas
from $115 a ton to $95 a ton, and withdrew 600 technicians. However, Soviet aid, despite its initial failure,
was, in one sense, an unqualified success: it had denied
the West a monopoly over economic contacts with sub-
Saharan Africa, and established a viable trading relationship with Guinea which continued to grow (see Tables 6.1
and 6.2). Nevertheless Soviet-Guinean relations had
reached a low ebb at the time of Khrushchev's fall.

---

proceeds goods which they reimported into Guinea, thereby
depriving the state of profit from these transactions.

TABLE 6.1

Volume of Soviet Trade with Guinea and Nigeria, 1959-71
(millions of roubles)

Year	Guinea			Nigeria		
	Exports	Imports	Total	Exports	Imports	Total
1959	0.8	0.7	1.5	--	6.6	6.6
1960	5.2	2.0	7.2	--	6.3	6.3
1961	24.5	3.8	28.3	--	--	--
1962	18.0	2.4	20.4	--	--	--
1963	12.7	2.1	14.8	--	--	--
1964	18.3	2.0	20.3	1.1	3.8	4.9
1965	8.7	3.2	11.9	2.9	5.2	8.1
1966	9.7	3.2	12.9	4.1	0.7	4.8
1967	6.5	2.6	9.1	9.7	8.2	17.9
1968	12.4	2.9	15.3	10.7	19.2	29.9
1969	7.9	3.1	11.0	15.0	22.0	37.0
1970	11.2	3.0	14.2	10.9	20.3	31.2
1971	31.2	5.0	36.2	15.7	41.0	56.7

Source: <u>Vneshnaya Torgovlya Soiuza SSR za 1959-71 Gody.</u>

TABLE 6.2

Soviet Trade with Guinea
(thousands of roubles)

	1970		1971	
	Quantity	Value	Quantity	Value
Exports				
Machines, equipment and means of transport	--	5,073	--	21,672
Equipment for enterprises engaged in output of nonferrous metals	--	--	--	15,475
Cranes	--	--	3	71
Equipment for food-processing industries	--	854	--	936
Trucks	83	461	497	1,887
Accessories and spare parts for trucks and garage equipment, including engines	--	901	--	195
Special automobiles	51	468	14	114
Air transport	--	209	--	447
Automobiles	10	13	37	55
Accessories and spare parts for automobiles, including engines	--	583	--	369
Oil and petroleum products	60.7 th. tons	1,769	70.5 th. tons	2,079
Steel	645 tons	81	1,780 tons	210
Tires	8.4 th.	284	15.2 th.	629
Cement	18 th. tons	196	36 th. tons	399
Condensed milk	722 th. tins	105	2,821 th. tins	368
Fresh and frozen fish	6,246 tons	1,140	3,000 tons	547
Cotton fabrics	7 mill. metres	1,097	20.6 mill. metres	3,499
Medication	--	9	--	102
Laundry soap	551 tons	73	1,104 tons	188
Household goods	--	35	--	216
Refrigerators	125	16	350	48
Printed products	--	9	--	6
Films	--	--	--	6
Total		11.2 mill. roubles		31.2 mill. roubles
Imports				
Bauxite	118.9 th. tons	542	211.4 th. tons	926
Palm seeds	1,312 tons	183	3,976 tons	544
Pineapples	5,196 tons	2,002	7,916 tons	3,049
Bananas	3,130 tons	270	3,112 tons	269
Mangoes	18 tons	6	733 tons	243
Total		3 mill. roubles		5 mill. roubles

Source: Vneshnaya Torgovlya Soiuza SSR za 1959-71 Gody.

156

Reevaluation of Aid After Khrushchev's Fall

Although Khrushchev is usually associated with an ex-
pansionist and somewhat indiscriminate policy in Africa,
there are some signs that he was aware of some of the
drawbacks inherent in Soviet foreign aid policies. As
early as 1958, he had said:

> While the Soviet Union and other socialist
> countries consider it their duty to help
> underdeveloped countries--we cannot say
> that our economic relations are based on
> mutual advantage. Generally speaking,
> from the commercial standpoint, our eco-
> nomic and technical assistance to under-
> developed countries is even unprofitable
> for us.[43]

Just before his fall, he also admitted that "when the Soviet Union helps the young developing countries, when it
gives them part of the wealth accumulated through its own
efforts, it restricts for a time its own opportunities."[44]

Nevertheless Khrushchev continued to lavish aid on
certain Third World countries and there is some evidence
that his handling of foreign aid was one of the contribu-
tory factors which led to his downfall.[45] A few days
after he was ousted, details of charges against him were
leaked to the Western press:

> Many of the journeys on which Comrade
> Khrushchev embarked in 1962 and later were
> decided upon without any prior consulta-
> tion with the other members of the Central
> Committee Praesidium or the Praesidium of
> the Supreme Soviet--Frequently the results
> of these missions did not accord with the
> interests of the Soviet Union--Very recent-
> ly a loan of $280 million was handed to the
> UAR and the order of "Hero of the Soviet
> Union" was given to President Nasser with-
> out prior consultation with the authorities
> involved in the Soviet Union.[46]

After Khrushchev was ousted, there was a general
realization that foreign aid must be based on a more
realistic appraisal of capabilities and commitments and
an admission that Soviet domestic economic priorities

must be recognized. An important editorial in <u>Pravda</u>, after Khrushchev's fall, signified the change in Soviet attitudes toward aid:

> Aid to the developing countries is ren-
> dered not from surpluses but at the ex-
> pense of diverting funds and materials
> from what would be most useful to the
> socialist countries themselves--Social-
> ist countries can only claim to be the
> vanguard of world revolutionary movement
> if they build up their own economic sys-
> tems--<u>at home</u>.[47]

The article went on to say that too much involvement in
the Third World might lead to a nuclear war, and too much
aid would represent a diversion of resources badly needed
at home.

Soviet foreign aid to Africa before 1964 had clearly
yielded meager economic and political results. Although
aid only accounted for about 0.36 percent of total Soviet
GNP, it became an important issue at this time during the
debate about the deteriorating economic performance of
the USSR.[48] Against the background of growing domestic
tensions about the allocation of scarce resources, and the
visible lack of political payoff, the whole question of
Soviet aid generated a political controversy dispropor-
tionate to the costs of the program.

While Soviet ideas about economic performance within
the USSR were undergoing a reevaluation in the mid-1960s,
the debate about economics spread to questions of foreign
aid. The full dimensions of this debate cannot be dealt
with adequately here,[49] but a brief survey of the main
questions will show how the Soviets, faced with the failures of aid programs such as those in Guinea, were forced
to rethink some of their hastily defined concepts.

The most important aspect of the reorientation of Soviet ideas on foreign aid was the redefinition of the criteria for Soviet aid. As early as 1961 Mikoyan had
stressed that Soviet aid should be made to yield better
returns.[50] Since 1962 a group of economists at the Institute of the Economy of the World Socialist System had been
working on indexes of the effectiveness of economic relations with the newly independent states. By 1965 they
were advocating that the USSR stop striving for self-
sufficiency in all branches of production and that it take
advantage of the international division of labor and base

its economic relations with the Third World on the principle of comparative advantage.[51] They suggested that Soviet aid and trade be based on the joint production of such items as petroleum, iron ore, cotton fibers, and ferrous metals. Planning should be coordinated to give the USSR a stable (and cheap) supply of needed raw materials, fuels, and some industrial products. At the same time it was assumed that the new states would benefit from production for the foreign market and expanding output of traditional products more than from aid projects designed to produce for the home market alone. Aid projects built mainly for political impact were also no longer to be supported. The economists finally published a book summarizing their conclusions in 1966,[52] and stressed that the main determinant of aid should be its capacity to bring solid economic returns to the USSR, not its ability to bring unlimited benefits to developing nations. Instead of the customary paeans to mutually advantageous cooperation, they discussed trade fluctuations and the problems of aid in a frank manner. The old slogans were absent, replaced by hard-hitting criticism.

The net result of these researches was to stress "productive cooperation" and "effectiveness" as the new criteria of Soviet aid.[53] In practice, however, it is difficult to be precise about how these principles affect either the form in which aid is given or the kind of projects for which it is designed. Productive cooperation envisaged a situation where the donor country plans and finances a project whose eventual production, exported to the donor country, would help toward paying off the loan. This would in part solve the repayments problem. A Guinean fruit and vegetable cannery built with Soviet aid in Guinea was cited as an example of productive cooperation.[54]

Although it is too early to draw definitive conclusions on how the pattern of Soviet aid has altered under the Brezhnev-Kosygin regime, it is clear that a concern for returns on aid has replaced the expectation of political payoffs. Ironically, despite the decreasing emphasis on the specific political goals of aid, economic considerations may ultimately bring political dividends. A study of Soviet aid to Guinea after 1966 and to Nigeria indicates that "businesslike" contacts can also be politically beneficial.

Guinea's Return to Favor

Despite the expulsion of the Soviet ambassador in 1961 and the cooling of Soviet-Guinean relations, there were Soviet projects in Guinea which remained to be completed, and after Khrushchev's fall, both President Toure and the new Kremlin leaders were willing to try again.

After the two-year hiatus in their relations and a moratorium on new aid commitments, the Soviets and Guineans renewed their contacts. They had signed an agreement on June 26, 1963, which stipulated that the USSR would set up a joint direct-labor business firm to finish delayed capital projects.[55] Guinea's economy was experiencing many problems but in its three-year plan, completed in 1963, the main successes were Soviet-built projects.[56] In the seven-year plan, initiated in 1964, Guinea gave priority to building an infrastructure, stressing hydroelectric power, and reintroducing state control of the economy, which pleased the Soviet government. In October 1965, Toure returned to Moscow after four years and tried to secure a promise from the Soviet leaders that they would finance the construction of a major dam on the Konkoure River. The undertaking would have involved an outlay of at least $250 million. The electricity output of the dam was to be 3,000-6,000 million kilowatts per year.[57] The Soviets did agree to finance a plant for processing alumina from extensive bauxite deposits. The French had refused to finance this, but it was of great potential importance for the future industrial development of Guinea. A subsequent aid agreement in September 1967 specifically allocated funds for projects already built, that needed extra resources to improve their functioning. Thus the food canning factory, that had been plagued by short supplies was backed up by a new tomato plantation.[58] Gradually the content of Soviet-Guinean aid agreements began to show a marked increase in concern both for the feasibility of projects and for their role in Guinea's overall economic growth.

Undoubtedly the most important aspect of Soviet-Guinean relations since the late 1960s has been their joint exploitation of bauxite and the USSR's growing involvement in Guinea's profitable mineral industry. In November 1969 the Soviets signed a contract with Guinea in which they agreed to establish a joint company, Obkea, to exploit bauxite deposits at Debele in the Kindia region. The USSR pledged 83 million roubles (2.3 billion Guinean sylis) to finance the operation.[59] A further

agreement was announced in September 1970 providing for
the construction of a 140-kilometer railway from Fridiabe
in the mining area, to Conakry on the coast, for the construction and improvement of port installations at Conakry
and for the construction of a mining town at Debele.[60]   In
December 1970 Moscow announced a major 30-year contract
under which Guinea will supply the Soviet Union with two
million tons of bauxite a year from the Kindia reserves.[61]
The 30-year stipulation shows a growing sense of realism
on the part of Soviet officials about the possibilities of
debt repayment, and the bauxite imports will be the main
means of repayment.

The bauxite operations have significant implications
both for the Guinean and the Soviet economy. Unlike earlier projects, this one was completed in record time. A
recent article in the Soviet industrial daily, Sotsialisticheskaya Industriya, written on the occasion of the
visit by Guinean Premier Lansana Beavogui to the USSR,
said that the mine would go into production on December
31, 1973.[62] The Debele operation has two giant construction sites separated by a ravine. One site includes the
administrative buildings, chemical laboratories, and repair facilities; the other the open-pit mine with a
crusher installation.[63] The Soviets lack large domestic
resources of high-grade bauxite and have been developing
lower-grade materials at a higher cost to build up an
aluminum industry that is now second only to that of the
United States. They are, therefore, very eager to develop
foreign sources of bauxite for their growing aluminum industry, and the new sales of bauxite will also increase
Guinea's supply of badly needed foreign exchange. The
reserves of the mine have been estimated at over 44 million tons. The bauxite will be shipped from Conakry to
the aluminum plant at Zaporozhye in the Ukraine.[64] Under
the loan agreement, part of the bauxite will be used by
Guinea to repay the Soviet investment, part will be sold
to the USSR on commercial terms, and part may be marketed
by the Guineans at their discretion.

The bauxite enterprise also marks a change from earlier Soviet-Guinean projects, because it seems to have
been constructed with few major problems. Although a
French journal claimed recently that the Soviet operation
had run into some difficulties,[65] Soviet commentators
praise the success of the project and point to its speedy
completion. Recently a Soviet writer, stressing the haz-
ards of climate and rocky terrain, said that he had been
struck on repeated visits to the Kindia site by the

"enthusiasm of the workers and the effective use to which the first-class Soviet machinery is put."[66] The Soviets, of course, may have glossed over difficulties in the press, but since they were quite candid about their disappointment with Guinean workers in the early 1960s, it is significant that they now have only praise for their 10,000 employees at the site. One of the Soviet technicians told the Soviet reporter: "It is very gratifying to observe the conscientious attitude of our Guinean comrades to work, their genuine concern for the standard of their work and for the success of the entire complex in general."[67]

The success of the Soviet-Guinean bauxite plant is particularly significant in view of the fact that until now Western companies have been most active in developing Guinea's vast bauxite reserves.* The USSR, therefore, is making inroads on a traditionally Western preserve. It is also training Guineans on the mining site in such skills as excavation, welding and foundry work, and electrical know-how. Apart from this technical training which is specifically oriented toward the bauxite project, the USSR has recently signed another agreement with Guinea aimed at technological cooperation in broader fields. It has promised to help Guinea establish a scientific research center, which will provide facilities for studies in oceanography, heliophysics, and hydroelectricity.[68] Credits have also been given for the construction of a sawmill and a large food preservation plant.[69] The USSR has given assistance in the creation of Guinea's national air line, Air Guinee, and is training Guinean pilots.[70] Soviet trade with Guinea has also increased markedly since 1970, and all indicators point to a continuing growth of economic contacts.[71] The new aid agreements with Guinea display a growing awareness of economic necessities and concern for real growth. Instead of the "impact" projects of the early 1960s, the USSR is now helping to build an important part of Guinea's needed industrial infrastructure.

The regeneration of Soviet-Guinean economic contacts has been paralleled by increasingly cordial political relations. Guinea's ruling Parti Democratique Guineen (PDG) was the only West African party to be invited to the 24th

---

*The World Bank, a Swiss Company Alusuisse, and various international consortia such as Halco Mining Inc. and FRIA (U.S., French, British, Swiss, and West German investors) have all been active in Guinea's bauxite production. Yugoslavia has also formed a joint company with Guinea for bauxite production.

CPSU Congress in 1971, and the recent visit by Premier
Beavogui to the USSR received extensive and favorable
press coverage. Kosygin and other members of the Politburo met the Guinean delegation at the airport and spent
several days negotiating with them.[72] A lengthy analysis
at the end of the talks stressed common views on major
foreign policy issues and Guinean gratitude for Soviet
aid.[73] Yet the recent praise of Toure's government in
the Soviet press is qualitatively different from the eulo-
gies of the early 1960s. Today largely as a result of
their sobering experiences with foreign aid, and the expulsion of the ambassador in 1961, Soviet experts are
willing to concede that Guinea is one of the states where
"the anti-capitalist slogans of many leaders of the national liberation movement" contributed to "the illusion
that a decisive commitment to socialism would be made."[74]
Nevertheless, despite the appreciation of the problems inherent in the Guinean body politic, Guinea still ranks
high in the Soviet appraisal of African states. Guinea's
PDG was recently described as a "revolutionary-democratic
Party"[75] and its foreign and domestic policy were singled
out approvingly: "In Western Africa, this republic . . .
has embarked on the road of non-capitalist development
. . . [and] has invariably adhered to an anti-imperialist
course. . . ."[76]
     Soviet approval of Guinea's domestic and foreign
policy is both a cause and result of the recent success
of Soviet aid projects in Guinea. The Soviet experience
of foreign aid in Guinea is an example of the full range
of mistakes that can be committed by a superpower when
preemptive political motivation is the prime criterion
for economic assistance. The Soviet Union, because it
paid more attention to anticipated political payoffs than
to the feasibility of projects in the late 1950s and early
1960s, committed countless errors through failure to appraise economic ventures prior to their implementation and
through a mistaken notion of the level of development of
their Guinean partners. In the late 1960s, a growing
sense of realism both about the influence of foreign aid
and about Guinea's potential meant that Soviet aid was
based on different, more profitable criteria, both economically and politically.

                 NIGERIA: THE NEW PRAGMATISM

     Soviet aid to Nigeria is an even more striking exam-
ple of the post-Khrushchev policy, because prior to 1967,

                            163

the USSR had virtually no economic or political ties with
that nation. Guinea had always been one of the USSR's
favored nations politically in West Africa, and after the
Ghana and Mali coups, the only state with left-wing leanings, in which the Soviet Union already had a stake. However, Nigeria was initially firmly in the Western camp,
and resisted repeated Soviet attempts to establish relations in the early 1960s. The USSR was only able to extend its influence to Nigeria when it appeared as the Federal Military Government's savior during the Civil War,
and supplied arms while other powers held back. The blos-
soming of Soviet-Nigerian relations in the last five years
shows how the Soviets have been able to eschew their traditional ideological criteria in the selection of allies
and have been primarily motivated by pragmatic economic
considerations in their foreign aid program.

Nigeria delayed the establishment of diplomatic relations with the USSR until 1961 and later on it restricted
the size of the Soviet mission in Lagos. Thereafter it
obstructed travel to the Soviet Bloc; it frustrated attempts to make use of Soviet aid and trade; and it blocked
the importation of Communist materials. In June 1961 the
Nigerian Minister of Finance led a high-level economic
mission to Moscow. As a result of this exploratory visit,
the two countries pledged to "conclude a trade and cultural agreement in the near future" and the USSR said it
would provide economic and technical assistance for organizing and processing agricultural projects and for
building training centers for Nigerians in industry and
agriculture.[77] However, this agreement never materialized,
partly due to Nigeria's suspicion of communism, and partly
due to the USSR's unwillingness to press aid on so unresponsive a recipient. In 1964 various other exploratory
moves were made but nothing concrete ever emerged.*

Although Nigeria was a predominantly agricultural
country, since 1952 industry had been developing, financed

----

*In the field of trade, relations were somewhat bet-
ter. In July 1963 the USSR and Nigeria concluded a trade
agreement intended to increase trade in a number of products, specifically columbite, which Nigeria had previously
been forbidden to export to communist countries under the
terms of the 1951 U.S. Battle Act. Trade continued to
increase, but Nigeria still ranked low on the list of
Soviet trading partners in Africa.

largely by foreign private capital. During the period of
the first national development plan (1962-68), which had
as its objective the attainment of a 4 percent rate of
growth in GNP, while consumption was only to increase at
the rate of 1 percent, the 4 percent rate of growth was
outstripped in the industrial sector in the early years,
reaching as much as 19 percent in the manufacturing sector. One of the main reasons for Nigeria's healthy economy since 1958 has been the production of oil. Clearly
Nigeria, unlike Guinea, offered more favorable prospects
for economic assistance since its rich endowments of
natural resources, unlike those in Guinea, were already
being successfully exploited prior to independence. The
USSR was well aware of Nigeria's economic potential but
was initially unable to gain an entree into the economy.

The USSR entered Nigeria under circumstances somewhat similar to those which prevailed in Guinea when the
USSR first established relations with Toure. In both
countries the former metropolitan power was denying its
ex-colony vital resources. In the case of Guinea, the
rift with France meant the removal of all economic aid.
In Nigeria, Britain's refusal to supply as much arms as
the government wanted gave the Soviets an ideal and more
dramatic entry into the former bastion of Western influe-
ence. When the Civil War broke out in Nigeria, the Soviet press maintained a cautiously neutral position. As
soon as it became obvious that Lieutenant-Colonel Odumengo
Ojukwu, leader of the breakaway Biafra, and Major-General
Yukubu Gowon, leader of the Federal Military Government
(FMG) had irreconcilable differences, the USSR discussed
the merits of each side's claims, without committing itself. Before the outbreak of the war, the USSR had concluded a cultural agreement with the Federal Government
in March, but at this time was still contemplating supporting Biafra. Biafra was also asking the Soviets for
arms. In July 1967, even after the outbreak of hostili-
ties, Moscow was careful not to manifest an obvious bias.
The USSR only committed itself when it became obvious
that the Federal Government had general support from
other powers and was likely to win.[78]

The USSR entered into economic relations with Nigeria
after Britain refused to supply Gowon with aircraft and
certain types of arms. When the Nigerians returned to
Moscow in late July to ratify the cultural agreement made
in March, this protocol was used as a means of negotiating
an arms deal. The Soviet Union began to supply Mig 17s to
Nigeria in August, and continued to supply equipment and

technicians during the Civil War. Both sides stressed that these arms deals were "strictly for cash on a commercial basis."[79] The terms of the agreement are not known, but in 1969 the New York _Times_ reported that in March 1969, Mig 15s had been purchased for cash and 7,000 tons of cocoa.[80] Whatever the precise terms, it was clear that both sides emphasized the "business-like" nature of the deals. The Nigerians were particularly adamant that they had no intention of changing their economy to a socialist one or of making political concessions to the USSR. Moscow also denied any possibility of Nigeria being on the "noncapitalist" path of development.

A recent Soviet article on economic relations with Nigeria stated quite frankly that "it has not been easy to establish Soviet-Nigerian economic cooperation."[81] The USSR finally overcame Nigerian suspicions of Soviet aid by giving the FMG military aid at a time when no other major power would commit itself to the Federal cause, and Britain was reluctant to go too far in its support. This unequivocal support paid off and allowed the USSR to enter the Nigerian economy. The USSR entered the Nigerian market on a firmer basis than it had in Guinea, namely as a supplier of arms. As the Nigerian ambassador in Moscow said after the war was over, victory over the Biafrans was the result of Soviet assistance, "more than any other single thing-- more than all other things together." He went on to say, "The important thing is that the Soviet Union made no noise about the assistance it has rendered Nigeria."[82]

Soviet nonmilitary aid to Nigeria has been directed at exploiting mineral wealth and developing the agricultural sector. In November 1968 an agreement was signed in Lagos, pledging Soviet credits of $140 million. The credits were primarily intended to build an iron and steel complex, initially rejected by the West and under study by the Soviet experts since 1967. No further details were given. In June 1970 the Soviets and Nigerians signed a protocol on geological prospecting and research in Nigeria for finding iron ore, coking coal, and fluxes for the projected metallurgical complex. This would last five years and cost 58 million pounds.[83] It was agreed that construction of the iron and steel project would begin in 1974.[84] Further agreements to this effect were signed in 1970 which specified more precisely the cost and scope of the steelworks and the prospecting. The steelworks were to produce 800,000 tons of steel a year. It is clear that the USSR is carefully investigating the costs and structure of the projects before committing itself to construction. In addition it has set up centers for the sale and servicing of Soviet machinery under joint Nigerian and Soviet ownership. These mixed companies are also becoming important in Soviet supplies of automobiles to Nigeria. Since 1968 over 2,500 Soviet motor vehicles have been sold in Nigeria, and the "Moskovich" car is an increasingly familiar sight in the streets of Lagos.[85] The USSR has also given a $20 million loan to build an 800 bed hospital in Enugu. Other negotiations underway are concerned with Soviet interest in developing the petrochemical industry in Nigeria, and possible training of the Nigerians for satellite communications development.[86] In 1972 over 1,000 Nigerian students were studying in the USSR, after years of lack of cooperation in this area.[87]

Soviet economic contacts with Nigeria have greatly increased over the last five years. Although it is too early to evaluate the results of this new aid program, it seems that the Soviet Union expects more economic dividends from this policy than was previously the case in other African nations. Nigeria's economy is remarkably resilient and has made a quick recovery from the dislocation of war, especially considering the fact that during the war oil supplies were cut off in Biafra. The Nigerian rate of growth during 1970-71 was 9.6 percent for the economy as a whole, exceeding the target of the four-year development plan. During 1970-71, it was about 12 percent. However, the oil sector contributed 5.7 percent to growth while agriculture only contributed 2 percent.[88] Soviet aid in Nigeria is therefore operating in a healthy economic climate which promises to improve. Nigeria's thriving economy is a much more attractive environment for economic assistance than was Guinea in the early years of independence, when economic crises were the norm. The USSR has given Nigeria credits for the construction of viable industrial and agricultural projects and has not wasted its resources on show projects, as it did in Guinea.

As yet neither side has voiced any complaints about the actual workings of Soviet aid, but the newness of Soviet assistance may account for this. On the basis of the past few years, it seems that the USSR is primarily interested in economic profitability in its aid to Nigeria and is not giving credits out of political motivation.

Before the Civil War Nigeria's economy was mainly privately controlled, but since 1970 Major-General Gowon has been changing the structure of the economy and government toward a more centralized, etatist state-controlled system. In October 1970 the new economic reforms stipulated

TABLE 6.3

Soviet Trade with Nigeria
(thousands of roubles)

	1970		1971	
	Quantity	Value	Quantity	Value
Exports				
Machines, equipment and means of transport	--	1,646	--	3,335
Aluminium wire	214 tons	146	1,425 tons	846
Equipment for geological prospecting	--	--	--	1,007
Trucks	329	809	52	177
Accessories and spare parts for trucks and garage equipment, including engines	--	193	--	359
Automobiles	62	70	236	231
Accessories for spare parts for automobiles, including engines	--	109	--	211
Motor scooters	202	26	--	--
Oil and petroleum products	1,000 tons	113	1,450 tons	229
Sheet glass	37 th. sq. metres	11	171 th. sq. metres	63
Refined sugar	25.7 th. tons	2,352	35.0 th. tons	3,678
Cotton fabrics	13.3 mill. metres	1,632	6.1 mill. metres	834
Medication	--	--	--	55
Bicycles	--	--	500	9
Printed products	--	11	--	20
Office accessories	--	7	--	1
Cement	115 th. tons	955	211 th. tons	1,756
Total		10.9 mill. roubles		15.7 mill. roubles
Imports				
Cocoa beans	26.4 th. tons	20,285	66.3 th. tons	34,940
Printed products	--	--	--	1
Total		20.3 mill. roubles		41.0 mill. roubles

Source: Vneshnaya Torgovlya Soiuza SSR za 1959-71 Gody.

that the state's interest in all industrial enterprises
with the participation of foreign capital had to be no
less than 55 percent, and in other spheres no less than
35 percent. Also the state was to play a far bigger role
in distribution, especially where foreign capital was predominant.

Gowon has also passed an Indigenization Decree which
stipulates that after March 31, 1974, 22 types of busi-
nesses will be completely barred to firms even partly
owned by aliens. A further 33 types will be barred to
aliens if the business does not exceed a specified turnover or paid up capital requirements. However, this increase in domestic control of the economy should not be
taken as a leftward turn.[89] The government wants to pro-
ceed with the drive for greater Nigerian participation in
the economy while simultaneously attracting more foreign
investment.[90] Nevertheless, the Soviet press has praised
the new measures.[91] One result of these new measures is
that public ownership is growing in the iron and steel
and petrochemical industries, all subsidized by the USSR.

Soviet aid to Nigeria may therefore ultimately prove
more profitable for Moscow than initially expected. The
USSR is becoming increasingly involved in Nigeria's lucra-
tive oil industry and in a time of energy crises, this may
prove to be important. State control is slowly making inroads in the oil industry, and in April 1971, the Nigerian
National Oil Corporation (NNOC) was set up, receiving
strong Soviet endorsement when it demanded an increase of
its share in foreign-owned oil companies.[92] Needless to
say, the Soviet press has consistently criticized "imperialist" foreign oil firms and their exploitation of
the Nigerian economy.[93] Nigeria's move to increase state
participation in its oil industry has received support
from the Organization of Oil Exporting Countries (OPEC).
It may be contemplating more radical public control of
the industry. When asked whether Nigeria was going to
nationalize its oil industry, Alhaji Shettina Ali Monguno,
Commissioner for Mines and Power, replied:

> Ours at the moment is a reasonable and pro-
> gressive participation in the oil industry.
> But national interest will always dictate
> the course of our foreign policy--we hope
> the oil companies in this country will also
> be reasonable.[94]

One of the main reasons for Nigeria's inability to
nationalize its oil industry is the lack of trained

indigenous manpower to run the industry, and this is where
the USSR has stepped in and is encroaching on the West's
former monopoly in the field. In 1972 the USSR and the
FMG signed an agreement under which the Soviet Union is
assisting Nigeria to establish an Oil Education Center at
Warri. The Center is run by the Soviet agency Technoex-
port. Nigeria is providing $3 million toward the con-
struction of the Center and the USSR is supplying experts
and teaching equipment for the Center, which will offer
courses to the Nigerian employees of the NNOC, and will
train 500 specialists at a time.[95] Moscow is also helping in other ways to train personnel for the "upper levels" of the national economy in order to support the government's policy of enlarging the state sector. In June
1973 a delegation of the Soviet Committee for Foreign
Economic Relations signed a contract in Lagos with the
Nigerians pledging Soviet assistance for the development
of the NNOC. The USSR, therefore, has entered the profitable Nigerian oil market as a partner promoting state-
controlled enterprises which are dedicated to lessening
Western domination of the market.

It would, however, be an exaggeration to depict the
USSR as taking over the Nigerian oil industry. The NNOC
currently has access to 1.75 percent of total oil output
although it hopes, with Soviet help, to increase this
share. Previously, the joint Shell/BP corporation had a
monopoly on oil refining at Port Harcourt, but now the
USSR and Rumania are training Nigerian technicians to re-
fine their own oil. Shell/BP, however, still controls the
industry and produces about 65 percent of the total oil
output.[96] Also the USSR is by no means Nigeria's largest
oil customer. The United States buys about 27 percent of
Nigeria's oil, with Britain and the West Indies taking 16
percent each.[97] However, in the present oil crisis, Nigeria's resources are especially in demand, because the
oil has a low sulphur content. Nigeria is the world's
sixth largest oil exporter, and in 1972, oil exports
earned $1.5 billion.[98]

Despite their participation in the state-controlled
NNOC, the Soviets seem to have no illusions about Nigeria's
internal development. The local entrepreneurial classes
are still thriving, and the government is encountering resistance from the large Western oil corporations as it
tries to encroach on their territory.

The Soviets are cautious about Nigeria's economic development. A recent Soviet article talks of the "positive" tendencies in Nigeria's economy and of "mutually

advantageous cooperation" between the two countries.[99] Soviet commentators admit that "Nigeria has changed to some
extent its attitude to the Soviet Union and other socialist
countries--relations between the two countries continue to
develop successfully,"[100] but they do not suggest that Nigeria is moving in the same direction as Guinea. For instance when Gowon announced his new economic program in
July 1971 _Pravda_ commented: "From this program it is not
sufficiently clear on which road Nigerian development will
travel, the capitalist or noncapitalist."[101] At the most
the USSR expects concrete economic dividends from its aid
policy and general friendliness from the Nigerian government. It has no illusions about incipient Nigerian socialism or about automatic Nigerian support for Soviet foreign
policy. Economic and political realism seem to be increasingly important in Soviet aid to sub-Saharan Africa.*

SOVIET FOREIGN AID IN PERSPECTIVE

There has definitely been a change of emphasis in Soviet foreign aid policies since 1958, as our examination
of Guinea and Nigeria suggests. However, it would be an
overstatement to say that the entire Soviet aid program
has been altered since Khrushchev. There are as yet too
many unknowns to paint such a neat picture. Even today
Soviet officials themselves contradict each other in their
pronouncements on aid. At the Twenty-fourth Party Congress, Zlemanov said:

> The USSR places its equitable and mutually
> advantageous ties with developing countries
> on immutable Leninist principles, without
> requiring for itself any economic advan-
> tages or political concessions.[102]

On the other hand V. Sergeyev, Vice-Chairman of the USSR
State Committee on Foreign Economic Relations, in the same
year, stressed that aid was not philanthropy and had to be
"well-justified economically."[103] Although the second
pronouncement is nearer the truth, the fact that the first
still has political sanction means that the USSR has not

---

*Nigeria maintained diplomatic relations with Israel
until October 25, 1973 and the rupture was due more to
African than Soviet pressures.

given up the declarative aim of giving aid as revolutionary humanitarianism, even if this is not evident in its
operational policy.

One area in which Soviet aid policies have not changed
is the field of multilateral aid, for which the USSR has
never shown much enthusiasm. After initially refusing to
contribute to any United Nations funds, the USSR began to
contribute to the UN's Expanded Program for Technical Assistance (EPTA) in 1954. Between 1954 and 1958, the USSR
gave $39.8 million to EPTA and the UN Special Fund, or 3
percent of the total, while the United States gave $622.2
million or 43 percent.[104] The Soviet Union used to com-
plain that the UN, dominated by "imperialist" powers, was
frustrating Soviet attempts to play a more active role in
multilateral aid.[105] The initial lack of Soviet support
for the UN aid agencies was largely a result of the predominant U.S. role in shaping and implementing these programs. Nevertheless, during the process of the creation
of the UN Capital Development Fund, which was established
in 1966 and which the United States opposed, the USSR
could have seized the initiative in shaping the new agency
to its liking. However, it took virtually no interest in
the enterprise and has remained basically opposed to multilateral aid. The United States has been a little more en-
thusiastic, but, to put things in perspective, UN aid forms
only about 2 percent of total aid to developing countries,
on the basis of bilateral and multilateral arrangements.[106]

Although all conclusions about the changes in Soviet
aid must be tentative, given the lack of data on projects
in progress, there are differences between early Guinea and
late Guinea and Nigeria to illuminate certain changing motivations in Soviet foreign aid. The granting of aid has
always been a product of two concerns--the desire to cultivate relations with new states whose political sympathy
was needed, and also the concern to expand economic ties,
both in terms of trade and aid. The latter was and is
still the lower priority. In the early years in Guinea,
for example, political considerations were uppermost. The
USSR has never expected that the giving of foreign aid
would bring communist governments to power, but it has
hoped that aid would prevent the West from preempting the
new states. Soviet aid has made neutralism a practical
alternative and has thus accomplished its chief political
aim. In the early 1960s, however, Khrushchev, with his
flare for improvization, was willing to lavish aid for
political prestige, regardless of economic merit. When
the projects built with Soviet aid began to fail, the

political heavy-handedness of Soviet officials, inexperienced in dealing with Africans, was thrown into sharp relief against the background of inappropriate aid. The Soviets learned their lesson the hard way, but slowly realized that the last thing these newly independent countries wanted was to be under a new neocolonial master and they began to reorient the political dimensions of their foreign aid to a more realistic basis.

With Nigeria, all the internal political expectations involved in initial aid to Guinea were absent. Gowon was not Toure, and had no pretensions to socialism. At the same time as Soviet economists realized that their early aid to Guinea had often been counter-productive because it was not geared to the needs of the Guinean economy, they began to stress criteria of feasibility, profit, and efficiency. The Soviets have become more concerned with insuring that they receive sufficient returns on their end. Implicit in the aid to Nigeria is the concept of give and take, absent in the Guinean case. Political motivation is not entirely absent, and the USSR has certainly increased its prestige with the FMG, but clearly economic considerations have played an important role in Soviet aid to Nigeria. Whatever political motivation there is, it is not of the crass variety, as in early years. Indeed, it would be unrealistic to imagine that any great power would give economic assistance to a developing nation without expecting some political dividends. The difference between Soviet aid under Khrushchev and under his successors is that the USSR has changed the expectations of political payoffs which it hopes to gain from foreign aid.

Experience with specific projects has also changed the character of the assistance given. In Guinea many of the early projects were inadequately researched prior to construction, and their scale was too vast for a small country. Soviet-Guinean working relations left something to be desired, by all accounts, and repayment schedules were unrealistic. The results were often frustration and chaos, and aid projects benefited neither the Guinean nor the Soviet economy. As a result of its problems in Guinea in the early 1960s, the USSR has learned from experience with projects which could not absorb capital aid deliveries on schedule or were generally unsuitable. It has also become more discriminating in its commitments to aid projects. Now, as in the case of the Nigerian iron and steel complex, Soviet technicians carry out elaborate feasibility surveys before any definite commitment is made, and the USSR extends fewer comprehensive lines of credit covering multiple, undesignated development projects. It also makes more allocations for specific projects than it did previously. The USSR is now cooperating with more mixed enterprises and in Nigeria has set up joint stock companies. Soviet specialists are still involved in agricultural projects, but in both these and in industrial projects they are now paying far more attention to training indigenous personnel to operate the enterprises once the Soviets leave.

Probably the most significant change is the growing Soviet involvement in the production of minerals--bauxite in Guinea, and oil and iron and steel in Nigeria.[107] These industries are not only vital for the development of the economies of these two countries, and potentially one of their greatest sources of wealth, but they are also important for the Soviet economy. These projects could turn out to be a source of considerable profit to both donor and recipient, and to the joint companies involved in these ventures. Repayment arrangements have also become more realistic. There is a growing emphasis on importing manufactured goods produced with Soviet aid, and less stress on traditional products.[108] A comparison of early Guinea with late Guinea and Nigeria shows that, although the form in which aid is given remains the same, the content of aid projects has definitely changed from "show" projects to those oriented toward feasible and profitable economic development.

The reorientation of Soviet aid is part of the general shift in Soviet foreign policy since the fall of Khrushchev and thus not only the product of specific experiences with projects. The Brezhnev regime has relegated the Third World, and particularly sub-Saharan Africa, to a lower position in the foreign policy hierarchy. Disillusionment with the internal problems of so many African states and the ephemeral nature of many of their governments has made the Soviets wary of too great an involvement in any African regime, lest they get burned, as they were in Ghana. Aid commitments have declined since the early 1960s and are more selective. Detente with the United States has lessened the importance of Africa as a Cold War chessboard and thus political dividends, particularly the desire for socialist regimes there, are less important. The conflict with China, however, and Sino-Soviet rivalry in Africa has ensured that the USSR continue its aid program to forestall any increase in Chinese influence in Africa. The increase in aid projects oriented toward profitability is one aspect of the USSR's concentration on its own technological development as its main

priority and its willingness to "do business" with any
country. The Soviet Union's general desire for more sophisticated technology seems to have extended to its willingness to appraise aid projects more thoroughly and ensure that they accrue some profits to the USSR.

Since foreign aid forms such a relatively small part
of total Soviet resources, changes in the direction and
composition of projects must of course be understood in
the context of their somewhat lesser importance to Soviet
leaders. The Soviet Union, like other developed nations
has become disillusioned with aid as a political lever.
So for the near future it seems that Soviet aid will continue to be bilateral, discriminating, concerned with economic results, and not particularly forthcoming. Whether
this kind of aid is what developing nations really need
is another question. At least aid will continue to bolster the USSR's prestige in Africa and possibly bring it
dividends without draining domestic resources beyond a
reasonable limit.

NOTES

1. For general works on Soviet foreign policy toward
sub-Saharan Africa, see Helen Desfosses Cohn, Soviet Policy
Toward Black Africa: The Focus on National Integration
(New York: Praeger Publishers, 1972); W. Raymond Duncan,
ed., Soviet Policy in Developing Countries (New York: Ginn
and Company, 1970); and Robert Legvold, Soviet Policy in
West Africa (Cambridge, Mass.: Harvard University Press,
1970).

2. Since there is no Soviet source which offers comprehensive figures for aid and commitments by country or
by year, any study of Soviet aid necessarily involves
drawing from a variety of Soviet and Western sources, and
patching available information together. This method inevitably has some loopholes, but the best available sources
are the Soviet Vneshnyaya Torgovlya Soyuza SSR za-god,
which are annual trade statistics published by the USSR
Ministry of Foreign Trade; the U.S. Department of State's
Bureau of Intelligence and Research's annual document Communist Governments and Developing Nations: Aid and Trade
in 19--; the British Economist Intelligence Unit: Economic Review of the French African Community; and Quarterly Economic Review of Nigeria (for Africa) and the French
weekly Marches Tropicaux et Mediterraneens (for Africa).

3. In 1923 a conference of People's Commissars on
Foreign Trade agreed to aid Eastern countries, but apart

from a loan of $8 million in 1932 and one to Afghanistan in 1927, aid was not forthcoming. Prior to 1955 the Soviet Union traded with only eight underdeveloped nations and the total volume of trade with sub-Saharan Africa was minimal. See Alexander Ehrlich and Christian R. Sonne, "Soviet Economic Activity," in Africa and the Communist World, ed. Zbigniew Brzezinski (Stanford: Stanford University Press, 1963).

4. Although this is the conventional view of Stalin's foreign policy, some authors disagree. Marshall Shulman in his book Stalin's Foreign Policy Reappraised (Cambridge, Mass.: Harvard University Press, 1963), claims that Stalin became interested in the developing countries shortly before his death, and Khrushchev's policies were therefore a continuation of his predecessor's.

5. Khrushchev, cited in Kurt Mueller, The Foreign Aid Programs of the Soviet Bloc and Communist China (New York: Walker and Company, 1967), p. 44.

6. For a comprehensive discussion of the theory of the noncapitalist path see Cohn, op. cit., chapter 6.

7. B. Pichugin, "The Seven-Year Plan and the Soviet Union's Foreign Economic Relations," International Affairs, no. 10 (Moscow, 1959): 71.

8. Vneshnyaya Torgovlya, no. 2 (1959): 12.

9. Cited in Sovremennyi Vostok, no. 7 (1959): 4.

10. There is some evidence that the Soviets present their views on aid differently depending on the audience at which their writing is directed. For instance one edition of a book which was oriented toward Eastern Europe stressed how aid would help the Third World become socialist. In the version of the same book intended for the developing nations, the Soviets emphasized that aid would help stimulate independent economies. See Nadia Derkach, "The Difference in Soviet Portrayal of their Aid to Underdeveloped Countries in English and in Russian," RAND Corporation Paper (Santa Monica, Calif.), p. 2853.

11. For a discussion of the question of comparative advantage see Joseph Berliner, Soviet Economic Aid (New York: Praeger Publishers, 1958), chapter 7.

12. See articles in Voprosy Ekonomiki of November 1965, February 1966 and April 1966 for a Soviet argument of this view.

13. Berliner, op. cit., p. 136.

14. Vasily Sergeyev, "The Soviet Union and the Developing Countries," New Times 3 (January 20, 1971): 18.

15. U.S. Department of State, Director of Intelligence and Research Memorandum, Communist Governments and Developing Nations: Aid and Trade, RSE-65, p. 8.

16. Ibid.

17. Sergeyev, op. cit., p. 18.

18. Ibid.

19. Under this arrangement, a foreign firm builds the plant, imports the necessary equipment, puts the plant in operation, trains indigenous personnel and then turns over the operating of the unit to the government for a fixed fee. See Ehrlich and Sonne, op. cit., p. 69.

20. Recently Secretary of State Kissinger was quoted as saying to Egyptian President Sadat, referring to Dulles' refusal to finance the Dam, "It was not one of our more intelligent decisions." New York Times, January 13, 1974, p. 10.

21. See U.S. Department of State Memorandum, op. cit., RSB-50, 1968, p. 6.

22. James Richard Carter, The Net Cost of Soviet Foreign Aid (New York: Praeger Publishers, 1969) claims that the net cost of Soviet aid is substantially lower than might appear from looking at data on aid extensions. There are considerable lags between aid promised and aid disbursed, he says, and price discrimination lessens the real cost of aid, since Soviet exports in the form of aid deliveries are overpriced by about 15 percent. Altogether he finds that between 1955 and 1968, the USSR ostensibly delivered $3.1 billion in goods and services to noncommunist developing countries; the net cost, however, was only about $680 million, after deducting what the USSR received in repayment of the loan-aid and the benefit of price discrimination. Nevertheless, while the net cost of aid to the USSR is probably less than its apparent cost, there may be some flaws in this calculation. See Joseph Berliner's review of the book in Slavic Review (March 1973): 177.

23. See U.S. Department of State Memorandum, RSC-65, pp. 5-7.

24. For a fuller description of these agencies, see Marshall Goldman, Soviet Foreign Aid (New York: Praeger Publishers, 1967), pp. 75-78.

25. For a detailed discussion of Soviet aims in Guinea, see Legvold, op. cit., pp. 56-67.

26. Ibid., pp. 58-59.

27. Eliot Berg, "The Economic Basis of Political Choice in French West Africa," American Political Science Review 54 (June 1960): 391-405.

28. Vneshnyaya Torgovlya, no. 10 (October 1959).

29. Pravda, March 3, 1960.

30. Sovremenny Vostok, no. 5 (May 1960).

31. Pravda, March 3, 1960.

32. Yuri Bochkaryov, "The Guinean Experiment," New Times, no. 24 (June 1960): 23-26.

33. N. Famara Keita, Guinea's Minister of Planning, cited in Pravda, April 7, 1960, p. 3.

34. William Attwood, The Reds and The Blacks (New York: Harper and Row, 1967) recalls that Soviet diplomats hated to travel in Guinean buses purchased from the USSR because they were insufferably hot. On one occasion the Soviet ambassador insisted on riding in his own car, while other diplomatic personnel suffered gallantly in the bus. Another anecdote recounted in the New York Times, August 20, 1960 was that a Soviet cement cargo bound for Conakry was rerouted to Monrovia because of inadequate landing facilities, and it arrived just before the rainy season. The cement, unloaded and left on the docks, was not surprisingly a hardened pyramid of cement when it was finally fetched. However, this tale seems to have been told about Soviet aid to many countries.

35. Marches Tropicaux et Mediterraneens, no. 874 (August 11, 1964): 1705.

36. Economist Intelligence Unit, Three-Monthly Review of the French African Community, no. 8 (March 1962): 16.

37. "Economic Notes," Africa Report (January 1961): 2.

38. In March 1972 hotels and cinemas in Guinea were returned to private enterprise because they had been so badly run by the state. See Africa Confidential 13, no. 5 (March 3, 1973).

39. Attwood, op. cit., p. 66.

40. Goldman, op. cit., p. 171.

41. His crime was his alleged connection with a plot to oust Toure, which the government claimed to have unmasked, and in which a group of communist teachers was implicated. However, the extent of Soviet involvement in this plot is doubtful. See Attwood, op. cit., pp. 76-77.

42. The Soviet press tried to gloss over the rupture with Guinea and did not mention Solod's recall in Pravda. In January Mikoyan went to Guinea and eulogized Toure at a Soviet trade and industry exhibition. See Mizan, January 1962. However, to put things in perspective, the French ambassador was expelled in 1965 and the U.S. ambassador in 1966 and both were later allowed in again.

43. Pravda, July 13, 1958, p. 4.

44. Moscow News, May 30, 1965, p. 4.

45. For an informative discussion of this problem, see Uri Ra'anaan, "Moscow and the Third World," Problems of Communism 14, no. 1, pp. 22-31.

46. See <u>Le Monde</u>, October 30, 1964 and the <u>Frank-furter Allgemeine Zeitung</u>, October 31, 1964.

47. "Socialism's Supreme International Duty," <u>Pravda</u>, October 27, 1965.

48. In the mid-1960s, the Soviet rate of growth began to decrease and the economy began to show signs of strain. See Abram Bergson, <u>Planning and Productivity under Soviet Socialism</u> (New York: Columbia University Press, 1968).

49. For an excellent discussion on the debate, see Elizabeth Kridl Valkenier, "Recent Trends in Soviet Research on the Developing Countries," <u>World Politics</u> (1968): 298-312. See also David Morison, "USSR and Third World: Questions of Economic Development," <u>Mizan</u> (December 1970): 124-52.

50. He said, "it will be necessary to make wide use of foreign trade as a factor for economizing in current production expenditures and in capital investment." <u>Pravda</u>, October 22, 1961, p. 8.

51. See especially L. Zevin, "Vzaimnaya Vygoda Ekonomicheskogo Sotrudnichestva Sotsialisticheskikh i Razvivayushchikhsia Stran" (Mutual Benefits in the Cooperation between the Socialist and Developing Countries), <u>Voprosy Ekonomiki</u>, no. 2 (February 1965): 72-83.

52. G. M. Prokhorov, ed., <u>Problemy Sotrudnichestva Sotsialisticheskikh i Razvivayushchikhsia Stran</u> (Problems of Cooperation between the Socialist and Developing Countries) (Moscow, 1966).

53. One author suggested that the USSR accept less profit for its share in joint enterprises than would a Western company but it should nevertheless secure a "fair" return on its investment. See Yu Shamrai, "Problemy Sovershenstvovaniya Ekonomicheskogo Sotrudnichestva Sotsialisticheskikh i Razvivayushchikhsia Stran" (Problems of Perfecting Economic Cooperation of the Socialist and Developing Countries), <u>Narody Azii i Afriki</u> 4 (August 1968): 10-13.

54. L. Zevin, "Some Trends in the Division of Labor between Socialist and Developing Countries," <u>Voprosy Ekonomiki</u>, no. 8 (1967): 91-92.

55. Previously the Guineans had insisted on retaining control over the construction of Soviet projects but this had led to such bottlenecks that in 1963 the Soviets persuaded the Guineans to transfer administrative control over the implementation of Soviet projects to Soviet technicians. See Legvold, op. cit., p. 158.

56. The stadium at Conakry was completed in 1964 (Tass Press Release, December 13, 1964); the hotel in 1964 (Pravda, October 2, 1964); the refrigeration plant in 1963 (Trud, March 22, 1963); the sawmill in 1964 (Tass Press Release, December 13, 1964); and the cannery at Mamou in 1963 (Tass Press Release, December 31, 1963). The completion of the projects also meant that Guinea now had to repay the USSR, and thus the success of the projects also meant a repayment problem.

57. The Soviet press never acknowledged this promise and indeed never built the dam but did supply Guinea with ten new trawlers. See Legvold, op. cit., p. 238.

58. Vneshnyaya Torgovlya 9 (September 1968): 20.

59. Marches Tropicaux (July 13, 1973): 2217.

60. Economist Intelligence Unit, Review of Former French West Africa, no. 4 (1970): 7.

61. Ibid. (December 1970): 6.

62. This is according to the chief engineer of the project, Anatoly Sinegovsky. See New York Times, November 23, 1973.

63. Ibid.

64. In 1973 the USSR imported more than 1.7 million tons of bauxite. Domestic bauxite production figures are estimated at about 4 to 5 million tons. See ibid.

65. See Marches Tropicaux (November 9, 1973): 3263.

66. V. Shishkovsky, "Guinea Looks Ahead," New Times 39 (September 1973): 15.

67. Alexander Logish, foreman of the drilling and dynamiting section at Benti, quoted in ibid., p. 15.

68. Economist Intelligence Unit, Review of Former French West Africa, no. 3 (1973): 10.

69. Ibid., no. 2 (1970): 5.

70. Vneshnyaya Torgovlya, no. 5 (1973): 26.

71. Guinea's main exports to the USSR are bananas, grapefruit, coffee, and bauxite; its main imports from Russia are machinery, equipment, and petroleum products. Also over half the cars in Guinea are Soviet-made. Ibid., p. 26.

72. See articles in Sotsialisticheskaya Industrya (November 1973): 16-21.

73. Ibid. (November 21, 1973): 3.

74. V. Tyagunenko, "Nekotorye Problemy Natsional'no-Osvoboditel'nikh Revolutsii V Svete Leninizma" (Certain Problems of the National-Liberation Revolutions in the Light of Leninism), Mirovaya Ekonomika i Mezhdunarodnoye Otnoshenia, no. 11 (1972): 114.

75. V. Solodovnikov, ed., Politicheskiya Partii Afriki (Political Parties of Africa) (Moscow, 1970). On

p. 18, he says, "The views of A. Sekou Toure do not contradict the ideas of expanding a mass base of support of
the revolutionary-democratic parties in the course of national construction. This process is actually taking
place."

76. Shishkovsky, op. cit., p. 15.

77. _Pravda_, June 10, 1961.

78. For a discussion of the factors which led the
USSR to support the Federal Military Government, See
Arthur Jay Klinghoffer, "The USSR and the Secession Question," _Mizan_, 10, no. 1 (January-February 1968): 64-70,
and Legvold, op. cit., pp. 311-30.

79. New York _Times_, August 24, 1967, p. 15.

80. Ibid., March 9, 1969, p. 5.

81. R. Alexeyev, "Nigeria on the Road of National
Development," _International Affairs_, no. 3 (Moscow, 1972):
62.

82. New York _Times_, January 21, 1970, p. 1.

83. Alexeyev, op. cit., p. 63.

84. _Africa Contemporary Record_, 1970-71, P. A 61.

85. _Pravda_, July 9, 1971.

86. _Tass_, September 16, 1971.

87. Nigeria now has the second largest number of
Third World students in Communist countries. See U.S.
Department of State Memorandum RSE-65, p. 11.

88. _Africa_ Annual 1973, p. 176.

89. For further details of the Indigenization Decree
see _Africa Confidential_ (April 21, 1972): 7.

90. Ibid. (June 16, 1972): 6.

91. See Y. Tsaplin, "Nigeria Moves Forward," _New
Times_ 34 (August 1973): 12.

92. _Tass_, March 9, 1973.

93. Y. Doletov, Moscow Radio, cited in _The USSR and
The Third World_, February 8-April 8, 1973.

94. _Africa Confidential_ 13, no. 13 (June 30, 1972): 7.

95. _Economist_ Intelligence Unit, _Quarterly Economic
Review of Nigeria_ (November 3, 1972): 13.

96. M. Zenovich in _Pravda_, April 12, 1973.

97. New York _Times_, November 23, 1973, p. 53. Gulf
Oil produces about 18 percent of Nigeria's oil, and Mobil
Oil about 10 percent.

98. Ibid.

99. Alexeyev, op. cit., p. 62.

100. Tsaplin, op. cit., p. 13.

101. M. Zenovich, _Pravda_, July 1, 1971.

102. Cited in _International Affairs_, no. 8 (Moscow,
1971): 9.

103. V. Sergeyev, "The Soviet Union and the Developing Countries," _ibid_., no. 5 (1971): 26. At the 24th Party Congress, the 1971-75 Five Year Plan stated that "development of stable external economic, scientific and technological ties with developing Asian, African and Latin American countries shall be continued on terms of mutual benefit in the interest of strengthening their economic independence." D. Chertkov, "The USSR and Developing Countries: Economic Relations," _International Affairs_, no. 8 (Moscow, 1972).

104. Robert S. Walters, _American and Soviet Aid_ (University of Pittsburgh Press, 1970), p. 171.

105. A. Nekrasov, "Soviet Aid: Past and Present," _International Affairs_ no. 3 (Moscow, March 1963): 83.

106. _Africa in Soviet Studies Annual_ (Moscow, 1968): 209.

107. According to the New York _Times_, December 1, 1968, the iron and steel project "appears to be the sort of prestige undertaking of which Soviet diplomats in the Third World have long been fond. Its economic viability, given the poor quality of Nigeria's iron ore and coal, is another question." However, not all commentators share this view.

108. Sergeyev, in a 1971 interview, stressed that credits are repayable in traditional exports or local manufactures, and this provides the recipient country with stable markets for their output and gives the USSR an additional source of supply to meet economic demand. _The USSR and the Third World_ 1, no. 3 (1971): 5.

7

NAVAL STRATEGY AND
AID POLICY: A STUDY OF
SOVIET-SOMALI RELATIONS
Helen Desfosses

Recent Western press commentary has evidenced increasing concern with Soviet aims and strategy in the Indian Ocean. References to the area as "a Soviet sea"[1] point to the intensity of the concern and also indicate the assumptions being made regarding the goals and effects of Soviet policy in this region. It is assumed that the USSR has achieved significant influence on the politics of the littoral states, that the search for such influence is part of a wide-ranging Soviet strategy to exclude the West from the area and its oil, and finally, that this "escalation" in Soviet naval presence relates to some long-range policy of achieving an offensive posture on the world ocean. However, an examination of the realities of Soviet-Indian Ocean posture reveals a much less dynamic and successful policy.

Analysis of the timing of the Soviet-Indian Ocean buildup, the nature of Moscow's aims, the actual degree of Soviet influence in key littoral states such as Somalia, and the nature of Soviet naval capabilities and strategy indicates that the Soviet expansion is more symbolically, rather than militarily, significant. Also it is accompanied by political influence that in no way approximates control. In fact the political and economic realities of the Indian Ocean countries suggest constraints, difficulties, and responsibilities for the USSR that significantly complicate the realization or extent of Soviet influence.

A discussion of the timing of the Soviet buildup in the Indian Ocean cannot be divorced from the question of the general shift in Soviet naval strategy which became discernible after the Cuban missile crisis and which was intensified after the accession to power of Brezhnev and

Kosygin. (In 1964 a policy of extending the operations of Soviet surface ships to the high seas became especially noticeable.) This shift stemmed, first of all, from the dramatic illustration of Soviet naval shortcomings afforded by the Cuban confrontation. The October 1962 crisis demonstrated to the USSR much more directly than ever before the capacity of the United States for naval conflict intervention and for challenging the USSR at strategic levels. Also the increased American investment in seaborne strategic delivery systems emphasized anew the untenability of continued Soviet concentration on land-based missile procurement.[2]

The development of U.S. capabilities was perhaps the major factor in promoting Soviet awareness of the strategic significance of the Indian Ocean. The USSR had extended military and economic aid to Indian Ocean states on its southern periphery (India, Indonesia, Afghanistan, and Iraq) in the 1950s. However, the strategic importance of the Indian Ocean itself was impressed upon the Soviet leadership by the deployment of the Polaris A3 missile in December 1964. The 2,500 nautical mile range of this missile not only implied the vulnerability of eastern regions of the USSR, but it also meant the increased attractiveness of northwest corners of the Indian Ocean for launching attacks on the highly developed areas of European Russia. While such geostrategic considerations might have affected the Soviet decision of late 1963 to extend the unconditional and large amounts of military aid to Somalia rejected by the West, they certainly influenced the Soviet diplomatic initiative at the United Nations in the last weeks of 1964. The Soviet memorandum "On measures for further easing international tension and restricting the arms race" included a proposal for nuclear-free zones in the Mediterranean and Indian Oceans. No mention was made of other seas, a fact that certain Western analysts find especially revealing of Soviet concern.[3]

The absence of favorable Western response to the memorandum did not trigger any noticeable increase in Soviet naval activity in the Indian Ocean. The ouster of Khrushchev and the priority of the Mediterranean in naval strategy (it remained the most important potential locus of submarine rocket attack) made Moscow particularly sensitive to the likely effect of Soviet expansion into an area long considered a Western preserve. In fact it was not until 1968 that the USSR began its much-publicized buildup, heralded by a cruise of several months duration by a _Kashin_ class destroyer, a cruiser, and a guided-missile

destroyer from the Soviet Pacific Fleet. The impact of
this action in the West was intensified by the multi-fleet
operations and port calls by several Soviet ships in the
ensuing months. Since 1969 there has been a continuous
Soviet presence in the Indian Ocean, typically consisting
of a rotating group of ten combatants and ten auxiliaries.[4]

Much has been made in the West of the near coincidence
between Britain's announcement of its planned withdrawal
from military commitments east of Suez and the initial
phase of Soviet Indian Ocean naval activity. However,
while the ramifications of this for Soviet policy were
certainly taken into account, there were other, more significant, factors which serve to present the British
statement as a precipitating, rather than causal, factor
in the Soviet Indian Ocean decision. The mid-1960s had
been an eventful period, witnessing the introduction of
multiple warheads for the Polaris A3 and the development
of the higher-payload Poseidon missile, the exigencies of
space recovery operations, the lessons of the Six-Day War
regarding the need to reduce the impact of the American
naval presence, the intensifying Sino-Soviet dispute, and
finally, the significant qualitative, and to a lesser extent quantitative, improvement in Soviet naval capabilities. The pressure of these events was such as to make a
Soviet expansion into the Indian Ocean highly probable;
the British decision accelerated the process.

SOVIET AIMS IN THE INDIAN OCEAN

While it could be pointed out that the number of Soviet vessels in the Indian Ocean is less than one-tenth
the number of Soviet ships typically away from home, it
would be more useful to focus our analysis on a point
made by T. B. Millar, Director of the Australian Institute for International Affairs: "The significance of the
Soviet vessels lies less in their quantity than in their
novelty, in the fact that they have so little competition
and in their being part of a collection or pattern of Soviet activities, strategic, political and economic."[5]

In order to evaluate this putative pattern in Soviet
activity, it is necessary to discuss Moscow's aims in expanding its naval presence and military-economic ties in
the Indian Ocean. While it is difficult to assess the
relative importance of various influences on Soviet
decision-making, the dominance of strategic concerns--
real or presumptive--in any country's policy process can

provide some useful clues. Similarly concern with security vis-a-vis members of the Great Power Triangle can also be assumed to be paramount in Moscow, Washington, and Peking. Viewed in this light, Soviet Indian Ocean policy emerges as a flag-showing effort designed to alert the United States, and secondarily, China, to a forward Soviet naval strategy and facilities concern. The USSR's actions in littoral states also represent an attempt to balance America's lingering concern with alliance-building in the Third World. For this still occurs in an era when the Nixon Doctrine and the dramatic summits in Washington, Moscow, and Peking have shifted the primary emphasis of superpower foreign policy to bilateral or tripartite agreements among its privileged ranks.

Finally we must consider what Thomas W. Wolfe has called the "interaction" phenomenon in Soviet and American naval decisions.[6] The interaction phenomenon has a technological and a policy aspect. Thus the technological achievements of the United States and the Peoples Republic of China have increased the importance of the Indian Ocean in Soviet security calculations. Several reports during the past year, for example, have mentioned China's construction of an instrumentation station in Dar-es-Salaam to monitor the test flights of ICBMs from China over the Indian subcontinent to an impact point in the Indian Ocean;[7] the Chinese might also be preparing naval facilities in Tanzania for tracking ships.[8] The 1965 U.S. announcement of the decision to develop the Poseidon missile also had ramifications for the importance of the Indian Ocean to Soviet strategists. The range and payload of this American missile narrowed the gap between the Indian Ocean and the Mediterranean in terms of attraction as a launching area (against both the USSR and the PRC). Two events since that time have further drawn the attention of strategists to the Indian Ocean: the Six-Day War and SALT I. The concentration of Soviet naval power in the Mediterranean since the 1967 Arab-Israeli war has meant that this area is very well defended, thus reducing its potential as an anti-Soviet launch area. Finally as certain analysts have noted, the SALT restrictions on offensive missiles (and the not unrelated research and development efforts at new submarine-tracking methods) could make the Indian Ocean vital to U.S. nuclear deterrence.

Regarding the policy aspect of the interaction phenomenon, it is, of course, true that any attempt to identify certain factors on the spiral of recent American-Soviet naval interaction as causal or reactive can create severe problems of evaluation and, perhaps, objectivity for the researcher.[9] However, it can be stated that long-standing Western assumptions of gaps in Soviet naval capabilities, and resulting American deployment and local interventionary moves could not fail to elicit an eventual corrective or forward Soviet response. The USSR's resolution of certain intramilitary disputes, budget allocation conflicts, and increasing, albeit varied, efforts to neutralize the Chinese military and diplomatic challenge, paved the way for some response in kind to what they perceive as possible U.S.-Chinese collusion in the Indian Ocean and America's heightened reliance on a "naval choice"[10] under the present Administration.

In the Soviet view there has been an increased Pentagon emphasis on the ocean as a strategic base; this has affected not only overall American planning, but also, more specifically, U.S. Indian Ocean strategy. The United States has been more active than the USSR in the Indian Ocean area in terms of the establishment of bases and port facilities, arms shipments, military advising and training, and ship visits.[11] Meanwhile the construction of a modern U.S. naval base at Diego Garcia[12] is seen as the lynchpin in a chain of Western bases stretching from the British island possessions of Aldabra and Farquhar off the southeast coast of Africa to the Cocos Islands off Australia. Soviet analysts further postulate that this Indian Ocean network is intended to link the Atlantic and Pacific military-political alliances.[13]

Moscow's reponse to the new dimensions of America's seaborne strategic capability in large part conditioned both its forward strategy in the Indian Ocean and its attempts to parlay resulting Western concern into an American decision to extend the SALT principle of equal security in strategic forces to the area of general purpose naval forces.[14] Washington has not done this. Indeed, the 1974 announcement that U.S. forces in the Indian Ocean would be improved indicates that the Soviets may have failed in their attempt to demonstrate their naval capabilities to achieve certain global security objectives, while not frightening the United States (and its allies) into a more determined Indian Ocean posture.[15] Soviet showmanship and propaganda have been so successful that many Western policymakers have adopted an exaggerated view of Soviet naval capacilities. The long-standing assessment of many analysts that the level of these capabilities dictates a greater value of the world ocean to Moscow as a stage than as a potential battleground has been overlooked.[16]

It is true that vast improvements have been made in the
past decade in the structure and capabilities of the Soviet
navy.[17] However, the USSR must still contend with a situation where its forward deployment strategy is based on a
real, yet limited, naval presence.[18] The qualitative aspects of her new surface vessels, the considerable build-up
in submarines, and the extensive high seas training provided
for her crews by such ventures as the Indian Ocean expansion
have not been able to overcome what one Western naval officer-
analyst has called "a lack of balance between its increasingly credible strategic forces and its qualitatively impressive
but quantitatively inferior lower-level combat force."[19] Recent reports regarding Soviet aircraft carrier construction
must be considered in evaluating this imbalance* (see Table
7.1). However, the expense involved in any extensive effort
seems to mitigate against any early Soviet realization of
the ability to challenge Western forces for command of the
high seas. Any Soviet effort would also be complicated by
the costly effects of the Soviet Union's geography, the need
to maintain four separate fleets and to contend with the
lack of direct free ocean access.

TABLE 7.1

Naval Balance

	Major Combatants	
	United States	USSR
Aircraft carriers	16	1
Helicopter carriers	7	2
Cruisers	9	25
Destroyers and escorts	211	204
Surface totals	243	232
Nuclear submarines	56	65
Diesel submarines	41	218
Submarine totals	97	283

Source: Adapted from The Military Balance, 1973-1974
(London: The International Institute for Strategic Studies,
1973) and information compiled by Dr. Richard Burt, Fletcher
School of Law and Diplomacy.

---

*The first Soviet aircraft carrier, the Kiev, is now
undergoing sea trials, while a second carrier is under construction. These ships will carry V/STOL (vertical short
take-off and landing) planes as well as helicopters.

These general limitations on Soviet naval capabilities have done much to condition Soviet Indian Ocean strategy. Geography, expense, and quantitative vessel limitations have worked to effect a Soviet policy that is a curious mix of a search for port facilities, propaganda (relatively muted but often uncontrollable in its effects), military and economic aid, and appeals for the denuclearization of the entire area. The search for port facilities has been a constant since the mid-1960s, as the closing of the Suez Canal turned a 3,200 n. mi. voyage even for the elements of the Black Sea fleet into one of over 11,000 n. mi. in order to reach areas off the southern Arabian coast.[20] Although this problem is one which the USSR shares with the United States, Soviet difficulties are compounded by the restrictions which the Dardanelles and Oresund Straits pose for the Black Sea and Baltic fleets, and those which fog and ice place on Pacific Fleet movements for much of the year.

However, the Soviet Union has not turned to bases in order to facilitate the maintenance of a permanent Indian Ocean presence.* While this may be partially attributable to the reluctance of certain littoral states to grant such rights, it is instructive that in almost two decades, the USSR apparently has not insisted on base acquisition as a precondition for continued relations. This is true even vis-a-vis Somalia and the People's Democratic Republic of Yemen, countries where Soviet influence is said to be predominant, and where bases would be essential if Soviet Indian Ocean maneuvers actually involved preparations to interdict oil shipments to the West.

It is, of course, true that the USSR has dredged and developed the harbors of Berbera, Somalia, and at Hodeida on the Yemeni coast for repair and refueling operations of its ships. It is also true that Soviet military aircraft use Yemeni and Somali airfields, and that Soviet personnel have installed a communications facility at Berbera. However, several factors caution against any interpretation

---

*Although the USSR has supplied India with over 1.2 billion dollars in arms aid it was thwarted in its apparent efforts to obtain "basing privileges" during the December 1973 consultations between Brezhnev and Prime Minister Indira Gandhi.

of these moves as a menace to the West or as other than an
attempt to inject the Soviet presence into what was previously a Western preserve. First of all there are still
over 3,500 Americans stationed at the giant U.S. telecommunications facility at Kagnew in Ethiopia (see Table 7.2),
while the British and American navies have port facilities
at several places along the East African coast. Second
the 1972 lesson of being expelled from its Egyptian base
might have increased the importance of Somalia to the Soviet military, but strategists are also wary of any dependence on the facilities of such volatile African and Middle
Eastern countries.[21] Thirdly although naval and air bases
can help to compensate for Soviet inferiority in aircraft
carriers or sustained air cover, they cannot redress the
vulnerability of Soviet supply lines.[22] Fourth the extremely variegated nature of the states in the Indian
Ocean littoral, plus the enormous area concerned, implies
the futility of the Soviets even attempting, through base
rights, to neutralize NATO's seaborne strategic missile
system.[23] Finally while the nature of Soviet naval capabilities and the geostrategic environment of the Indian
Ocean area mediate against any offensive Soviet posture
in subregions such as the Horn, the nature of domestic
politics in a country like Somalia also constitutes a
hindrance.

   Even if one were to accept the debatable point that
the Soviets aim at controlling the country, rivalries
within the Somali military government represent a con-
straint of significant proportions. The evidence suggests cleavages between pro-Soviet and pro-Chinese factions, between pro-Western and pro-Communist groups, between those who favor war or detente with Ethiopia, and
between those who favor encouraging Great Power military
and economic aid competition and others who fear its effects on Somali sovereignty. President Siad Barre has
reacted to these conflicting pressures by opting for the
classic zigzag policy course. For example 1970 witnessed
the expulsion of the Peace Corps and the proclamation of
Somalia as a socialist state; 1972 witnessed Siad's visits to both Peking and Moscow,[24] while the friendly reception accorded the new U.S. ambassador indicated some effort at improving Somali-American relations.

   The USSR's response to Siad's maneuvers at times suggests Soviet deference to Somali demands rather than Soviet control. Although the Soviets retain their dominant
position as advisers to the Somali armed forces and as the
country's main aid supplier, these positions have not
brought proportional influence. References in the Soviet

media to Somali "reactionaries"[25] provide some indication
of policy disagreements, as do reports by high-level Washington sources that the USSR has been troubled by mounting
Somali demands for MIG-21s. In fact the Soviets face the
same dilemmas in planning their military aid program toward
Somalia as they do in their economic assistance efforts:
how to have leverage without responsibility, how to advise
without becoming implicated in Somalia's border disputes,
how to give enough assistance to impress Siad (and to some
degree, military governments elsewhere) without intensifying the fears of anti-Soviet factions, and how to keep the
level of Great Power competition in the Horn from threatening the general thrust of peaceful coexistence.

TABLE 7.2

Soviet Military Personnel in Less Developed
Countries in 1972

Country	Number of Military Personnel
Afghanistan	200
Algeria	1,000
Egypt	5,500*
India	200
Iraq	500
Somalia	400
Sudan	100
Syria	1,100
Yemen (Aden)	200
Yemen (Sana)	100
Other	150
Total	9,450

*This number does not include an estimated 7,500
Soviet military personnel who were assigned to Soviet
operational units in Egypt. These troops were withdrawn
at Egypt's request in mid-1972, along with most Soviet
military advisers and technicians.

Source: Communist States and Developing Countries:
Aid and Trade in 1972 (Washington, D.C.: U.S. Department
of State, 1973), p. 13.

The pressure of such multiple dilemmas has produced many situations where the Soviets have reacted to, rather than originated, developments,[26] and where they have assumed an aid burden higher than their apparent "aid for facilities" formula would entail. The USSR has so far granted almost $90 million in economic aid and $50 million in military aid to Somalia, making the country the largest Soviet aid recipient in Tropical Africa. Furthermore there is substantial evidence of Soviet vulnerability to increased levels of Somali involvement with the People's Republic of China. For example the 1971 Chinese loan offer of $110 million elicited a favorable Soviet response a few months later to a previously rejected dam construction project and to the issue of reopening discussions on new arms shipments. In 1971 the USSR also agreed to cancel Somali debts totaling over $2 million and to extend the debt repayment schedule by five years.[27] Informed analysts feel that these offers reflect a Soviet desire to appear responsive without assuming additional commitments to the military. They also reflect a degree of Soviet control over the evolution of its relations with Somalia that is far from all-encompassing.

This minimal control also extends to the matter of Somali disputes with Kenya, and especially, Ethiopia. The extent of the conflict is of significant concern to the USSR. As Somalia's major arms supplier, she could be implicated in violence which might upset the delicate balance in the Horn or threaten the sovereignty of Ethiopia, an important American ally and Western communications center. Thus, even though Somalia confronts the second largest army in Black Africa (35,000 men) and perhaps the largest air force (2,100), ten years of Soviet military assistance have seen the development of only a 17,000-man Somali army and a 350-man air force (see Table 7.3). Somali requests for sophisticated equipment have frequently been denied, while much of what has been granted seems to be geared more toward promoting an image of Soviet responsiveness than toward developing a viable Somali defense system[28] (see Table 7.4). Similarly Moscow's aid policies have aimed at securing port facilities rather than bringing about anything even approaching parity between Somalia and Ethiopia in terms of armed forces, equipment, or volume of military and economic assistance. By its policies and diplomatic efforts, the USSR has attempted to minimize the level of conflict between the two African countries and between the superpowers who are their sponsors.

TABLE 7.3

Security Forces in Somalia and Ethiopia

	Somalia	Ethiopia
Army	17,000	35,000
Air force	350	2,100
Navy	300	1,380

TABLE 7.4

Military Equipment

	Ethiopia	Somalia
Army	50 M-41 medium tanks 20 M-24 light tanks	150 T-34 medium tanks*
Air force	37 combat aircraft	21 combat aircraft

Navy	1 coastal minesweeper
	5 patrol boats
	4 harbor defense craft
	4 landing craft
		4 P-6 motor torpedo
		   boats
		6 P-4 motor torpedo
		   boats

*The oldest Soviet model

Source: The Military Balance, 1973-1974 (London: The International Institute for Strategic Studies, 1973).

Another indication of the limited character of Soviet Indian Ocean policy vis-a-vis the Horn is that while the USSR has attempted to establish itself as Somalia's patron, it has not made the rejection of deals with the United States or the People's Republic a precondition of the relationship's continuance* (see Table 7.5). Nor has the USSR attempted to preempt or even challenge America's relationship with Haile Selassie's regime or that of China

---

*The Chinese are reported to have offered Somalia an arms deal in 1973, provided that they did not accept similar aid from other powers.

with Nyerere's government. It is perhaps a reflection of
the changed character of superpower relations since the
Moscow, Peking, and Washington summits that, although the
Horn is strategically important vis-a-vis the Middle East
(an area that has been deemed a compelling arena by the
Tripolar Club), each superpower seems to have staked out
its base in the Horn. There appear to have been no strong
efforts by any power to preempt another's position.

TABLE 7.5

Aid to Somalia and Ethiopia, 1954-73
(in millions of U.S. dollars)

	Somalia	Ethiopia
Economic aid		
United States	79	249
Soviet Union	90	18
People's Republic of China	110[a]	84[b]
Military aid		
United States	--[c]	200
Soviet Union	55	--[c]
People's Republic of China	na	na

[a]Offered in 1971.

[b]Offered in 1972.

[c]Negligible.

Note: na = not available.

Some explanation for this is no doubt provided by
the muting of Cold War postures and the superpower preoccupation with domestic and/or intra-alliance difficulties that the past few years have witnessed. However,
another more compelling explanation derives from strategic
considerations. While a strategic presence in the Horn
and the Indian Ocean is significant, this region remains
somewhat peripheral to the superpowers' larger interests.
Naval considerations do not figure prominently in the
security efforts of the People's Republic of China; meanwhile, many experts argue that the area is not vital to
Western nuclear deterrence.[29]

THE USSR AND OIL TRADE

In recent months concern about the energy situation
has been accompanied in the press and in many Department
of the Navy analyses by emphasis on the strategic importance of the Persian Gulf region and Indian Ocean shipping
lanes, and by fear that these might be eyed by Soviet military leaders as excellent potential pressure points for
crippling the West. At times the commentary has suggested
not only the attractiveness of such an option to the Kremlin, but that the Soviet search for port facilities, its
policy toward Iraq's conflict with Kuwait, and its general
maneuvers in the Indian Ocean and its littoral state are
steps in Moscow's plan to control the route for shipment
of oil from the Gulf. However, the cursory references to
U.S. security interests in President Nixon's April energy
message to Congress,[30] conversations with State Department
energy officials, and recent Defense Department leaks to
the press[31] suggest that high-level concern about Soviet
plans to interdict oil shipments might be largely confined
to the Navy. Furthermore a brief review of certain economic and geostrategic realities indicates the justifica-
tion for the more moderate perspective.

Although it has been clearly stated since the days of
Khrushchev that one of the primary missions of the Soviet
Navy in wartime would be to disrupt the shipping of oil
and other cargoes to the West, there are many geographical
and strategic problems that would mitigate against the ac-
tualization of such a policy. This applies especially to
the Indian Ocean, where any blockading Soviet force, surface or submarine, would have to cover the entire several
hundred mile wide Cape of Good Hope passage, operating
without air cover and under threat of attack from the
Simonstown air base in South Africa. Such problems would
not only hinder Soviet attempts at interdiction, but at a
more limited harassment of Western vessels as well. In
the absence of any real prospects for success, embarking
on a harassment policy would almost certainly entail serious escalation if the USSR aimed at demonstrating global
military might.[32] Meanwhile Soviet ships would provide
hundreds of potential hostages for NATO forces.

The economic ramifications of any Soviet move against
Western oil supplies would also be severe. The operations
of the Soviet merchant marine, which contribute significantly to the Soviet economy, would almost certainly be
disrupted in retaliation, as would the marketing of Soviet
oil, the largest single source of foreign exchange for

the USSR. Furthermore Moscow's promotion of a triangular oil arrangement, whereby it seeks to import energy resources from the Persian Gulf while exporting Siberian reserves to Japan and the West, would be thwarted. The supplier countries would be angered by the interruption of their shipments to Western markets, which are much more significant both in volume and in provision of hard currency than the typically small Soviet barter deals. Good trade relations with Japan would be sacrificed, removing the major growth area in Soviet east-of-Suez trade.*

Similar considerations affect an evaluation of Western speculation that the USSR might attempt to substitute its own market as a replacement for disrupted Western ones. Such conjecture overlooks the long-standing Soviet policy of maintaining self-sufficiency in oil;[33] it also ignores the payment, storage, and processing problems that would loom large. Relative to the United States alone, the USSR consumes only one-third as much oil and in contrast to the United States, must dispose of a sizable export surplus. Furthermore virtually all of the oil procured by the USSR from Middle Eastern countries has been based on a barter arrangement; the Soviet Union can provide neither the hard currency nor the sophisticated goods that the producer states have been acquiring in such large quantities. Finally Soviet storage tanks and tankers† are almost totally committed to the Soviet export trade, and its refinery capacity remains extremely limited.

Thus a review of strategic, geographical, and economic realities strongly suggests that the USSR could not expect to successfully interdict oil shipments to the West. The evidence further indicates that Moscow has a sizable stake in the continuation of a stable world petroleum trade. To move against this trade would endanger Brezhnev and Kosygin's policy of promoting detente with the United States, Japan, and Western Europe; it would also run counter to an increasingly obvious regime goal of improving the USSR's trade position.

---

*Trade with the entire Third World constitutes only 11.3 percent of Soviet overseas trade.
†Soviet tanker capacity is less than 3 percent of total world tonnage.

SOVIET INFLUENCE

To argue that the evidence suggests that the Soviet Union's expansion into the Indian Ocean is not based on the goals or capabilities of threatening Western security, interdicting oil supplies, or controlling littoral states is not, of course, to support a Moscow Radio claim[34] that the build-up is primarily attributable to increased fishing and oceanographic research activity. By intruding into what was an exclusively Western preserve, the USSR has served notice of her improved naval capabilities and her determination that Soviet security concerns should be considered in Western policy-making regarding yet another of the world's oceans. She has also joined the ranks of powers who are not abstractions to Indian Ocean littoral states, but whose views, to varying degrees, must be considered in formulating domestic and foreign policy.

The capacity of the Soviet government to engage in gunboat diplomacy and to dispense significant amounts of military and economic assistance in exchange for facilities cannot but affect political calculations in states plagued by poverty, ethnic rivalries, and frequent violent regional disputes. However, it should be noted that Western recognition of the delimiting effects of Soviet Indian Ocean presence on the potential of Western interventionary actions must also be mirrored in the Kremlin. Similarly growing American awareness of the uncertainty of any correlation between Great Power aid input and Third World policy output is shared increasingly by Soviet officials and analysts.[35]

Of course, the superpowers have not abjured the search for influence. For the USSR, such activity provides a means of maintaining a certain global balance, indicating the compatibility between Communism and Islam, and obtaining support for Soviet positions on disarmament, denuclearization, etc. Soviet Indian Ocean activity also helps to counter Chinese influence on governments and liberation movements in the littoral states, and to convince key countries like Egypt that the USSR is powerful enough to best protect Egyptian aims vis-a-vis the state of Israel.

However, the absence of insistent Russian pressure to reopen the Suez Canal, the withdrawal of Soviet pilots from the Yemeni civil war once their identity was revealed, and Soviet efforts to maintain good relations not only with the two Yemens, but with Somalia's neighbors as well, suggest Moscow's unwillingness to pay too high a price for influence in terms of regional stability and Soviet involvement. These moves also indicate Soviet hesitancy to base its strategic and/or foreign policy goals on any assumption of continued influence, or even good relations, with a single area state.

Similarly, the leveling off of the number of Soviet ships in the Indian Ocean since 1970,* the repeated Soviet appeals for denuclearization and the extension of the "spirit" of the Moscow agreements to naval affairs, and the Soviet agitation among Third World countries for support of those proposals, indicate that Soviet naval aims and expectations in the Indian Ocean are relatively limited. It is galling, to be sure, that the USSR has been able to parlay a minimal naval presence into a prominent influence on the future of this important ocean in superpower security calculations. However, as Alastair Buchan, Director of London's Institute for Strategic Studies, recently pointed out:

> To take fright at the prospect of . . .
> Soviet ships in the Indian Ocean . . . is,
> first, to be guilty of a form of hubris
> which will bedevil our thinking about the
> new pattern of international equilibrium,
> namely, that the high seas are an exclusive
> Western possession; secondly, to act as an
> unpaid public relations officer for Fleet
> Admiral Gorshkov.[36]

The worldwide projection of Soviet naval power has ended the long-standing American ability to intervene virtually unchallenged in national or regional conflicts.[37] However, the United States realizes, as Secretary of State Henry A. Kissinger has pointed out, that "there is a great danger of looking at the developments in this [Indian Ocean] area in terms of a strategy that is more appropriate to the previous century than now."[38] The United States can continue to reap whatever lingering benefits of gunboat diplomacy that remain, as the deployment of the carrier Hancock during the 1973 Arab-Israeli War indicated; however, it will also exert its influence to help resolve those regional conflicts that have increased the destabilizing potential of burgeoning superpower naval capabilities.

----

*Note, however, that the Soviets did despatch more ships to the area in October 1973 in response to the deployment of the American carrier Hancock.

198

NOTES

1. New York _Times_, November 17, 1970.
2. C. G. Jacobsen, _Soviet Strategy-Soviet Foreign Policy_ (Glasgow: Macelhose, 1972), p. 123.
3. Geoffrey Jukes, _The Indian Ocean in Soviet Naval Policy_, Adelphi Papers, No. 87 (1972), p. 7.
4. According to Adm. Elmo R. Zumwalt, the U.S. Chief of Naval Operations, the number of Soviet ships in the Indian Ocean is now three times that of the United States. Boston _Sunday Globe_, June 3, 1973.
5. New York _Times_, November 13, 1970.
6. Thomas W. Wolfe, _Soviet Naval Interaction with the United States and Its Influence on Soviet Naval Development_, Rand Report (Santa Monica, Calif., October 1972), p. 4913.
7. New York _Times_, March 20, 1972.
8. _Military Review_, Fall 1972.
9. Charles B. McLane, _Soviet-Middle East Relations_ (London: Central Asian Research Center, 1973), p. 8.
10. G. I. Svyatov, "The United States Navy," _SShA_, no. 9 (September 1972); trans. _USA_ (Joint Publications Research Service 57211, October 10, 1972), p. 14; also, Anatoliy Gromyko and A. T. Kosokhin, "The World Ocean in American Politics," _SShA_, no. 11 (November 1970); trans. _USA_ (JPRS 54676, December 10, 1971), p. 16.
11. New York _Times_, June 18, 1973.
12. The Nixon administration announced plans to expand the harbor, construct fuel storage facilities, and extend the 8,000 foot runway to 12,000 feet. In this way, the base could accommodate aircraft carriers and B-52 bombers. New York _Times_, March 13, 1974.
13. B. L. Teplinsky, "The World Ocean and US Military Strategy," _SShA_, no. 10 (October 1972); trans. _USA_ (JPRS 57398, November 1, 1972), p. 17.
14. Svyatov, op. cit., p. 148; Teplinsky, op. cit., p. 26. Also, see the interview with Leonid Brezhnev in the _Canberra Times_ (Australia), June 14, 1971, cited in Jukes, op. cit., p. 23.
15. Jukes, op. cit., p. 11.
16. Stephen Kime, "The Rise of Soviet Naval Power in the Nuclear Age," unpublished Doctoral Dissertation, Harvard University, 1971, p. 319.
17. According to Wolfe, op. cit., p. 36, these improvements have been very noticeable in the Soviet effort "to optimize its capabilities against superior Western surface forces by a combination of surface, subsurface, and air-launched anti-ship missiles."

18. Jacobsen, op. cit., p. 123; Kime, op. cit., p. 134.

19. Kime, op. cit., p. 319.

20. Note that this situation would be reversed by the projected 1974 reopening of the Suez Canal. However, according to the Washington Post (January 26, 1974), "some defense planners do not believe the Soviet Union would be able to transfer many more ships from the higher priority areas of the Atlantic, Pacific and Mediterranean. Nor do they believe that the Suez Canal--which US Sixth fleet units can also use--and the Red Sea are safe waterways in a crisis since both are easily blocked."

21. Michael McGwire, "The Mediterranean and Soviet Naval Interests," International Journal 18, no. 4 (Autumn 1972): 551.

22. Curt Gasteyger, "Moscow and the Mediterranean," Foreign Affairs 46, no. 4 (July 1968): 680-81.

23. Robert Herrick, Soviet Naval Strategy (Annapolis, Md., 1968), p. 111.

24. Reportedly the Chinese have been invited to construct the strategic 650-mile Beled Wen-Burao highway and the sports center in Mogadiscio--both projects that Moscow wanted. Soviet Analyst, August 3, 1972.

25. Moscow Radio Peace and Progress, January 26, 1971. Also a Washington Post report of December 18, 1973 indicated that Somali officers and soldiers trained in the USSR are often viewed as politically unreliable and are deactivated upon returning home.

26. See Uri Ra'anan, The USSR Arms the Third World: Case Studies in Soviet Foreign Policy (Cambridge, Mass., 1969), p. 10.

27. Mogadiscio Radio, March 4, 1971.

28. Wynfred Joshua and Stephen P. Gibert, Arms for the Third World (Baltimore: Johns Hopkins Press, 1969), p. 46.

29. According to the Stockholm International Peace Research Institute, the ongoing development of a new generation of sub-launched missiles in the USSR and the United States (with ranges such that any part of the enemy's territory can be reached from one's own off-shore waters) renders a "nuclear disengagement in the Indian Ocean hardly a great sacrifice for either." World Armaments and Disarmament SIPRI Yearbook 1973 (Stockholm, 1973), p. 395.

30. New York Times, April 20, 1973.

31. New York Times, June 18, 1973.

32. Jukes, op. cit., p. 20; Kime, op. cit., p. 221; Herrick, op. cit., pp. 131-36.

33. Premier Aleksei Kosygin reaffirmed the advantage of this policy in a speech in Minsk. Sovetskaya Belorossiya, November 17, 1973.

34. Moscow Radio (in English to South and Southeast Asia), December 17, 1970.

35. Helen Desfosses Cohn, "Soviet-American Relations and the African Arena," Survey 86, no. 1 (Winter 1973): 161-63.

36. Alastair Buchan, Power and Equilibrium in the 1970s (New York: Praeger, 1973), p. 19.

37. Thomas W. Wolfe, The Soviet Quest for More Globally Mobile Military Power, Rand Report 5554 (Santa Monica, Calif.: December 1967), p. 16.

38. Office of Media Services, U.S. Department of State, "Transcript of a Press Conference held November 21, 1973 by Secretary of State Henry A. Kissinger," p. 10 (Mimeo.).

8

ON THE LIBERATION OF
AFRICAN LIBERATION MOVEMENTS
Michael H. Glantz
Mohamed A. El-Khawas

For a good number of years, many students of African
liberation movements have tended to reduce the cause of
revolutionary movement impotence to internal ethnic problems. As an example of this school of thought, one Soviet
observer noted that

> The extreme backwardness of social rela-
> tions, the ill-defined social differentia-
> tion, the political backwardness of the
> peasants who are the main force behind the
> movement but the majority of whom are
> still under the sway of tribal or other
> prejudices, make revolution exceedingly
> difficult. Traditional factors . . .
> [are] decisive in African politics.[1]

Such interpretation is partly correct because of the lega-
cies of tribal and ethnic differences in African history.
It is true that Africa, past and present, has suffered
from tribalism more than any other continent, particularly
throughout the early years of independence. Currently
leaders of independent African states have been wrestling
with various political, social, and economic problems,
many of which have been either directly or indirectly related to ethnic and tribal differences.
    The leaders of revolutionary movements in the yet un-
liberated southern African countries are faced with similar, but more complicated, problems due to the nature of
the struggle and the vulnerability of their claim for
leadership. For these reasons anyone interested in the
understanding of liberation movements cannot afford to

ignore the negative implications of ethnic and tribal differences on the conduct of revolutionary struggles in Africa.

Yet another important aspect has been ignored by many scholars, that is, the impact of regional and global political cleavages on the revolutionary movements in Africa, including such international cleavages as the cold war and the Sino-Soviet dispute, but also including possible ideological and/or personality differences among African leaders and/or countries. It is the thesis of this chapter that movement ties with external powers have often embroiled these movements in the larger cleavages, even to the extent that their revolutionary effort becomes "stalled."

The significance of such cleavages stems in part from the fact that internal armed struggle often has to depend on outside sources for material support, particularly for arms and personnel training. In a context where the countries able to provide assistance have differing ideological and political views they would like to further, the offers of material aid and support that a liberation movement receives are usually tinged with partisan political pressures of greater or lesser subtlety.

The Sino-Soviet ideological rift provides some illustration. As many observers have argued, this larger conflict has inevitably had harmful repercussions on the conduct of the liberation struggles in Africa, particularly in that nationalistic groups and individuals within these groups have sometimes been forced to choose between support from Peking or support from Moscow. Since 1965 China has denied material and moral support to any movement that chose to side with the Soviet Union. This was contrary to its earlier policy, which had aimed at maintaining contacts with all competing revolutionary factions within the same country while also encouraging unity among them. In the early 1960s, for instance, Peking had urged the Pan-Africanist Congress (PAC) and the African National Congress (ANC) to form a united front within South Africa. However, when the South African Communist Party, which was affiliated with the ANC, chose to side with Moscow, China moved to channel its material aid only to the PAC. Ideological conflict between the two communist powers also furthered divisions among revolutionary movements within Namibia (South West Africa) when South West Africa Peoples' Organization (SWAPO) became the recipient of Soviet assistance; in response, China put all its weight behind South West Africa National Union (SWANU). Sino-Soviet disputes also had a divisive impact on the International Conference in Support of the Liberation Movements of Portuguese Colonies and Southern Africa, which was held in Khartoum, the Sudan, in January 1969. The pro-China movements--such as Pan-Africanist Congress (PAC), Zimbabwe African National Union (ZANU), Uniao Nacional para a Independencia Total de Angola (UNITA), and Comite Revolucionario de Mocambique (COREMO)--boycotted the meetings. They considered the conference to be an attempt to control the liberation struggles in Africa in order to further American-Soviet detente and dominance over world affairs. On the other hand, the pro-Soviet movements--such as African National Congress (ANC), Frente de Libertacao de Mocambique (FRELIMO), Movimento Popular de Libertacao de Angola (MPLA), Partido Africano da Independencia da Guine e Cabo Verde (PAIGC), South West Africa Peoples' Organization (SWAPO), and Zimbabwe African Peoples' Union (ZAPU)--took a different stand and attended the conference which they considered to be a productive meeting.[2]

Because liberation movements typically have not received material aid from western Europe or the United States of America, they have had to rely solely on the Soviet Union, China, Cuba, and eastern Europe for the supply of arms they need to carry out their armed struggles. This places the communist countries in a strategic position by which they might influence the direction of the liberation struggles. If they were united in their revolutionary outlooks, they could provide massive support to particular nationalist groups. Similarly they could swing their support so as to encourage greater unity among competing revolutionary factions. Conversely divisions within the communist camp might have an adverse effect, particularly when aid is extended in line with ideological stance.

The African revolutionary movements are thus quite susceptible to such pressures because of their urgent need for external assistance. Another source of susceptibility, however, lies in their own organizational weaknesses. In particular internal dissension within movements, while perhaps inevitable in view of their almost impossible odds, nevertheless fosters a volatile environment in which leaders may be changed or in which new factions may develop at any time. As a result little long-term organizational stability is achieved and, in turn, the ideological positions of any movement are often not regarded as firm. Consequently contending major powers often find it fruitful to monitor closely the internal changes within movements.

Some amount of disagreement among revolutionary leaders is to be expected as to how best to liberate their

country. The international political environment in which
these leaders operate, however, has made it relatively easy
for dissident factions to break away from a parent organization and to receive encouragement, wittingly or unwit-
tingly, from outsiders. External support also enables
leaders of independent revolutionary movements to compete
with each other for such assistance. Moreover the existence of such divisive external pressures may frequently
exacerbate leadership differences and personality clashes
among revolutionary leaders. Support from external powers
can be an important source of autonomy for any dissident
faction or leader. In the absence of internal sources of
assistance, it is usually crucial that a movement turn to
outside assistance; because of a movement's own internal
instability--and because of the multiplicity of possible
external donors--the likelihood is great that external aid
will develop political uses. This circumstance particularly applies to revolutionary leaders in their conflict
with the state leaders they are trying to overthrow. However, dissident revolutionaries can also play on global
and regional cleavages in order to get support for their
own faction's efforts to "spin off" from or to stay independent of other movements seeking to liberate the same
target state.

It should also be noted that, in a divided revolutionary world, the role of host states--neighboring or
nearby countries that offer sanctuary to revolutionary
groups--cannot be underestimated. Their importance lies
not only in the amount of aid they give to the liberation
movements, but also in provision of training camps, sanctuary, and a means for channeling outside assistance.[3]
Yet host countries can also have negative impact on the
conduct of the revolutionary struggle. For example because Zambia allows both Rhodesian liberation movements
(ZAPU and ZANU) to maintain sanctuaries and headquarters
on its soil, it is to some extent sanctioning and reinforcing the differences between these rival groups. At
the very least, by allowing both movements to operate from
its land, Zambia has removed pressure from these movements
to form a united front and to combine their scarce resources in order to liberate their country.

From another point of view, however, the political
leaders in Zaire may have simply contributed to the continued existence of the rivalries among Angolan revolutionary leadership--Holden Roberto (GRAE/FLNA), Agostinho
Neto (MPLA), and Jonas Savimbi (UNITA)--by their decision
to allow exclusive sanctuary to the GRAE/FLNA. Such

action may also be detrimental to revolutionary unity since it could force greater separation--both ideological and geographical--between factions. Indeed the MPLA eventually did move its headquarters from Kinshasa to the Congo (Brazzaville)--a host country which has frequently been at odds with Zaire on ideological matters.

These examples suggest that political cleavages existing in regional and international spheres could easily enable revolutionary leaders from within the same movement or in different movements within the same country to rival each other for external support and positions of power, thereby fragmenting the liberation movement and inevitably weakening the revolutionary struggle.

IMPACT OF "EXTERNAL CLEAVAGES"

In the study of African liberation movements, this side of the "external cleavages" has so far been overlooked. For this reason, there is a need to examine, impartially but systematically, several examples of the impact of the African and global cleavages on the revolutionary struggle in Africa. Because of the relatively large number of revolutionary movements in Africa, the discussion in this chapter will be limited to an examination of the impact of regional and international cleavages on the liberation struggle in Portuguese Africa and in Southern Rhodesia which are as follows:[4]

Angola	GRAE/FLNA (Governo Revolucionario de Angola no Exilo Frente Nacional de Libertacao de Angola)
	MPLA (Movimento Popular de Libertacao de Angola)
	UNITA (Uniao Nacional para a Independencia Total de Angola)
Guinea (Bissau)	PAIGC (Partido Africano da Independencia da Guine e Cabo Verde)
	FLING (Frente de Luta pela Independencia Nacional da Guine)
Mozambique	FRELIMO (Frente de Libertacao de Mocambique)
	COREMO (Comita Revolucionario de Mocambique)

Southern Rhodesia	ZANU (Zimbabwe African National Union)
	ZAPU (Zimbabwe African Peoples' Union)
	FROLIZI (Front for the Liberation of Zimbabwe)

It should be kept in mind that several of the liberation movements are fragile coalitions of smaller political parties. For example FRELIMO was created by a merger of UDENAMO, MANU, and UNAMI in June 1962. After several leaders had been expelled from the parent organization they formed new parties such as UDENAMO-Monomatapa, UDENAMO-Mozambique, MANU, MANCO, and UNAMI; these new political factions eventually merged into one large organization—COREMO—in June 1965.[5] The GRAE in Angola is also a coalition of smaller parties which have aligned with Holden Roberto's Bakongo-based UPA.

One of the major reasons several movements exist for each country is because of leadership differences (many authors refer to such differences as "squabbles"). These differences have manifested themselves in at least two ways. Either they have resulted in the defection of one or more leaders from the parent movement, as was the case with COREMO, thus leading to the creation of a spin-off movement seeking to liberate the same country. Or there existed at the outset of the violence phase of revolution, two or more movements with two or more sets of leaders, organizations, followers, tactics, ideologies, and external supporters. Neither set of leaders wanted to become subordinate to the other set and, as a result, rivalries ensued. It appears that for both categories just mentioned the primary objective of the liberation of the target country was replaced by the desire of each revolutionary group to maintain its identity and autonomy from the others. Undoubtedly the existence of independent, external sources of support has tended to reinforce the differences between the leaders of the contending revolutionary factions. To support this view Table 8.1 is presented.

Several conclusions can be drawn from Table 8.1. First, in all cases, there are two or more revolutionary movements working for the liberation of the target country. Such a lack of a united front could place the revolutionary struggle in jeopardy since their limited resources are not mobilized to defeat their common enemy and occasionally are used against each other. For example there are reports of armed clashes between movements such as GRAE-MPLA and ZAPU-ZANU.[6] Thus it increases animosity among the rival groups

TABLE 8.1

National Liberation Movements in Portuguese Africa and Rhodesia

Target Country[a]	Revolution Group(s)	Spin-Off (S) or Independent (I)[b]	Sanctuary	Primary Sources of External Aid	ALC-OAU Recognition
Angola	GRAE/FLNA	I	Zaire	Zaire	Yes
	MPLA	I	Zambia	USSR	Yes
	UNITA	S	Angola	China	No
		(GRAE)			
Guinea (Bissau)	PAIGC	I	Guinea	USSR-China	Yes
	FLING	I	Senegal	Senegal	No
Mozambique	FRELIMO	I	Tanzania	USSR-China	Yes
	COREMO	S	Zambia	China	No
		(FRELIMO)			
Southern Rhodesia	ZAPU	I	Zambia	USSR	Yes
	ZANU	S	Zambia	China	Yes
		(ZAPU)			

[a]Target country refers to the country which is to be liberated.

[b]Spin-off or Independent refers to the origin of the revolutionary movement. If the movements for a particular target country developed independently from one another and maintained their autonomy, they are classified as independent. If the movement is the result of a split that has occurred in a parent movement, then it is considered to be a spin-off movement.

Sources: Kenneth W. Grundy, Confrontation and Accommodation in Southern Africa (Berkeley, Calif.: University of California Press, 1973), p. 155; Bruce D. Larkin, China and Africa 1949-1970 (Berkeley, Calif.: University of California Press, 1973),

within the same country and diverts their attention away from their ultimate goal which is the liberation of their land. Secondly Table 8.1 shows that liberation movements have to depend heavily on the communist countries for material and financial assistance since no aid was forthcoming from the West. The communist involvement in the African revolutionary struggle is a matter of life and death.

All liberation movements, except GRAE and FLING, are recipients of assistance from the Soviet Union and/or China. Soviet material and moral support have been extended to the parent movements such as MPLA, the PAIGC, FRELIMO, and ZAPU, while the Chinese have supported the three spin-off movements in Angola, Mozambique, and Southern Rhodesia-- UNITA, COREMO, and ZANU, respectively.[7] It seems that China has encouraged dissenters to break away and to form their own organizations. In return for material and personnel training, China has generally insisted that the recipient groups must sign a statement condemning Soviet revisionism and Western neocolonialism. Some movements have managed to avoid signing the statement and have antagonized Moscow by asking Peking to channel its aid through the Organization of African Unity (OAU). In fact both FRELIMO and PAIGC have managed to receive aid from both China and the Soviet Union. One reason is that both movements have been relatively successful in carrying out their armed struggle against Portugal. Another contributing factor is that there has been no serious challenge to their leadership inside the territories; both COREMO and FLING are small movements and their influence has not been felt yet in the struggle to liberate their countries.

Bruce Larkin hypothesized the following motivations for Chinese involvement in African liberation movements. His hypotheses tend to be supported by the information presented in Table 8.1 shown earlier:

1. If a nationalist organization becomes friendly to the Soviet position in the Sino-Soviet dispute, China will probably aid a competing nationalist organization if a viable one exists.
2. If two organizations are competing for influence in an exile community and one accepts Soviet aid, China will cultivate the other one.
3. If a group is the only radical nationalist movement conducting effective operations in a territory, China will give aid to that group even if the Soviet Union also gives it aid. (The case of South West Africa suggests a qualification to this hypothesis. If China has identified

herself with one group, which becomes ineffective but maintains a bare or nominal existence, and if Soviet support has gone to a competing group, China may continue to give her support to the first group.)

4. If two or more movements in a territory refuse to unite and yet refrain from mutually exclusive claims, China will attempt to maintain relations with persons or factions within both groups.[8]

One might conclude, then, that China's concern has been less with the success or failure of a specific liberation movement than with its competition with the USSR. It is apparent that China has responded to Soviet initiatives among revolutionary leaders by seeking other revolutionary leaders to support or other movements to aid.

Another important source of aid is the African Liberation Committee of the Organization of African Unity (ALC-OAU) which functions to coordinate assistance both from African countries and from outside the continent, and to grant recognition as well as legitimacy to selected revolutionary movements. Since ALC-OAU recognition is dependent upon demonstrated success in the military activities in the territories, Soviet and Chinese assistance have become essential in order to initiate successful military campaigns during the early years of the movement's life. The OAU recognition makes it possible for these movements to receive aid from ALC-OAU. In Guinea (Bissau) and in Mozambique, only one national liberation movement has been recognized and assisted by the ALC-OAU; in Angola and Rhodesia, multiple recognition prevails. It should be pointed out that ALC-OAU has worked closely with host nations that border on target countries. It has allowed these host governments to administer assistance to the liberation movements that operate from within their borders.

One must assume that the overriding objective of most African liberation movements is to liberate the target country from white minority rule. Yet it appears that external involvement in these liberation movements is having a negative effect on the attainment of that goal. In their drive for control over tactics, strategy, and ideological commitment of the revolutionary movement, leaders within a movement compete with each other for external, independent sources of support.

Let us review separately the situations in each of the Portuguese colonies and in Southern Rhodesia. Two general issues underlying this study include: whether the Sino-Soviet competition to capture the leadership in the

Third World has affected the revolutionary struggle on the African continent; and whether the OAU and the African host states have had any influence on the conduct of the liberation struggles in Africa.

Angola

Holden Roberto's personal friendships over time with such leaders in Zaire as Adoula, Bomboko, and Mobutu have given his movement, the GRAE, a prominent place in the liberation of Angola. The GRAE is the only movement to receive sanctuary in Zaire. Zaire's leaders have sought to merge other rival factions into the GRAE on an unequal basis, that is, members of rival factions were asked to join the GRAE as individual members and not as a bloc. Such demands, however, have forced other movements to seek sanctuary elsewhere. For example the MPLA moved its headquarters from Kinshasa to Brazzaville and, later, to Lusaka.

It might be argued that Zambia has been responsible for the balkanization of the Angolan liberation movement by allowing UNITA, led by Jonas Savimbi who left the Kinshasa-based group of Holden Roberto in 1964, to establish headquarters and to have sanctuary in Zambia, while the Zambian government permitted the MPLA the same conveniences. In 1968 UNITA was banned from Zambia because of their raids on the Benguela Railroad which has been vital for the export of Zambia's copper via Angola to the port of Lobito for shipment overseas. The banning of UNITA caused Savimbi to move his headquarters first to Cairo and later inside Angola. This ban denied him access to training areas for guerrillas and to a means for importing arms through Zambia for transfer into Angola.[9] It can be concluded that President Kaunda was willing to allow UNITA to use his country as sanctuary as long as they refrained from attacking the railway whose disruption could cause severe economic problems for Zambia. When this gentleman's agreement was violated by UNITA, Kaunda had to give priority to his country's economic needs. Thus Zambia has proven to be sensitive to economic pressure--a matter which cannot help the revolutionary struggles in Southern Africa and especially in Angola. The ALC-OAU has also reinforced existing cleavages between Angolan liberation groups by having extended recognition and support at one time or another to the GRAE and to the MPLA, although this was done in accordance with the ALC policy of recognizing and assisting only one movement per territory. Time and time again the ALC-OAU has been forced to withdraw recognition and aid from a given liberation movement when it has failed to maintain an active fighting force. Under these circumstances the ALC-OAU would shift its recognition to another liberation movement in the same country which has carried out successful military campaigns against the enemy. In doing so the OAU has not contributed to the reduction of intergroup rivalries, but in fact has exacerbated them.

Finally the states which have served as the principal sources of aid and support for the three Angolan movements have further reinforced existing cleavages among these groups. GRAE, for example, has received no aid from China. Their aid from the Soviet Union was interrupted following the 1964 Congolese rebellion which resulted in the rupture of diplomatic relations between Kinshasa and Moscow. For this reason, GRAE has had to rely for the most part on Zaire's aid in order to continue its guerrilla campaigns against Portugal. GRAE has been given exclusive access to Angola's border with Zaire. In return it has assisted the Zairois army in preventing the pro-Soviet MPLA fighters from crossing Zaire en route from their bases in Congo (Brazzaville) to fighting zones in northern Angola. On the other hand the MPLA has received support from the Soviet Union, while UNITA has become a recipient of China's aid.[10] China's involvement in Angola had been an apparent response to the Sino-Soviet competition to capture the revolutionary leadership in Africa. It is apparently part of a practice by Peking to support spin-off movements in southern Africa--such as COREMO (Mozambique) and ZANU (Rhodesia)--and to encourage them to side with China. With the existence of so many sources of external support, each with its own favored recipient, there has been no compelling reason, for example, for Angolan revolutionary factions to give up their desire to stay independent from other factions and to lead eventually a united liberation movement.

Guinea-Bissau

The PAIGC was founded in the mid-1950s in Bissau, the capital of Portuguese Guine. Amilcar Cabral, founder of the party supported by aid from the Soviet Union, established a sanctuary in the Republic of Guinea. Sekou Toure, President of Guinea, allowed the PAIGC to establish

military bases along its border with Portuguese Guine.
The PAIGC, under Cabral, was able to maintain a high degree of control over its own affairs within the Republic
of Guinea. Leopold Senghor, President of the neighboring
Republic of Senegal, had not been on good terms with the
ideologically more radical Guinean regime. His hostility
to Toure carried over to liberation movements supported by
Tour.[11] Gibson noted that

> The fears of . . . Senghor concerning the
> revolutionary militancy of Sekou Toure's
> regime in the neighboring Republic of
> Guinea naturally extended quickly to the
> leftist PAIGC, which was backed by Conakry.
> Hence, the Senegalese Government was more
> than willing to support, if not actively
> foster, rivals to the PAIGC.[12]

There exists in Senegal a very large community of Porgu-
guese Guinean refugees estimated to be as large as 65,000.
This community had been represented, generally speaking,
by a number of smaller groups, many of which joined together in 1963 to form FLING. (FLING claimed to be an African party designed to liberate Portuguese Guine. No
reference was made by them to liberate the Cape Verde
Islands.) Eventually by 1967 the relatively inactive
FLING was overshadowed by military successes of the PAIGC
within Guine. Senghor, forced to rethink his antipathy
toward the PAIGC, signed an agreement with that movement
and allowed it to establish a sanctuary and military base
along its border with Portuguese Guine. Despite the obvious improvement in Senegalese-PAIGC relations, complaints of harassment were still made by the PAIGC cadre
as late as 1970. Nonetheless, Senegal has become an important sanctuary to the PAIGC.

It should be pointed out that PAIGC is one of the two
African liberation movements that has received aid from
both the Soviet Union and China. This is probably because
the PAIGC has been relatively successful in its military
campaigns in Guinea (Bissau) and is now in control of a
significant part of the territory. In addition PAIGC is
the sole liberation force conducting effective operations
against the Portuguese inside the territory.[13] Because
PAIGC is apparently close to achieving its goal, neither
China nor the Soviet Union can afford to lose its friendship at this time.

Mozambique

There are now two movements which seek to liberate Mozambique from Portuguese control--FRELIMO and COREMO. FRELIMO, founded in 1962, is the older of the two and has established sanctuary, training camps, and headquarters in Tanzania. It has been officially recognized by the ALC/OAU and is the recipient of its aid and support. FRELIMO received support from both the USSR and China.

COREMO is a spin-off of FRELIMO. The leaders of this movement were at one time or another high ranking members of FRELIMO but had been expelled by the Central Committee of FRELIMO. In order to continue their efforts, the expelled leaders needed to establish another organization working for liberation on their own. For example, after having been expelled from FRELIMO, Gumane and Mobundu (former Deputy Secretary General and Secretary General, respectively) formed a new revolutionary party in Cairo. Gwambe (a former treasurer of FRELIMO) formed a new party in Uganda. Eventually these splinter parties regrouped into a coalition party known as COREMO.[14] On the origin of COREMO, Gibson has written that

> The Zambians hoped to effect the reunification of the Mozambiquan nationalist movement, but Mondlane walked out of the talks after the others had refused to disband their groups and join FRELIMO as individuals. The remaining delegates then united their five organizations in the new COREMO.[15]

COREMO was allowed to establish its headquarters and sanctuary in Zambia with Zambia thereby admitting COREMO's right to exist. Once the split among Mozambiquan revolutionary leaders had taken place, the Chinese supported COREMO. Without damaging their relationship with FRELIMO, Peking had no difficulty in extending aid to COREMO since the spin-off group generally operated in the southern part of Mozambique. For the most part the parent organization has stayed out of this area, directly across from the Zambian borders. It is expected that China would continue to provide aid to both FRELIMO and COREMO as long as the two groups operate in different geographical regions and as long as they are physically separated by a buffer zone. There are signs that Peking has increased its volume of aid to the liberation movements in southern Africa,

including FRELIMO, following the Cultural Revolution.
FRELIMO, which used to receive the bulk of its aid from
Moscow, is now getting more weapons from China. A recent
defector to Portugal, Jose Alves Dias Muganga, a former
member of FRELIMO Central Committee, stated: "Today the
party is commanded by Communist China, although the Soviet
Union, not wishing to lose completely the control it formerly had, still continues to supply much war material."[16]
Under these circumstances, FRELIMO leadership would be
divided ideologically between Chinese and Soviet doctrines.
Thus external aid has been used to reinforce cleavages not
only between leaders of two separate movements in the same
country but also the leadership within a single movement.

Southern Rhodesia

Similar occurrences can be seen in the case of Southern Rhodesian liberation movements. ZAPU and ZANU maintain headquarters and sanctuary in Zambia, each has training camps in Tanzania, and each has been officially recognized by the ALC-OAU. It can be argued that Kaunda of
Zambia supported and, in fact, sanctioned the split in the
Rhodesian liberation movements when he allowed the two
rival parties to establish their headquarters in Lusaka.
Reinforcing the separation of these two groups is the fact
that they receive assistance from Moscow or Peking. Since
the Soviet Union aids ZAPU and has no interest to subsidize another revolutionary group in Rhodesia, ZANU has no
alternative but to seek assistance from China.

In 1967 when ZANU applied for membership in the Afro-
Asian Peoples' Solidarity Organization (AAPSO), ZAPU, the
rival movement, was able to block its admission by accusing ZANU's leaders of being "pro-Peking extremists," thus
counting of the "pro-Moscow" majority votes.[17]

The extent to which rival groups have put aside their
main objective--liberation--and have replaced it with the
objective of the persistence of the revolutionary movement, ideology, and/or leadership was referred to by
Grundy when he wrote that

> The physical struggle between ZAPU and
> ZANU [has been very disruptive]. Occa-
> sional reports have appeared of press-
> ganging among Zimbabwian refugees in the
> African township of Lusaka. At one point
> Zambia authorities expelled 52 Rhodesians

to Tanzania. Zambia became particularly
alarmed with the strong-armed methods used
in search of potential guerrillas, particularly when ZAPU and ZANU preyed upon Zambian citizens. Dar-es-Salaam has also seen
its share of internecine threats, fights,
and assassinations between competing nationalist movements and within them as
well.[18]

Yet despite the pettiness of revolutionary in-
fighting, Kaunda and the ALC-OAU have been unable to
force these movements to cooperate with each other on a
long-term basis. As long as these movements have independent sources of support, they have no reason to give
up their autonomy by merging on an equal basis with any
other movement. For almost nine years, the ALC-OAU repeatedly but unsuccessfully attempted reconciliation between the two movements. Their leaders however showed no
sign of compromise: ZAPU refused to acknowledge that ZANU
had any followers inside Rhodesia, while ZANU rejected any
proposal to form a political organization headed by Joshua
Nkomo. It was not until after violent clashes in ZAPU in
1970 that its leaders sought reconciliation with ZANU.
This offer was accepted by ZANU, but failed to produce immediate results because of the ideological and tribal
splits within ZAPU. Concerned over their failure to bring
about unification, Kaunda warned "they have to choose between coming together or forfeiting Zambia's readiness to
accommodate them." Shortly thereafter it was announced
that members from ZAPU and ZANU had merged to form the
Front for the Liberation of Zimbabwe (FROLIZI). Kaunda
gave his blessing to the new organization, in the hope
that the bulk of both ZAPU and ZANU would join FROLIZI.
However, when this failed to happen, he began to pressure
ZANU leaders including Herbert Chitebo as well as J. Z.
Moyo's faction of ZAPU, all of whom had so far refused to
join the new movement. Such pressure resulted in the
formation of the joint ZAPU-ZANU military command that
seems to be effective in carrying out commando raids
against Rhodesia.[19]

REVOLUTIONARY ALLIANCES

An interesting consequence of the need for allies by
revolutionary factions and the fact that they have been
unable to join with other groups from the same country,

is the alliance system that nationalist movements have
worked out with similar revolutionary groups from other
countries. It is designed to provide them with a vehicle
to share information; to jointly publicize their cases
abroad; to coordinate their military operations as much
as possible; and to solicit more aid.

Ideologically akin revolutionary movements in the
Portuguese territories--PAIGC, MPLA, and FRELIMO--joined
together in the early 1960s to form the Conference of Nationalist Organizations of the Portuguese Colonies (CONCP).
An obvious exclusion from this group was Holden Roberto's
GRAE. In another attempt at alliance SWAPO formed a working relationship with UNITA in July 1964 but this alliance
caused the MPLA to put pressure on SWAPO to sever its ties
with UNITA and to support the MPLA. Recent reports indicate that MPLA and SWAPO are cooperating in Angola.

> These pressures were crudely applied at
> the 1969 Khartoum conference of Moscow-
> line liberation movements. . . . Here,
> in addition, leaders of the ANC called
> privately for an alliance with SWAPO
> similar to their party's tie-up with
> ZAPU.[20]

In 1967 ANC and ZAPU announced the formation of a
"military alliance between their two movements and . . .
proclaim[ed] that their forces were already engaged in a
long-term operation that was designed to carry them
through Rhodesia and the Republic of South Africa."[21]
After their first joint military adventure in Wankie,
Rhodesia, had turned into a disaster, ZANU leaders began
to express a desire to change tactics for the use of the
ANC guerrillas. They argued that

> the greatest help we can get from ANC is
> for ANC to wage intensive guerrilla war-
> fare in South Africa. If ANC can pin down
> the whole South African force inside South
> Africa, then Zimbabweans shall be left
> with Smith alone without South African
> aid. As it is now, the ANC and [ZAPU] al-
> liance has made it easy for Smith and
> Vorster to unite and concentrate their
> forces to slaughter Zimbabweans.[22]

Their alliance however has grown weaker because of successive military failures, tension, and ethnic feuds--

matters which have weakened the fighting spirit and resulted in desertion from ZANU's rank and file.

Although these alliances are small and have very
little military significance, their existence is a testi-
mony to the need for regional coordination in order to
carry out successful revolutions in southern Africa. It
seems that alliances among revolutionary movements such
as the one that exists between ZANU and FRELIMO may prove
to be a major step on the road to independence. As areas
in adjacent countries become liberated, new sanctuaries
may become available to an allying revolutionary movement.
These alliances among revolutionary movements from different territories are taking place in spite of external involvement and not because of it. What the revolutionary
groups are unable to get from other movements seeking to
liberate the same target or from external sources, they
are getting from ideologically akin revolutionary movements which are operating in adjacent territories.

Recently determined efforts have been made to convince leaders of movements seeking to liberate the same
country to merge their forces, energies, and resources.
For example Zambia had brought about a fragile reconciliation between ZAPU and ZANU. It appears that the new movement, the Front for the Liberation of Zimbabwe (FROLIZI),
has not attracted most of the leaders of both ZAPU and
ZANU.[23] There has also been a fragile reconcilation between the MPLA and the GRAE. Although attempts at reconciliation have proven futile in the past, this should not
discourage external revolutionary supporters from making
more efforts to bring about unification of liberation
movements within a single country because such unity will
facilitate and speed up the process of liberation in the
remaining white-minority-ruled territories in southern
Africa.

SUMMARY AND CONCLUSION

Two major factors have been examined to determine the
degree of contribution to the failure or success of the
liberation struggles in Africa. First it has been argued
that Sino-Soviet rivalry has caused a sharp division in
the rank and file of revolutionary leadership in southern
Africa. In their competition for Third World leadership,
Moscow and Peking have directly encouraged dissension
among nationalist leadership within the same country;
they have made it possible for dissenters to break away

from the parent organizations and to form their own revolutionary factions. Such spin-off movements would have
been unlikely to come into existence if the Chinese or Soviets had not made material and moral assistance available
to them. Thus it can be said that the Chinese and Soviet
activities can be detrimental to the liberation cause in
Africa. Undoubtedly revolution could not be served properly if there is division among revolutionaries and if
their limited resources are not pooled together to carry
out an effective armed struggle against their common enemy.
For instance the invitations issued only to the pro-Moscow
movements of the CONCP to attend a conference in support
of the struggles of the Peoples of the Portuguese Colonies
in Rome in 1970,[24] could hardly serve the revolutionary
struggles in southern Africa. On the contrary it was
likely to increase hostility and to sharpen ideological
differences between liberation movements belonging to the
same country. Secondly host states and, to a lesser degree, the ALC-OAU, have furthered the fragmentation of
the revolutionary struggles in Africa. This has been done
by extending recognition and material support to several
factions seeking to liberate the same country. For the
most part they have failed to exert enough pressure on
various revolutionary groups to reconcile their differences and to unite behind their cause. Being aware of
the seriousness of this problem, several African leaders
such as Kaunda and Nyerere have made numerous attempts to
effect reconciliation. The OAU efforts in this direction
should not be disregarded. For instance the OAU sponsored
a conference at Moshi in 1967 to reconcile differences between FRELIMO and COREMO in order to bring about a united
front against Portuguese colonialism in Mozambique. The
conference however broke up when COREMO turned down a
FRELIMO offer for 6 out of the 15 places on a newly struc-
tured central committee.

It should be pointed out that revolutionary leaders
are also trying to bring about unity among revolutionary
rank and file not only in a single country but also with
their counterparts in the southern Africa region. Last
year the MPLA and FNLA buried their animosity and joined
to form the Supreme Council for the liberation of Angola.
However, UNITA was left out of the Council, despite the
fact that Savimbi had expressed his interest to join it.[25]

In the final analysis, global and regional supporters
of African liberation movements should review the role of
their involvement in liberation movements. Assuming that
their primary objective is the liberation of African people

from white minority rule, the aid that they give must reflect that aim. Chinese-Soviet competition has caused those governments to support competing revolutionary factions to the detriment of revolutionary solidarity. Zambia and Tanzania have also fostered cleavages among revolutionary factions by permitting several factions from the same country to operate independently from each other. Zaire's leaders have sought to foster the predominance of the GRAE in the Angolan liberation struggle. Senegalese leaders have allowed their personal rivalries to interfere with the objective of gaining independence for Guine-Bissau. Even the ALC-OAU has not pursued a rational policy toward African liberation movements because they have given recognition and support to more than one movement from the same country.

Once African liberation movement leaders appreciate to a greater extent the fact that external sources of assistance have sought to further their own ideological interests at the cost of national liberation, they may see the need to bring about national unity among the revolutionary rank and file in order to carry out a successful armed struggle in a given country. Thus when liberation movements have liberated themselves from internal rivalries fed by such external cleavages, their chances for revolutionary success will have been greatly improved.

NOTES

1. R. Legvold, Soviet Policy in West Africa (Cambridge, Mass.: Harvard University Press, 1970), p. 276.
2. Bruce D. Larkin, China and Africa 1949-1970 (Berkeley, Calif.: University of California Press, 1973), pp. 187-88.
3. Paul M. Whitaker, "Arms and the Nationalists," Africa Report (May 1970): 12-13.
4. Kenneth W. Grundy, Guerrilla Struggle in Africa (New York: Grossman Publishers, 1971), pp. 189-99.
5. Ronald H. Chilcote, Portuguese Africa (Englewood Cliffs, N.J.: Prentice Hall, Inc., 1967), p. 121.
6. Grundy, op. cit., p. 130.
7. Kenneth W. Grundy, Confrontation and Accommodation in Southern Africa (Berkeley, Calif.: University of California Press, 1973), pp. 192-95.
8. Larkin, op. cit., p. 190.
9. Basil Davidson, In the Eye of the Storm: Angola's People (Garden City, N.Y.: Doubleday, 1973), pp. 241-42.

10. Whitaker, op. cit., p. 13.

11. Basil Davidson, The Liberation of Guine (Middle-sex, England: Penguin, 1969), pp. 86-90.

12. Richard Gibson, African Liberation Movements (New York: Oxford University Press, 1972), p. 261.

13. Larkin, op. cit., p. 189.

14. Eduardo Mondlane, The Struggle for Mozambique (Middlesex, England: Penguin, 1970), pp. 130-33.

15. Gibson, op. cit., p. 288.

16. The Christian Science Monitor, December 31, 1973.

17. Gibson, op. cit., p. 177.

18. Kenneth Grundy, "Host Countries and the Southern African Liberation Struggle," Africa Quarterly (April/June 1970): 15-24.

19. Gibson, op. cit., pp. 176-84.

20. Ibid., p. 138.

21. Ibid., p. 165.

22. Ibid., p. 166.

23. Africa Report (May-June 1973): 15.

24. Gibson, op. cit., pp. 241-42.

25. The Washington Post, December 25, 1973.

9

CHINESE AND SOVIET
AID TO AFRICA:
AN AFRICAN VIEW
Thomas Nsenga Kanza

AFRICA IS A CONTINENT

It is worthwhile to refresh the reader's memory by
reminding him that Africa is one of the five continents,
comprising over 40 different and independent states with
a total population of over 200 million inhabitants. It
is the third largest continent in the world after Asia and
North America. It is 5,200 miles from Tangiers in the
Mediterranean to Capetown in South Africa--approximately
the same distance as that from Panama City to Anchorage
in Alaska. It is 4,600 miles from Dakar in Senegal (West
Africa) to Cape Guardafrei, the easternmost point of the
African Horn--only 65 miles less than the airline distance from New York to Moscow. Africa is over three times
the size of the continental United States of America.[1]
Although the outside world sees Africa as an immense country with people who are alike, there are in Africa practically the same problems and the same human intrigues
that exist elsewhere.

It is wishful thinking to believe that Africa and
Africans could be so blessed that they don't have to face
the same social, human, and racial problems as elsewhere.

The same Africa which is today an important continent
in the world for various reasons, good or bad, was not
long ago known as the backyard of Europe, the "living
museum." Since World War II, the continent has changed
into a "busy political laboratory, experimenting with all
the theories and ideals of the rest of the world."[2]

The continent has changed and continues to change.
Today, more than ever before, Africa is helping and will
be helping to shape history. Together with Asia and

Latin America, the former "Dark Continent" of Africa will
help to correct the vision of a European and American-
centered world. Anything happening in Africa is a change,
an evolution for the African people. Ex Afrique semper
aliquid novi,* wrote Pliny the Elder 2,000 years ago. After the first shocks--psychological, social, political,
cultural, and human--provoked by the contact between European and African civilizations, one could say that there
are new discoveries being made on both sides and the confrontation between old Western and new African thinking
is bound to provoke revolution in the years to come. This
revolution will be part of universal revolution and will
be beneficial to all since the world is getting smaller
and smaller every day with the progress of technology.

HUNGRY NATIONS

The newly independent countries in Africa, Asia, and
Latin America are known under many names which vary from
time to time and from place to place. Names such as backward nations, undeveloped nations, underdeveloped nations,
less developed countries, emerging countries, poor countries, developing countries, newly developed countries,
and the Third World are some of those used. I prefer the
name suggested by William and Paul Paddock, that is,
"Hungry Nations."[3]
This term seems to be more precise and proper than
any of those mentioned above; it expresses the needs and
the current state of these countries as well as the needs
and the aspirations of their inhabitants. All these nations, whether in Latin America, Asia, or Africa, are
hungry for many things and their day-to-day struggle is
against hunger in many forms.
To quote the Paddock brothers, these nations "are
hungry for food, they are hungry for stability, they are
hungry for international prestige, for education, for
health, housing, culture, etc. In short, they are hungry
for the twentieth century."[4]
The opposite of these hungry nations would be those
countries known as developed, industrialized, or rich
countries; they could be called "comfortable nations,"[5]
in the sense that their resources have been developed to
the point where their populations "live in an environment
capable of supporting their modern desires."[6]

---

*"There is always something new from Africa."

The problem facing the world today is not one of aid or assistance to the Third World, be it from the West or from the communist world, but what are and what will be the relations between the comfortable nations and the hungry ones? How sincere are the peoples of the comfortable nations in their aid and assistance to the hungry nations for the development of the latter?

It is often said that these hungry nations are poor, that they have no resources. This is not true and I agree with W. and P. Paddock, who wrote that no country lacks resources for its development and each country has tangible and intangible resources which could and can be properly used for its development and prosperity. The tangible resources are of three types: the air, the land, and the water which are found in every single country of the world but in varied form, varied proportion, and arrangement. The intangible resources of a nation are difficult to define; the Paddock brothers have mentioned the character, the history, and the multiple virtues of the people of every nation. To ensure the prosperity of a country, one requires on the one hand favorable proportions of the three tangible resources (air, land, and water), and on the other, the best use of these resources by the citizens of the country--at the right economic moment--for full development.[7] This is so true that "no two nations, no two provinces have the same combination of land, water and air resources; consequently, no two nations, even among the rich ones, have the same wealth, nor the same level of prosperity."[8]

When one considers seriously the main theme of our book, one intends to summarize the theme, from the African point of view, as follows:

How sincere is Western aid to Africa?
How sincere is Chinese and Soviet aid to Africa?
How sincere is the Western world vis-a-vis the Chinese and/or Soviet world and vice versa?

These are academic questions for academic seminars. Academic discussions are excellent for the comfortable nations; the hungry nations are so hungry that they have no time and cannot afford the luxury of arguing about the motivation behind all aid or assistance, be it from the West or the Chinese and Soviet world.

Before going further one would like to state certain realities which are generally accepted by all groups concerned: the Western world, the Chinese and Soviet world,

and the hungry nations of Africa. Firstly Africa's links
with the West are very strong, and it will be a great mistake to dismiss or underestimate this fact. These links
are cultural, economic, monetary, military, philosophical,
and so on.

Secondly there is no pure charity in any aid given to
Africa; from the African point of view, the motivation of
Chinese and Soviet aid is as political as that of Western
aid to Africa. The West and the Chinese and Soviet world
are providing financial help to Africa in vast amounts and
their respective aims are economic, political, military,
etc. In short one would say their aims are everything but
charitable.

Therefore only in this perspective can one look at
the Chinese and Soviet aid to Africa as a challenge, or
better still, a threat to the West.

THE AFRICAN REVOLUTION

The African views on the capitalist system and Western imperialism are well known. The political leaders of
the hungry nations in Africa are not particularly fond of
Western economic imperialism in their countries. Nevertheless this imperialism, which is a danger threatening
Africa, also appears to be a necessary evil if Africa is
to achieve economic development and the creation of an
environment capable of supporting the modern desires of
the African people.

Until now the Africans were only aware of the existence of Western imperialism defined as essentially a
form of financial control with ramifications extending
into the realms of politics, defense, and diplomacy. This
imperialism is a refined form of colonialism conducted by
international financial trusts originating principally in
the Western European countries and the United States. It
is not even neocolonialism but international colonialism.
Most countries in Africa fought against national European
colonialism and find themselves today under international
colonialism.

But more and more the Africans have learned the existence of another form of imperialism which starts off on
the ideological level, but pervades economics, politics,
and diplomacy. This new imperialism, at first limited to
a very few states, has taken on international proportions
in the last two decades. It has not had financial trusts
and cartels at its disposal with which to create capital-
istic monopolies. The concentration of capital by the

225

state, accompanied by the concentration of political power and ideological control in the hands of a few leaders in the party apparatus, has brought about an ideological monopoly, whose activities and ambitions are likewise worldwide.

Most of the hungry nations of the world are facing the pressure of these two international colonialisms: the capitalist and the communist. The historical, social, cultural, and ideological transformations which are taking place in the capitalist and communist countries make it clear that the leaders of the hungry nations in general, and the African leaders in particular, will have to develop or create a new and original doctrine which is not a poor copy of either capitalism or communism.

Neither communism nor capitalism will do. It is absolutely vital for the African peoples to look beyond. Both these doctrines are equally self-centered, and neither of them constitutes an ideal toward which the multitribal and multiracial society of Africa should aspire. Moreover the differences between them in practical terms are diminishing steadily. The communist world, on the one hand, cannot prevent the development of social classes; communist leaders and intellectuals are beginning to wonder whether a classless society is possible. The capitalist world, on the other hand, is finding it necessary to introduce social, economic, and political reforms in the shape of a disguised proletarian revolution which would better serve the interests of capitalism. The two systems are approaching each other and may well end up as two sides of the same coin. "Once communism has achieved power it tends to reshape the rest of the world in its own image rather than interpret it,"[9] says Milovan Djilas. No less is true of capitalism. As the two worlds are at present in a position of almost equivalent power, they will sooner or later have to face the naked political realities; that they either have to agree that coexistence is of great urgency, or destroy each other and thus hasten the end of mankind. Has it not been said that two great powers who cannot destroy each other must eventually come to terms? Consequently, an African system--socialist or collectivist--may appear, without necessarily becoming communist or taking any other existing pattern. Most African political leaders or intellectuals who are aware of the existence of the two forms of "international colonialism," that is, Western imperialism or communist imperialism, have adopted a firm attitude of positive neutrality in their thinking and a policy of nonalignment in their actions.

For them, the drawing of an "equals" sign between the communist and the Western countries has become an important policy for survival, since, as Julius Nyerere remarks, both Western and Communist Bloc countries are engaged in "the second scramble for Africa."

Many Africans--leaders or intellectuals--tend to become Marxist Socialists rather than pro-Soviet or pro-Chinese Communists. They agree with the Black American writer Richard Wright that:

> Communism has won its battles only by appealing to the Western sense of justice and exploiting the traditional ambitions of the Westerner. Indeed, it can be said that it owes its strength essentially to the stupidity of the West, to its narrow-mindedness and its absurd racial jealousies. In short, to the fact that the West has renounced its own ideals.[10]

The Africans have learned that their problems are, in fact, different from those of the Soviet Union and its allies of the People's Republic of China, and they have already started to have what Abdoulaye Ly called "an intellectual approach to revolution"[11] which is less emotional and more pragmatic.

The comfortable nations of the West might look at Sino-Soviet aid to Africa as a challenge or a threat; but for Africans, the struggle for development and the attitude of positive neutrality and nonalignment will go on.

Aime Cesaire, the eminent statesman and scholar from Martinique and the father of "Negritude," wrote:

> I have come to the conclusion that our paths and those of Communism do not entirely converge, nor can they do so. As I see it, the most crucial point is that we, coloured men, have at this precise moment of history suddenly become aware of our uniqueness as a race and are ready to accept at every level and in every sphere the responsibilities that result from this realisation. By this I mean the uniqueness of our "position in the world," the uniqueness of our tumultuous history, punctuated as it has been by terrible upheavals, and the uniqueness of our cultural life, which we wish to live in an

increasingly genuine way. This means that
our paths for the future, politically as
well as culturally, are not yet laid down.
We still have to seek them out and this
labour of discovery concerns us alone.
Our struggle, the struggle of the colonized
against colonialism, the struggle of the
coloured races against racism, is far more
complex, or rather completely different
from that of the French (European or American) worker against French (European or
American) capitalism. It cannot in any way
be considered a part or fragment of this
struggle.[12]

The revolution which is taking place in Africa today
is a mental revolution; the revolution of the mind, the
reconquest of the right to think, to choose, to plan, and
to act in true freedom. Many leaders and many intellectuals in Africa still believe, rightly or wrongly, that
the problems of their hungry nations can be more effectively and adequately solved by the Marxist Socialist method
or approach, but they are no longer under the delusion
that the solution to the particular problems of the African countries can be found in foreign political parties
or in political decisions inspired by foreigners.

AFRICA TODAY

Economic Field

Virtually all African states which have recently
gained their national sovereignty help to enrich the outside world, both capitalist and communist, at the expense
of African poverty. Although they are nominally independent, they find it impossible to give their national and
continental economic development the necessary impetus
and acceleration.

They are still in a period of transition, and this
period is in danger of becoming permanent, a cul-de-sac
of stagnation and decline. We agree with W. W. Rostow
when he wrote that the duration and vicissitudes of the
transition between a traditional society and a modern society depend essentially on the degree to which these societies channel their talents, their energies, and their
resources into a national effort of modernization, and

not toward any other possible nationalist objectives. Generally speaking such a channelization and direction will have to be effected principally by the political leaders.[13]

In many African states overseas trade is not in the hands of the indigenous population, the principal consumers, but has remained the preserve of expatriates and foreign companies. The overwhelming majority of wholesalers who import goods for sale on the home market are either foreign settlers or foreign concerns. In spite of independence, overseas trade remains the private hunting-ground of the old rulers and their associates. The entire machinery is a remote-controlled monopoly. In some cases ministries function like a government within a government. Many decisions, especially relating to the export and import of capital and goods, are made by foreigners. Petty competition between African states--particularly those which produce the same primary and export products--has enabled international firms to manage much of Africa's external trade for their own benefit.

Compared with the situation before independence, national production per capita has fallen steeply in many African states. The cost of living is far above the wages paid to the nation's workers; the gap is continually widening between the "haves" (the ruling elite, the nouveaux riches, foreign "technical advisers") and the "have nots," who are the broad masses.

The African states are still undecided about which economic system they should adopt, although such a choice is fundamental to national development, planning, and economic expansion. They are increasingly finding themselves faced with an absolute choice: should they adopt the traditional capitalist method, which means, in effect, dependence on foreign capital and subordination of their own development to the special interests of monopoly capitalism? Or should they take the socialist road and plan their development rationally in the general interest of Africa and its people?

In the economic field, Africa is caught in a most vicious paradox. It includes states ruled by socialists with capitalist conceptions and others led by bourgeois politicians proclaiming scientific socialism and Marxism. Fortunately this mental confusion is practically confined to rulers with an insatiable need for slogans to maintain a hold on power. The working class itself is increasingly aware of the social injustice, sacrifices that brought them nothing, and severe limitations of liberty.

Military Field

In the military field one observes that, apart from
South Africa and one or two other African states, all the
African national armies are controlled or advised by foreigners from either capitalist or communist countries.
The day is perhaps approaching, but has certainly not yet
arrived, when the African military chiefs will get together
to plan and discuss a military strategy for the defense of
Africa; indeed, to make any military decisions which will
not be known by experts abroad less than 24 hours later.
There can be no state secrets when those who draw up and
keep those secrets are themselves not nationals of the
country concerned. The foreign staff in the various African national armies are doubtless loyal to the African
governments which they temporarily serve, but they also
remain loyal, faithful, and attached to their own mother
countries. They may not willfully betray the cause which
they happen to be serving, but there may be times when
they will be subject to irresistible pressures in a conflict of interests between their countries of employment
and origin.

African government remains dependent on foreign countries, and particularly on the West, for the purchase and
supply of arms and ammunition, military training of officers and men, the organization, and reorganization of national security forces. Any war conducted by "the armies
of Africa" against the white minority in Rhodesia, against
the South African racists, against the Portuguese colonialists, will probably remain a verbal struggle, a "talking
war." Africa speaks of armed revolution, but it lacks the
independent means to engage in such a war and still less
to pursue it to final victory.

Moral support and soul-stirring verbal solidarity
seem, alas, to constitute the maximum support that Africa
and certain sympathetic non-African countries are able to
offer, abundantly, to those who are still colonized, or
to the "freedom fighters" in South Africa, Namibia, and
Zimbabwe.

The communist countries deliberately supplied the
African states with small doses of military aid when the
latter hoped for sufficient aid to free themselves from
Western military control and supervision. Unfortunately
for Africa, the donors of this symbolic aid demand a degree of gratitude and commitment in inverse proportion
to the aid actually received. On the diplomatic level,
the supply of arms to the African countries by any military

bloc provides that bloc with a powerful lever to force
these countries into political alignment with it.

Those Africans who are still fighting to liberate
their country have, by now, learned to plan their struggle
in accordance with the actual material means at their disposal and not to count on illusory or symbolic aid, military or financial, which the external world, whether from
elsewhere within Africa or from outside, might promise or
provide . . . later!

SOVIET POLICY TOWARD AFRICA

Without going into the history of the Soviet Union's
interest in Africa, one would say that Soviet policy in
Africa has been conducted on two levels and with two objectives.[14]

On the upper level, dealing with the authority of the
African states, the Soviet Union exerts pressure on African governments to oppose Western policies and support
Soviet policies. On this level, Soviet policy is directed
not at competing with but at defeating Western influence
and gaining the support of the African states in the international sphere and their vote at the United Nations
and other international forums or meetings.

This pressure on the national authority in the African states is accompanied by Soviet economic and military
aid. Officially this is not connected with any political
aims whatever, but many African leaders have discovered
that this economic and military aid cannot be called disinterested assistance and is part of the long-term aim of
the Soviet policy in Africa.

On the lower level, dealing with the African people
and masses, the Soviet Union appeals for a solidarity and
common front against Western imperialism, Western racism,
and Western colonialism. The short-term objective here
is the Soviet Union's search for clients and allies for
the expansion of International Socialism and Communism.

For the last two decades the Soviet Union has learned
that sometimes, and quite often, there are contradictions
and conflicts between the two policies. In dealing with
the African states, the Soviet Union has become opportunistic and realistic. Earlier Soviet policy in Africa was to
assist progressive elements, groups, or states, in the hope
of making them permanent friends and allies of the Soviet
Union and the socialist group in general.

231

Today Soviet policy has ceased being concerned only
with the so-called progressive, revolutionary, or anti-
Western elements. The Soviets are no longer sectarian
and they became opportunistic and realistic to avoid self-
isolation. The Soviets have learned how to estimate and
evaluate their chances of success and their limitations,
the means at their disposal and the local situation in
Africa.

This suggests that there is no longer a clear-cut Soviet strategy regarding the African continent in general,
but permanent vigilance to exploit in favor of the Soviet
Union and the socialist ideology any situation which shows
signs of opposition to Western imperialism, to Western influence in general, and to Chinese influence in particular.

In Africa today the Soviet Union watches for any small
phenomenon which shows signs of being directed against local and foreign "monopoly capital" that is Western or Chinese in origin.

More and more the Soviet Union's policy could be described as tolerant vis-a-vis the Western influence in
Africa in the name of peaceful but competitive coexistence, and aggressively active vis-a-vis the Chinese influence.

CHINA'S POLICY TOWARD AFRICA

China's active political interest in Africa falls
into three main periods.[15]

From 1949 to 1955 China had no obvious divergence
from the Soviet line and China could not then afford to
oppose the Soviet Union; moreover, only a handful of African states were independent by 1955. The second period
covers the period between the Bandung Conference in 1955
and 1959. During this period, China fought to improve
her relations with the world, hoping to consolidate her
economic and political independence; by doing so, she was
also preparing the ground to compete with the Soviet
Union for influence in the Third World. Since 1959 and
the early 1960s there has been an increasingly open struggle in Africa and elsewhere in the world between orthodox
or Soviet-oriented communism and Mao-tse-tungism or
Chinese-oriented communism.

China's policy toward Africa is pragmatic, with
various long-term objectives. First of all China is
aware of all the mistakes and failures of the Eastern
communist countries in Africa; secondly the Chinese are

banking on the solidarity and unity of views between all
"colored people" of the world against the dominant white
race of West and East Europe and the United States; thirdly the Chinese are not in a hurry, they know that time is
on their side. They therefore follow a line of assisting
the African peasant masses, rather than seeking to win new
allies by making expedient friendships with African leaders. This effort to reach out toward the masses is undertaken with the approval of African leaders, to whom
China's successes, by her own efforts, have been demonstrated.

In her policy toward Africa, China hopes to pave the
way for a new alliance of the hungry nations and colored
peoples against the existing alliance of the comfortable
countries--capitalist and socialist--whose populations
happen generally to be white.

China's economic aid and military assistance seem
motivated by the solidarity and unity in struggle, not
only against Western imperialism and influence, but also
Soviet imperialism. Here one would correctly say that
China is excluding herself from the camp of imperialist
nations and she would like to identify with the hungry
nations. China is one of the very few hungry but superpower nations, and as W. A. C. Adie wrote, "the Chinese
are just as paternalistic and race-conscious towards Africans as the European Communists."[16] No doubt China exerts greater attraction for African leaders than the Soviet Union. China's approach to African problems is emotional and psychological. China is seen as a poor country
of colored people permanently fighting to preserve her independence against capitalist imperialism and Soviet imperialism. For tactical and political reasons, many Africans seem to agree with China that they are also fighting
the same war and facing the same problems. There is no
doubt that in the years to come Africans will cease to
identify China with the hungry nations and discover that
the philosophy of "peaceful and competitive coexistence"
has been extended from the present two to three or four
superpowers--and that China is one of them.

CHINESE AND SOVIET AID: CHALLENGE OR
THREAT TO THE WEST?

As I mentioned earlier, no country in the world,
even the so-called backward or undeveloped country, lacks
resources, the tangible and the intangible ones. I am in

agreement with the Paddock brothers that every country is or was "backward until sometime, if ever, something happens that increases productivity and thus enables the people to acquire the means for starting their country forward on the road of progress, development and prosperity."[17]

"When elephants fight," says an African proverb, "the grass gets trampled."

Africa is the battlefield on which military blocs, financial forces, and ideological groups battle for their advantage to the detriment of Africans. The battle is no longer between two elephants but many elephants—powerful, determined, and cynical.

Mental decolonization in the minds of the people and economic decolonization on the part of the states are the two forms of revolution which have to be fought in Africa.

How far will Western, Chinese, or Soviet aid help accelerate these two African revolutions? In other words does Western, Chinese, or Soviet aid, in their respective forms, help accelerate or delay the African countries' development effort to change their status of the "hungry nations"?

I believe that Chinese and Soviet aid might be a challenge to the West, in the sense that it forces the Western world to question both the motivation and the format of its aid (economic, military, and technical) to the developing countries of Africa.

This Chinese and Soviet aid might also become a threat to Western countries which are determined to perpetrate "economic colonialism" in Africa by trying desperately through all means in their power "to keep Africa with the West" and to maintain Africa within the orbit of Western imperialism.

For the Africans, Chinese and Soviet aid is seen neither as a challenge nor as a threat to the West, but as a useful and helpful stimulus which is necessary for the awakening of the consciences of Western countries; for us, Chinese and Soviet aid to Africa is a stimulant to the West and vice versa.

It is time that both the Western and the Communist world learned to plan their economic aid and other assistance to the hungry nations with a view to securing their own self-interest but in the spirit of feeding those who are hungry.

For both East and West, the means of political motive rated higher priority than the ends of the development goal for the developing nations. The hungry nations of the world are now devising their own strategy of development, learning from practical experience and trial and error. These experiences vary from nation to nation; they vary according to resources--tangible and intangible--at the disposal of nations and the use made of these resources with the aid and assistance of the outside world. The road to development by trial and error is not a fast road, nor scientific enough for modern times. But as this seems to be the only road to emancipation, the outside world must give Africa what she has long been denied: the time to experiment on her own with less foreign interference, and with sincere aid for development unsullied by motives of self-interest.

Africa as a whole is gripped as if in a vice. She is bound hand and foot. To the north there is Europe, who will do anything to safeguard her interests in Africa; to the south, the racist states ruled by white minorities will fight to the death to preserve their rights, their privileges, their race, and their riches, amassed on the sweat and blood of Africans. These racists rest secure in the knowledge that they will not be abandoned by their cousins in Europe and America--bound by the ties of "kith and kin," as Ian Smith said when he rebelled against the British.

We would like to borrow a quotation from Confucius which should be pleasing and useful to those concerned with the future of the African continent, the prosperity of the hungry nations, and the happiness of its peoples: "The character of the ruler is like wind, and the character of the common people is like grass, and the grass bends in the direction of the wind."

The future of Africa does not, for the time being, depend so much on the millions of Africans who constitute its masses, but it rests largely in the hands of those who govern the African states, some with the consent of the people, others without that consent.

All African countries are rich in tangible resources (air, land, and water) and the ruling class in Africa (politicians, intellectuals, businessmen, technicians, and so on) constitute the intangible resources. At the moment this ruling class is like the wind and it is greatly responsible for the direction and the speed of the country's development.

Unfortunately the members of this ruling class are often blinded by foreign doctrine and foreign pressures from the Western as well as from the Communist world. Few African leaders and their counterparts outside Africa

will go down in history as great leaders, unless, as
Emmanuel d'Astier says, they discover

> a new kind of humanism which is not simply
> for the sole benefit of the privileged
> classes. . . . They must realise that al-
> though social and economic change can be
> retarded, accelerated or set in motion by
> heads of government, the form it takes
> can only be determined by increasingly
> vast human groups becoming aware of change
> and being able to assess and participate
> in it.[18]

The African leaders have fewer excuses than their
colleagues in Western Europe or in the United States because, as I said earlier, leaders in Africa hold practically unlimited power for unlimited periods. They are
the only ones to blame if this power is not properly used
to create the conditions necessary for their country's
and their people's benefit. The African masses, who are
like the grass in the Confucian parable, know that the
development of their various countries may be activated
or stultified by powerful influences, forces, and pressures outside Africa. It is relevant to remind human
agencies behind these phenomena that there is a limit to
hunger. There is a point of no return when the fury of
the storm that could be provoked could never be held back.
As Maurice Duverger says: "The balance sheet of any government measures not only its actions, but also the reactions it provokes."[19]
Chinese and Soviet aid to Africa may be a challenge
or a threat to the West: this is the Western point of
view. Africa being kept within the orbit of the Western
control could also be a challenge or a threat to the East:
this is the Communist point of view.
For the Africans, economic aid, whether Chinese, Soviet or Western, is necessary; and moreover, it should be
given in a form and with the desire to further true development of the hungry nations and consequently prevent
these nations and their peoples from reaching the point
of no return which might provoke "unpleasant" surprises
and reactions.

NOTES

1. Paul Bohannan and Philip Curtin, _Africa and Afri-cans_ (New York: Natural History Press, 1971), p. 17.

2. A. Sampson, _Common Sense about Africa_ (New York: Macmillan Co., 1960), p. 14.

3. W. and P. Paddock, _Hungry Nations_ (Boston: Little, Brown & Co., 1964).

4. Ibid., p. 18.

5. Ibid.

6. Ibid.

7. Ibid., p. 21.

8. Ibid.

9. Milovan Djilas, _La Nouvelle Classe Dirigeante_ (Texte francais de Andre Prudhommeaux, Paris: Plon, 1957), p. 1.

10. Richard Wright, _Puissance Noire_ (Paris: Ed. Correa, 1955), p. 12.

11. Abdoulaye Ly, _Les Masses Africaines et l'Actuelle Condition Africaine_ (Paris: Ed. Presence Africaine, 1956), p. 18.

12. Aime Cesaire, _Lettre a Maurice Thorez_ (Paris: Ed. Pres. Africaine), pp. 7-9.

13. W. W. Rostow, _Les Etapes de la Croissance Eco-nomique_ (Paris: Editions du Seuil, 1960), p. 46.

14. D. L. Morison, "Soviet Policy Towards Africa," _The Soviet Bloc, China and Africa_, ed. Sven Hamrell and Carl Gosta Widstrand (London: Pall Mall Press, 1964), pp. 30-42.

15. W. A. C. Adie, "Chinese Policy Towards Africa," _The Soviet Bloc, China and Africa_, op. cit., pp. 43-46.

16. Ibid., p. 44.

17. Paddock, op. cit., p. 18.

18. E. d'Astier, _Les Grands_ (Paris: Gallimard, 1961), p. 212.

19. M. Duverger, _De la Dictature_ (Paris: Julliard, 1961), p. 183.

237

APPENDIX A:
COMMUNIST STATES AND
DEVELOPING COUNTRIES:
AID AND TRADE IN 1972

This is the Bureau of Intelligence and Research's annual report on the economic and
military relations of the Soviet Union,
East Europe, and the People's Republic of
China with the less developed countries of
the non-Communist world. The report includes economic and military aid and technical assistance data through the end of
1972, and complete trade statistics
through 1971.

ABSTRACT

The aid and trade programs of the Soviet Union, the
East European countries, and the People's Republic of
China in the less developed countries (LDCs) of the non-
Communist world continued in 1972 without any new initiatives of special note. Political considerations remained
paramount, although it is equally obvious that in Soviet
and East European calculations economic self-interests
play an increasingly important role. For China, foreign
aid is a means of fostering an image of a world power,
garnering attention and support among a host of smaller
countries, and visibly challenging the Soviet Union.
Chinese efforts in these directions are especially noticeable in sub-Saharan Africa.

Denying any special obligation or commitment to help
the less developed world, the Soviet Union to date has
ignored the Western trend toward aid multilateralization
and has tied Soviet aid to purchases in the USSR more
tightly than any Western donor has tied its aid. Furthermore, Soviet aid in the form of grants is practically non-
existent, and its financial terms for credits are harder
than average terms from Western official sources.

While the volume of Soviet aid deliveries in 1972
was maintained at the $400 million level of the past

Reprinted with the permission of the U.S. Department
of State. An updated version will be published in late
1974, and can be obtained from the State Department.

several years, repayments by the LDCs have continued to mount steadily. Net Soviet aid outflow in 1972 was only $140 million, an amount equal to less than 0.05 percent of estimated Soviet GNP. There is no indication that this trend will be reversed anytime soon.

Aid extended by the Soviets in 1972 fell to $581 million from $865 million in 1971. The 1972 aid was accounted for by four countries in the USSR's aid target area--the Near East and South Asia--and by Chile. No new aid was committed to any African or non-Communist East Asian country.

The East European countries, on the other hand, expanded their efforts somewhat in 1972 and extended credits of $645 million, compared to $468 million the previous year. While the East Europeans often emphasize commercial-type credits, as opposed to project-oriented Soviet commitments, their aid efforts are generally directed to the same countries and regions favored by the Soviets.

China maintained in 1972 its bid for an internationally recognized role in aid to the LDC world. China's commitments of $499 million added eight countries to the roster of LDCs which have received Communist economic aid pledges since 1954. While aid to Africa continues to be of considerable interest to the Chinese, relatively substantial aid extensions were made in 1972 to Near East and South Asian countries, as well as to Malta, Chile, and Guyana. Chinese aid continues to be very attractive: interest-free and repayable over 10 to 20 years after grace periods of 5 to 10 years.

New military assistance to the LDCs fell off very sharply in 1972. This is largely a Soviet-dominated activity, but extensions by the USSR amounted to only $310 million in 1972, almost $1 billion less than in 1971. Like economic aid, most military assistance is provided to Near East and South Asian countries.

With regard to technical assistance, the number of Communist economic technicians in the LDCs in 1972 rose moderately to a little more than 39,000. The increase was attributable to a further influx of Chinese personnel into African countries, largely in connection with construction of the TanZam Railroad. On the military side, the number of Soviet personnel in the LDCs during 1972 declined drastically and by the end of the year probably numbered less than 5,000. This was the result of the requested departure of most Soviet advisers and technicians from Egypt in mid-year.

Communist country trade with the LDCs in 1971 was un-
impressive in performance. By value, total turnover rose
less than 5 percent, from 1970's $5.9 billion to $6.2 billion in 1971, representing $3.3 billion in Communist ex-
ports and $2.9 billion in imports from the LDCs. The
trade surplus of $400 million was shared almost equally by
China and the East European countries, while the Soviet
Union for the second consecutive year registered a small
deficit.

Although trade with the Communist states, on a percentage basis, is relatively high for such countries as
Egypt, Sudan, and Syria, globally the Communist states account for only about 5 percent of LDC trade. Since Communist aid deliveries count as LDC imports, and repayments
as exports, it is not surprising that the Near East and
South Asian region accounted for 60 percent of aggregate
LDC-Communist country trade.

Explanatory Notes

1. The term "Communist countries" as used in this
research study is a convenience only; it refers collectively to the Soviet Union; the East European countries of Bulgaria, Czechoslovakia, East Germany, Hungary, Poland, and
Romania; and the People's Republic of China. Only where
specified does the term include Albania, Cuba, Mongolia,
North Korea, and North Vietnam.

2. The term "less developed countries" refers to the
non-Communist world and specifically includes the following:

(a) All countries of Africa except the Republic of
    South Africa;
(b) All countries in East Asia except Japan;
(c) Malta, Spain, and Portugal in Europe;
(d) All countries in Latin America except Cuba; and
(e) All countries in the Near East and South Asia.

3. The term "extension" refers to a commitment or
formal declaration of intent to provide goods and services. Extensions are generally on the basis of medium-
or long-term credits (five years or more) and are only
infrequently outright grants (approximately five percent
of the total since 1954). Short-term credits are not
included in the scope of this study. Downpayments, where
required, are not included in the aid figures.

4. The term "drawings" refers to actual delivery of goods or use of services.

5. Data are revised periodically to include new information and therefore may not be exactly comparable with data presented in previous INR annual reports on this subject.

ECONOMIC ASSISTANCE

Economic Assistance Totals $1.7 Billion in 1972

The Soviet Union, the East European countries, and the People's Republic of China in 1972 extended a combined total of just over $1.7 billion in new economic aid to the less developed countries (LDCs) of the non-Communist world.* These new extensions were fractionally below the total of $1.8 billion recorded in 1971. (See Table A.1.) Less developed countries in the Near East and South Asian region were again the primary recipients of Communist country assistance.

Collectively, the East European countries were the principal Communist aid donors in 1972. They extended $645 million--approximately 37 percent of the total--in agreements with 11 LDCs. Four of these countries--Iraq, Algeria, Syria, and Peru--accounted for 80 percent of total East European extensions worldwide. For the East Europeans, 1972 marked the highest level of aid commitments in a single year since their aid programs began nearly 20 years ago.

Soviet pledges to the LDCs, on the other hand, were off nearly one-third from 1971 and amounted to only $581 million. No new aid was committed to any African nation; and, apart from $144 million extended to Chile, all of the remaining aid was earmarked for Afghanistan, Bangladesh, Syria, and Turkey.

The Chinese foreign aid program continued at the relatively high level of the past several years and the $0.5 billion in extensions was spread out over 14 less developed countries, including the first Communist economic aid to Burundi, Dahomey, Malagasy Republic, Rwanda, Togo, Malta, and Guyana.

---

*See also RECN-39, "Communist Economic Aid to the LDCs Still a Fraction of Western Efforts," June 6, 1973.

TABLE A.1

Communist Economic Credits and Grants[a] Extended to Less Developed Countries, 1954-72 and Years 1971 and 1972 (in millions of U.S. dollars)[b]

Area and Country	1954-72 Total	USSR	East Europe	China	1971 Total	USSR	East Europe	China	1972 Total	USSR	East Europe	China
Total	15,023	8,229	4,095	2,699	1,806	865	468	475	1,725	581	645	499
Africa	3,359	1,252	785	1,322	586	192	99	295	419	0	209	210
Algeria	759	421	246	92	229	189	--	40	150	--	150	--
Burundi	20	--	--	20	--	--	--	--	20	--	--	20
Cameroon	8	8	--	--	--	--	--	--	--	--	--	--
Central African Republic	6	2	--	4	2	2	--	--	--	--	--	--
Congo	35	10	--	25	--	--	--	--	--	--	--	--
Dahomey	44	--	--	44	--	--	--	--	44	--	--	44
Equatorial Guinea	1	1	--	--	1	1	--	--	--	--	--	--
Ethiopia	203	102	17	84	84	--	--	84	--	--	--	--
Ghana	235	93	102	40	--	--	--	--	--	--	--	--
Guinea	259	168	25	66	--	--	--	--	--	--	--	--
Kenya	66	48	--	18	--	--	--	--	--	--	--	--
Malagasy Republic	9	--	--	9	--	--	--	--	9	--	--	9
Mali	138	60	23	55	--	--	--	--	--	--	--	--
Mauritania	28	3	--	25	20	--	--	20	--	--	--	--
Mauritius	34	--	--	34	--	--	--	--	34	--	--	34
Morocco	128	88	40	--	--	--	--	--	--	--	--	--
Nigeria	45	7	38	--	24	--	24	--	--	--	--	--
Rwanda	22	--	--	22	--	--	--	--	22	--	--	22
Senegal	7	7	--	--	--	--	--	--	--	--	--	--
Sierra Leone	28	28	--	--	--	--	--	--	--	--	--	--
Somalia	203	66	5	132	110	--	--	110	2	--	2	--
Sudan	299	64	153	82	115	--	75	40	--	--	--	--
Tanzania	289	20	13	256	1	--	--	1	7	--	7	--
Togo	45	--	--	45	--	--	--	--	45	--	--	45
Tunisia	143	34	73	36	--	--	--	--	36	--	--	36
Uganda	31	16	--	15	--	--	--	--	--	--	--	--
Zambia	274	6	50	218								

	1	2	3	4	5	6	7	8	9	10	11	12
Europe	45	0	0	45	0	0	0	0	45	0	0	0
Malta	45	--	--	45	--	--	--	--	45	--	--	45
East Asia	741	154	306	281	57	0	0	57	0	--	0	0
Burma	125	15	26	84	57	--	--	57[c]	--	--	--	--
Cambodia	134	25	17	92	--	--	--	--	--	--	--	--
Indonesia	482	114	263	105	--	--	--	--	--	--	--	--
Latin America	1,171	448	590	133	259	41	174	44	331	144	98	89
Argentina	54	45	9	--	--	--	--	--	--	--	--	--
Bolivia	56	30	26	--	27	2	25	--	--	--	--	--
Brazil	312	85	227	--	--	--	--	--	--	--	--	--
Chile	423	238	120	65	136	39	95	2	227	144	20	63
Colombia	7	2	5	--	5	--	5	--	--	--	--	--
Ecuador	15	--	15	--	--	--	5	--	--	--	--	--
Guyana	26	--	--	26	--	--	--	--	26	--	78	26
Peru	223	28	153	42	86	--	44	42	78	--	--	--
Uruguay	45	20	25	--	--	--	--	--	--	--	--	--
Venezuela	10	--	10	--	--	--	--	--	--	--	--	--
Near East and South Asia	9,707	6,375	2,414	918	904	632	195	77	930	437	338	155
Afghanistan	911	826	12	73	5	5	--	--	166	121	25	45
Bangladesh	99	74	25	--	--	--	--	--	99	74	--	--
Egypt	1,975	1,198	671	106	338	196	142	--	--	--	--	--
Greece	84	84	--	--	--	--	--	--	--	--	--	--
India	1,975	1,593	382	--	--	--	--	--	--	--	--	--
Iran	997	562	435	--	--	--	--	--	10	--	10	--
Iraq	1,013	549	419	45	304	222	37	45	200	--	200	--
Nepal	82	20	--	62	--	209	--	--	--	--	--	--
Pakistan[d]	857	474	74	309	209	--	--	--	--	--	--	--
Sri Lanka	229	38	62	129	32	--	--	32	54	74	10	44
Syria	665	317	287	61	--	--	--	--	222	84	93	45
Turkey	548	534	14	--	--	--	--	--	158	158	--	--
Yemen (Aden)	85	14	16	55	16	--	16	--	158	--	--	--
Yemen (Sana)	187	92	17	78	--	--	--	--	21	--	--	21

[a] Only about 5 percent of total economic aid represents grants.

[b] Converted at official exchange rates.

[c] Unused portion of 1961 $84 million credit that was reactivated in 1971.

[d] Includes Bangladesh prior to 1972.

243

Near East and South Asian Countries
Still Favored

With $930 million in aid commitments, the LDCs in the Near East and South Asian area remained, as in most previous years, the major Communist aid recipients. Both Iraq and Syria received pledges in excess of $200 million, and Turkey and Afghanistan each had offers of over $150 million. The area as a whole accounted for 54 percent of total Communist aid extensions in 1972.

Compared to 1971, Africa's share of total aid in 1972--$419 million in commitments--declined from 35 percent to 24 percent. The largest single African recipient again was Algeria with $150 million. Of the remaining ten African countries that received Communist aid in 1972, five were new to recipient roles and in each instance China was the donor country.

Apart from $45 million in Chinese aid to Malta, the remaining $331 million of global Communist aid was extended to Latin American countries, primarily Chile. No aid was provided by any Communist donor to any non-Communist country in East Asia.

Soviet Extensions

Total Soviet aid extensions in 1972 amounted to $581 million and were directed to only five countries: Chile, Afghanistan, Bangladesh, Syria, and Turkey.

The $144 million of credits to Chile was for development projects and machinery and equipment purchases. In the case of Afghanistan, Soviet aid extensions of $121 million are for support of that country's Fourth Five-Year Plan (1972-77) and include the following projects: oil refinery and pipeline, prefabricated housing plant, irrigation canals, expansion of two power plants, a flour mill, and telephone transmission lines. Aid extensions of $74 million to Bangladesh are to be used for the purchase of agricultural, construction, and shipbuilding equipment; aircraft; ships; and food supplies. In Syria, Soviet extensions of $84 million are earmarked for oil, railroad, electrification, agricultural, and water resource projects. The remaining $158 million of aid extensions was committed to Turkey for further expansion of the Iskenderun steel mill. Moscow also agreed to build a thermal power plant and hospital in Yemen (Aden) under an economic agreement, the value of which was not announced.

No Soviet aid extensions were made in 1972 to any LDC in
Africa or East Asia. (See Table A.2.)

East European Extensions

Total East European aid extensions of $645 million in
1972 were made to countries in Africa, Latin America, and
the Near East and South Asia.
Of $209 million of commitments to Africa, Algeria re-
ceived $100 million in credits from Romania and $50 million from Czechoslovakia to purchase machinery and equipment. Romania also extended a $50 million credit to Zambia
for machinery and equipment purchases. Tanzania and Somalia
were recipients of minor East European credits of $7 million
and $2 million, respectively.
In Latin America, the East Europeans committed a total
of $98 million to Chile and Peru. A $20 million credit to
Chile was provided by East Germany for purchase of machinery and equipment, and to Peru Hungary extended $30 million
for machinery and equipment and Poland committed $48 mil-
lion for development of a coal complex and a fishing port.
The bulk of East European aid--$338 million--was
pledged to Near East and South Asian countries. Czechoslovakia extended $25 million to Bangladesh for capital goods
purchases; Bulgaria committed $10 million to Iran for min-
ing and other machinery and equipment; and Iraq received
extensions of $100 million from Poland and $50 million from
Czechoslovakia to finance machinery and equipment purchases,
and a Hungarian credit of $50 million for capital goods,
including oilfield and refinery equipment. Other aid to
the region consisted of a $10 million credit from Hungary
to Sri Lanka to purchase pharmaceutical and aluminum processing equipment, and an extension of $93 million from
Romania to Syria to cover purchases of machinery and equipment for petrochemical, chemical, and various light industries. (See Table A.3.)

Chinese Extensions

Total 1972 Chinese aid extensions of $499 million
were provided to 14 LDCs located in several of the regions.
Africa accounted for $210 million of the total exten-
sions: Burundi ($20 million), Dahomey ($44 million),
Malagasy Republic ($9 million), Rwanda ($22 million), and
Togo ($45 million) all became first-time recipients of

TABLE A.2

Soviet Economic Credits and Grants[a] Extended to Less Developed Countries, by Year
(in millions of U.S. dollars)

Area and Country	1954-64	1965	1966	1967	1968	1969	1970	1971	1972	1954-72
Total	4,033	193	1,244	269	374	476	194	865	581	8,229
Africa	760	28	77	9	0	135	51	192	0	1,252
Algeria	231	--	1	--	--	--	--	189	--	421
Cameroon	8	--	--	--	--	--	--	--	--	8
Central African Republic	--	--	--	--	--	--	--	2	--	2
Congo	10	--	--	--	--	--	--	--	--	10
Equatorial Guinea	--	--	--	--	--	--	--	1	--	1
Ethiopia	102	--	--	--	--	--	--	--	--	102
Ghana	93	--	--	--	--	--	--	--	--	93
Guinea	73	--	3	--	--	92	--	--	--	168
Kenya	48	--	--	--	--	--	--	--	--	48
Mali	59	--	--	--	--	1	--	--	--	60
Mauritania	--	--	--	3	--	--	--	--	--	3
Morocco	--	--	44	--	--	--	44	--	--	88
Nigeria	--	--	--	--	--	--	7	--	--	7
Senegal	7	--	--	--	--	--	--	--	--	7
Sierra Leone	--	28	--	--	--	--	--	--	--	28
Somalia	57	--	9	--	--	--	--	--	--	66
Sudan	22	--	--	--	--	42	--	--	--	64
Tanzania	--	--	20	--	--	--	--	--	--	20
Tunisia	34	--	--	--	--	--	--	--	--	34
Uganda	16	--	--	--	--	--	--	--	--	16
Zambia	--	--	--	6	--	--	--	--	--	6
East Asia	147	3	4	0	0	0	0	0	0	154
Burma	15	--	--	--	--	--	--	--	--	15
Cambodia	21	--	4	--	--	--	--	--	--	25
Indonesia	111	3	--	--	--	--	--	--	--	114
Latin America	30	15	85	55	2	20	56	41	144	448
Argentina	30	15	--	--	--	--	--	--	--	45
Bolivia	--	--	--	--	--	--	28	2	--	30
Brazil	--	--	85	--	--	--	--	--	--	85
Chile	--	--	--	55	--	--	--	39	144	238
Colombia	--	--	--	--	2	--	--	--	--	2
Peru	--	--	--	--	--	--	28	--	--	28
Uruguay	--	--	--	--	--	20	--	--	--	20
Near East/South Asia	3,096	147	1,078	205	372	321	87	632	437	6,375
Afghanistan	553	11	1	5	127	--	3	5	121	826
Bangladesh	--	--	--	--	--	--	--	--	74	74
Egypt	1,002	--	--	--	--	--	--	196	--	1,198
Greece	--	84	--	--	--	--	--	--	--	84
India	1,020	2	571	--	--	--	--	--	--	1,593
Iran	41	--	289	--	178	--	54	--	--	562
Iraq	184	--	--	--	--	121	22	222	--	549
Nepal	20	--	--	--	--	--	--	--	--	20
Pakistan[b]	44	50	84	--	67	20	--	209	--	474
Sri Lanka	30	--	--	--	--	--	8	--	--	3C
Syria	100	--	133	--	--	--	--	--	84	317
Turkey	10	--	--	200	--	166	--	--	158	534
Yemen (Aden)	--	--	--	--	--	14	--	--	--	14
Yemen (Sana)	92	--	--	--	--	--	--	--	--	92

[a]Grants are believed to represent less than 5 percent of the total.

[b]Includes Bangladesh prior to 1972.

East European[a] Economic Credits and Grants[b] Extended
to Less Developed Countries, by Year
(in millions of U.S. dollars)

Area and Country	1954–64	1965	1966	1967	1968	1969	1970	1971	1972	1954–72
Total	1,264	588	228	118	166	430	188	468	645	4,095
Africa	200	79	0	47	56	11	84	99	209	785
Algeria	22	--	--	--	--	--	74	--	150	246
Ethiopia	12	5	--	--	--	--	--	--	--	17
Ghana	82	20	--	--	--	--	--	--	--	102
Guinea	25	--	--	--	--	--	--	--	--	25
Mali	23	--	--	--	--	--	--	--	--	23
Morocco	5	30	--	--	5	--	--	--	--	40
Nigeria	--	14	--	--	--	--	--	24	--	38
Somalia	3	--	--	--	--	--	--	--	2	5
Sudan	--	10	--	47	--	11	10	75	--	153
Tanzania	6	--	--	--	--	--	--	--	7	13
Tunisia	22	--	--	--	51	--	--	--	--	73
Zambia	--	--	--	--	--	--	--	--	50	50
East Asia	267	3	24	0	0	12	0	0	0	306
Burma	2	--	24	--	--	--	--	--	--	26
Cambodia	5	--	--	--	--	12	--	--	--	17
Indonesia	260	3	--	--	--	--	--	--	--	263
Latin America	188	0	43	15	10	11	51	174	98	590
Argentina	4	--	--	--	5	--	--	--	--	9
Bolivia	--	--	--	--	--	--	1	25	--	26
Brazil	184	--	43	--	--	--	--	--	--	227
Chile	--	--	--	--	5	--	--	95	20	120
Colombia	--	--	--	--	--	--	--	5	--	5
Ecuador	--	--	--	5	--	5	--	5	--	15
Peru	--	--	--	--	--	6	25	44	78	153
Uruguay	--	--	--	10	--	--	15	--	--	25
Venezuela	--	--	--	--	--	--	10	--	--	10
Near East/ South Asia	609	506	161	56	100	396	53	195	338	2,414
Afghanistan	7	--	5	--	--	--	--	--	--	12
Bangladesh	--	--	--	--	--	--	--	--	25	25
Egypt	252	255	--	22	--	--	--	142	--	671
India	250	22	68	10	--	32	--	--	--	382
Iran	15	125	--	10	75	200	--	--	10	435
Iraq	--	--	--	14	--	125	43	37	200	419
Pakistan[c]	28	--	28	--	--	8	10	--	--	74
Sri Lanka	10	42	--	--	--	--	--	--	10	62
Syria	30	55	59	--	25	25	--	--	93	287
Turkey	8	--	--	--	--	6	--	--	--	14
Yemen (Aden)	--	--	--	--	--	--	--	16	--	16
Yemen (Sana)	9	7	1	--	--	--	--	--	--	17

[a]Bulgaria, Czechoslovakia, East Germany, Hungary, Poland, and Romania.

[b]Grants are estimated to be less than 5 percent of the total.

[c]Includes Bangladesh prior to 1972.

economic aid from a Communist country. China's commitment
to the Malagasy Republic is for a tourist complex and rice
supplies, while its aid to Rwanda is for road improvement
and a cement plant. In addition, Mauritius accepted its
first Chinese assistance ($34 million), as did Tunisia
($36 million).

In Europe, Malta received its first Communist aid
commitment from China; the $45 million is allocated for
the construction of a drydock and chocolate and glass factories.

In Latin America, China extended a total of $89 mil-
lion: $63 million to Chile, partially for food imports;
and $26 million to Guyana (its first Communist aid) for
such contemplated projects as a textile mill, a highway,
a glass factory, and a brick and tile plant.

The remaining $155 million of 1972 Chinese aid exten-
sions was accounted for by Near East and South Asian countries: $45 million to Afghanistan for agricultural proj-
ects; $45 million to Syria for two yarn factories, a sta-
dium, and expansion of a Chinese-built textile mill; $44
million to Sri Lanka; and $21 million to Yemen (Sana).
(See Table A.4.) In addition, China signed an economic
agreement with Yemen (Aden), the value of which was not
announced.

Cumulative Aid Extensions Total $15 Billion

The Communist country economic aid programs, com-
mencing in 1954 in the case of the Soviet Union and the
East European countries, and in 1956 for China, totaled
slightly more than $15 billion by the end of 1972. Of
this total, the Soviets accounted for nearly 55 percent,
with extensions of $8.2 billion. The East European coun-
tries have committed $4.1 billion of credits, or 27 per-
cent of the total, and the People's Republic of China,
which has maintained a higher aid profile in the past
three years, increased its share of total extensions to
18 percent, or $2.7 billion. (See Figure A.1.)

Since 1954, Near East and South Asian countries have
received nearly 78 percent ($6.4 billion) of total Soviet
aid extensions; and within the region eight countries--
Afghanistan, Egypt, India, Iran, Iraq, Pakistan, Syria,
and Turkey--have accounted for nearly three-quarters of
all Soviet assistance globally. As a region, Africa has
been of secondary importance to the USSR, accounting for
15 percent ($1.3 billion) of Soviet aid, of which one-third

TABLE A.4

Chinese Economic Credits and Grants Extended to
Less Developed Countries, by Year
(in millions of U.S. dollars)

Area and Country	1956-64	1965	1966	1967	1968	1969	1970	1971	1972	1956-72
Total	734	59	119	50	56	0	709	473	499	2,699
Africa	285	15	41	22	0	0	454	295	210	1,322
Algeria	52	--	--	--	--	--	--	40	--	92
Burundi	--	--	--	--	--	--	--	--	20	20
Central African Republic	4	--	--	--	--	--	--	--	--	4
Congo	25	--	--	--	--	--	--	--	--	25
Dahomey	--	--	--	--	--	--	--	--	44	44
Ethiopia	--	--	--	--	--	--	--	84	--	84
Ghana	40	--	--	--	--	--	--	--	--	40
Guinea	26	--	30	--	--	--	10	--	--	66
Kenya	18	--	--	--	--	--	--	--	--	18
Malagasy Republic	--	--	--	--	--	--	--	--	9	9
Mali	52	--	3	--	--	--	--	--	--	55
Mauritania	--	--	--	5	--	--	--	20	--	25
Mauritius	--	--	--	--	--	--	--	--	34	34
Rwanda	--	--	--	--	--	--	--	--	22	22
Somalia	22	--	--	--	--	--	--	110	--	132
Sudan	--	--	--	--	--	--	42	40	--	82
Tanzania	46	--	8	--	--	--	201	1	--	256
Togo	--	--	--	--	--	--	--	--	45	45
Tunisia	--	--	--	--	--	--	--	--	36	36
Uganda	--	15	--	--	--	--	--	--	--	15
Zambia	--	--	--	17	--	--	201	--	--	218
Europe	0	0	0	0	0	0	0	0	45	45
Malta	--	--	--	--	--	--	--	--	45	45
East Asia	165	16	43	0	0	0	0	57*	0	281
Burma	27	--	--	--	--	--	--	57*	--	84
Cambodia	49	--	43	--	--	--	--	--	--	92
Indonesia	89	16	--	--	--	--	--	--	--	105
Latin America	0	0	0	0	0	0	0	44	89	133
Chile	--	--	--	--	--	--	--	2	63	65
Guyana	--	--	--	--	--	--	--	--	26	26
Peru	--	--	--	--	--	--	--	42	--	42
Near East/ South Asia	284	28	35	28	56	0	255	77	155	918
Afghanistan	--	28	--	--	--	--	--	--	45	73
Egypt	85	--	--	21	--	--	--	--	--	106
Iraq	--	--	--	--	--	--	--	45	--	45
Nepal	40	--	20	--	2	--	--	--	--	62
Pakistan	60	--	--	7	42	--	200	--	--	309
Sri Lanka	41	--	--	--	--	--	12	32	44	129
Syria	16	--	--	--	--	--	--	--	45	61
Yemen (Aden)	--	--	--	--	12	--	43	--	--	55
Yemen (Sana)	42	--	15	--	--	--	--	--	21	78

*$57 million of the 1961 Chinese credit to Burma was reinstated in 1971.

FIGURE A.1

Communist Economic Credits and Grants Extended
To Less Developed Countries, 1954-72

ASSISTANCE EXTENDED
BY RECIPIENT

Share of Total

ASSISTANCE EXTENDED
BY DONOR

Share of Total

Source: U.S. Department of State.

($421 million) has been directed to Algeria alone, the remainder scattered among 20 other African nations. Total extensions of $448 million to Latin America are predominantly accounted for by Chile ($238 million), and the remaining $154 million was extended to East Asia (primarily Indonesia) in the earlier years of the Soviet aid program.

East European aid, more trade-oriented than that of the Soviet Union or China, has also been targeted (nearly 60 percent) in a few Near East and South Asian countries, particularly Egypt, India, Iran, Iraq, and Syria. These five countries account for almost 55 percent of total East European global aid.

China, in sharp contrast to the USSR and East Europe, has directed nearly one-half of its total aid extensions to 21 African countries, primarily Tanzania and Zambia, in connection with the TanZam railroad project, and Somalia. At the same time, one-third of Chinese aid has also been committed to the Near East and South Asia, where the major recipients have been Pakistan, Sri Lanka, and Egypt.

Less Than One-Half of Total Communist Aid Drawn Since 1954

As of the end of 1972, the Soviet Union had delivered to the LDCs $4 billion of the $8.2 billion of economic aid offered since 1954. This calculates to a drawdown ratio of approximately 49 percent, an improvement over recent years. In fact, aid deliveries have averaged $400 million or more in each of the past four years, compared to about $300 million annually during 1965-1968. (See Table A.5.) The drawdown ratios of East European and Chinese aid are generally believed to be substantially less than that of the USSR, but, in the case of China, that situation should improve with the rapid progress being made toward completion of the large TanZam Railroad project.

There are several reasons for the relatively slow implementation of Communist aid by the LDCs. In general, the Communist countries do not provide commodity aid, a type of assistance which can be effected rapidly by LDCs. In contrast, project aid, which the Soviets emphasize, is not implemented rapidly in the LDCs because they lack adequate skilled and professional personnel, possess primitive infrastructures, and often do not have funds sufficient to finance the local costs of the projects.

TABLE A.5

Net Flow of Soviet Economic Aid to the
Less Developed Countries, 1954-72
(in millions of U.S. dollars)

	Deliveries of Economic Aid[a]	Estimated Repayments[b]	Net Outflow[c]
1954-64	1,195	155	1,040
1965	315	80	235
1966	270	105	165
1967	300	125	175
1968	300	150	150
1969	400	175	225
1970	410	185	225
1971	420	250	170
1972	400	260	140
Total 1954-72	4,010	1,485	2,525

[a]Based on annual issues of the Ministry of Foreign Trade, USSR, Vneshnyaya Torgovlya SSR (International Relations Publishing House, Moscow), with adjustments for grant aid and commodity assistance.

[b]Interest and principal on deliveries made under credit.

[c]Includes grant aid, estimated to be less than 5 percent of the total aid delivered.

Repayment of Soviet Aid*

Estimated repayments (principal plus interest) by the LDCs from 1954 through 1972 on $4 billion of Soviet aid deliveries (including small amounts of grant aid) amount to nearly $1.5 billion. The repayments estimated to have fallen due in 1972 continued to rise and reached a record level of approximately $260 million (see Table A.5). Estimating that approximately three-fourths of the cumulative repayments represents amortization, the total

---

*Detailed estimates on deliveries, repayments, and net aid flows are not available for the East European and Chinese aid programs.

outstanding debt of the LDCs to the Soviet Union amounted
to $2.7 billion at the end of 1972.

Net Outflow of Soviet Aid

The 1972 LDC repayments of some $260 million for So-
viet aid further reduced the net amount of such aid in
that year ($400 million delivered) to $140 million, or
about 35 percent of actual deliveries. This net flow is
one of the smallest for Soviet aid since the mid-1960s
and is off more than one-third from the average of the
past three years. (See Table A.5.) As a percentage of
estimated gross national product, Soviet net aid outflow
to the LDCs was less than 0.05 percent in 1972.

Communist Aid Terms

Most Communist country economic assistance to LDCs
is in the form of project aid, although commercial-type
credits for the purchase of equipment and machinery and
other products have been more common in the East European
programs than in the case of Soviet aid. This is especially true of the assistance offered to Latin American
countries. Generally speaking, Soviet project aid requires repayment over 12 years at 2.5 percent interest,
while commercial-type credits are usually for 8-10 years
at 3 to 3.5 percent interest. The East European countries
usually have provided their aid on somewhat harder terms
than have the Soviets. In both cases, however, commercial-
type credits frequently require downpayments by the LDCs
of anywhere from 10 to 20 percent.
Chinese economic assistance is offered on much more
liberal terms. This aid is interest-free, with repayments spread over 10 to 20 years following grade periods
of 5 to 10 years. Soviet and East European grace periods
are usually for one year after project completion or delivery of goods. In almost all instances, aid is closely
"tied" to donor goods and the assistance is repayable in
LDC goods and materials or in local LDC currencies depos-
ited in blocked accounts which the aid donor country may
draw against to finance imports of its choosing. In the
Near East and Africa, it is understood that the Soviets
and the East Europeans are increasingly tying repayment
of aid to oil and/or gas if the recipient is a producer
of such fuels.

FIGURE A.2

Communist Exports To and Imports From Less Developed Countries: Value of Trade, 1967-71

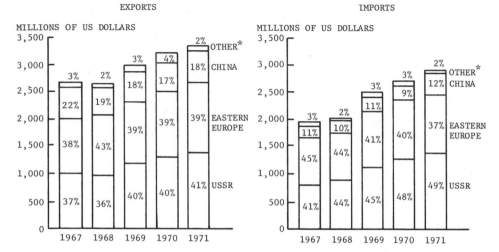

*Including trade of Albania, Cuba, Mongolia, North Korea, and North Vietnam.

PERCENT DISTRIBUTION, 1971

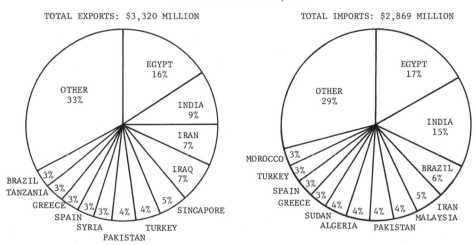

Source: U.S. Department of State.

Grant aid plays a very minor role in the programs of the Communist countries, although all of them on occasion provide some aid of this nature, especially in the humanitarian field, such as hospital construction, medical supplies, etc. Less than five percent of Soviet economic assistance is grant aid, while the percentage for China is somewhat more.

TECHNICAL AND ACADEMIC ASSISTANCE

Modest Increase in Economic Technicians in LDCs

More than 39,000 economic technicians from Communist countries are estimated to have worked in the less developed countries for a period of one month or more during 1972. This estimate represents an increase of about 12 percent over the number of technicians similarly employed in the LDCs in 1971, and includes persons working under both commercial contracts and aid agreements. The increase of more than 4,200 persons in 1972 was primarily accounted for by increased arrivals of Chinese personnel employed in the LDCs, particularly in connection with the construction of the TanZam Railroad in Africa. (See Table A.6.)

For the second consecutive year, the People's Republic of China provided in 1972 the greatest number of economic technicians* to the less developed countries. The Chinese share of the total number of Communist technicians employed in the LDCs rose from about 53 percent in 1971 to 56 percent in 1972. The Soviet share (virtually unchanged in absolute number of persons) declined from 32 percent in 1971 to less than 29 percent in 1972. In contrast, the East Europeans increased their presence somewhat in Africa and accounted for 15 percent of the worldwide total, the same percentage share as in 1971.

Communist country technical personnel continued in 1972 to be heavily situated in Africa and to a lesser but still very important extent in the Near East and South Asia. African countries accounted for nearly 71 percent of all Communist economic technicians in the LDCs--a

---

*The Chinese "technicians" working on the TanZam Railroad may include fairly substantial numbers of common laborers or workers.

percentage share far exceeding the African share of Communist aid commitments. This anomaly results from the large number of Chinese personnel constructing the TanZam Railroad, the continued employment of East European technical laborers on a contractual basis, and the large numbers of East European administrative and professional personnel employed, especially in North Africa. In 1972 the African countries were host to more than 90 percent of all Chinese economic technicians in the LDCs, 64 percent of all the East Europeans, and nearly 34 percent of Soviet personnel. The Chinese presence is greatest in terms of sheer numbers in Tanzania, while the East Europeans are concentrated in Algeria and Libya and the Soviets in Algeria.

Twenty-eight percent of all Communist economic technicians were working in 1972 in the Near East and South Asia, primarily in Afghanistan, Egypt, India, Iran, Iraq, and Syria. This region accounted for nearly 65 percent of all Soviet technicians in the LDCs and one-third of the East Europeans, but less than nine percent of Chinese personnel. The presence of Communist technicians in East Asia as well as in Latin America continued to be nominal, although a few Chinese technicians were noted in Latin America for the first time.

Decrease in LDC Technical Trainees Departing for Communist Countries

An estimated 2,330 trainees from the less developed countries departed for training in Communist countries in 1972, a decrease of 15 percent compared with 1971. This number, however, brings to nearly 23,500 the total number of LDC personnel who have gone to the Communist states for technical training since such trainees were first accepted in 1956.

The largest number of technical personnel again went to the Soviet Union, which received about 58 percent of the total departees. The East European countries hosted the remaining 975 trainees. No trainees were known to have gone to China during the year. (See Table A.7.)

The Communist technical training programs are intended primarily to provide LDC personnel with the technical and administrative skills required for implementing Communist-assisted development projects. Consequently, practically all of the technical trainees come from those LDCs in which Communist aid projects are underway or are in advanced stages of preparation. In 1972, therefore,

TABLE A.6

Communist Economic Technicians in the Less Developed Countries,* 1971-72

	Total		USSR		East Europe		China	
	1971	1972	1971	1972	1971	1972	1971	1972
Total	35,050	39,295	11,025	11,200	5,425	5,930	18,600	22,165
Africa	24,700	27,840	4,200	3,760	3,300	3,805	17,200	20,275
East Asia	225	75	150	25	75	20	--	30
Latin America	225	350	75	190	150	130	--	30
Near East/South Asia	9,900	11,030	6,600	7,225	1,900	1,975	1,400	1,830

*Minimum estimates of persons present for a period of one month or more.

TABLE A.7

Technical Personnel from Less Developed Countries Receiving
Training in Communist Countries,* 1971-72

	Total		USSR		East Europe		China	
	1971	1972	1971	1972	1971	1972	1971	1972
Total	2,745	2,330	1,310	1,355	1,435	975	0	0
Africa	170	535	90	280	80	255	0	0
East Asia	0	0	0	0	0	0	0	0
Latin America	10	50	10	20	0	30	0	0
Near East/South Asia	2,565	1,745	1,210	1,055	1,355	690	0	0

*Minimum estimates, rounded to the nearest five, as of December 1971 and
December 1972.

nearly three-quarters of the trainees were from countries in the Near East and South Asia; and, except for 50 from Latin America, all the remainder were from Africa. Again, no trainees were sent from East Asian countries in 1972.

No Significant Increase in Number of LDC Academic Students in the Communist Countries

During 1972, 24,065 students from the less developed countries were in Communist states for academic training (see Table A.8), including the first contingent in China since before the Cultural Revolution in 1966.

African nationals accounted for nearly one-half of the total number of students present in Communist countries in 1972, the same approximate share this area sent during the past decade. They were followed in numbers by Near East and South Asian nationals, who made up about 36 percent of the total; Latin American students again represented about 12 percent of the total. As in previous years, only about 3 percent came from the East Asian countries. With more than 1,700 students, Syria led the list of LDCs with students in the East for their academic training, followed by Nigeria, Algeria, Sudan, Egypt, and Cyprus, each with over 1,000 students enrolled in Communist educational institutions. Combined, these six countries accounted for more than 30 percent of the total.

Of the 24,065 LDC students in the Communist countries in 1972, approximately 14,500 were studying in the Soviet Union and virtually all of the remainder were in East European schools. Since the introduction in 1956 of the Communist academic training program for nationals from the LDCs, about 56,000 students from these countries have gone to Communist countries for training. The distribution between Soviet and East European educational institutions has been roughly 55-45. The number of LDC students who have enrolled in Chinese schools has been of relatively little significance.

While few of those students who have returned to their homelands after training in the Communist countries are believed to have attained positions of influence, LDC officials seem generally satisfied with the overall quality and character of the education the students have received. Increased demands for trained personnel in the LDCs and limited educational opportunities in the West (except for Latin Americans) probably will assure continuing competition among LDC students for the limited places available to them in Communist educational institutions.

TABLE A.8

Numbers of Academic Students from Selected Less Developed
Countries Being Trained in Communist Countries
as of December 1972

Total	24,065
Africa	11,715
Algeria	1,300
Botswana	30
Burundi	130
Central African Republic	175
Chad	100
Congo	485
Dahomey	100
Ethiopia	500*
Gambia	60
Ghana	185
Guinea	450
Ivory Coast	55
Kenya	500
Mali	420
Mauritania	110
Mauritius	90
Morocco	195
Nigeria	1,325*
Rwanda	100
Senegal	185
Sierra Leone	510
Somali	685
Sudan	1,175
Tanzania	480
Togo	85
Tunisia	350
Uganda	210
Upper Volta	80
Zaire	150
Zambia	255
Other African countries	1,240
East Asia	675
Burma	100
Indonesia	340
Laos	110
Other East Asian countries	125

(continued)

259

TABLE A.8 (continued)

Latin America	3,005
Bolivia	130
Brazil	150
Chile	260
Colombia	115*
Costa Rica	165
Ecuador	175
El Salvador	15
Guatemala	5
Nicaragua	115
Peru	185
Uruguay	20
Venezuela	45
Other Latin American countries	1,625
Near East and South Asia	8,670
Afghanistan	960*
Bangladesh	205
Cyprus	1,005
Egypt	1,110
India	480
Iraq	520
Jordan	535
Kuwait	15
Lebanon	430*
Nepal	300
Pakistan	30
Sri Lanka	130
Syria	1,735
Yemen (Aden)	680
Yemen (Sana)	450
Other Near East and South Asian countries	85

*Increase over the number cited in last year's report reflects the availability of new information on students rather than a large number of new enrollments.

MILITARY ASSISTANCE

Total new military assistance commitments by the Communist countries to the less developed countries fell off sharply in 1972 from the record highs of 1970 and 1971. As in all previous years, the Soviet Union again was the largest single donor of military arms and equipment, and accounted for most of the aid credits extended. The Soviet extensions in 1972 totaled slightly more than $300 million, a decrease of nearly 80 percent from the $1,365 million extended the previous year. (See Table A.9.)

TABLE A.9

Annual Soviet Military Aid Extensions to
Less Developed Countries, 1955-72
(in millions of U.S. dollars)

Total	8,475
1955-60	1,285
1961	830
1962	415
1963	390
1964	875
1965	260
1966	450
1967	515
1968	465
1969	330
1970	985
1971	1,365
1972	310

Cumulatively, the Soviet Union has extended nearly $8.5 billion in military aid since 1955 to more than two dozen LDCs in Africa, East Asia, and the Near East and South Asia. These aid extensions have been highly concentrated geographically: almost 80 percent ($6.7 billion) has been provided to Near East and South Asian countries. Within that region six countries--Afghanistan, Egypt, India, Iran, Iraq, and Syria--have accounted for all but $170 million of the area total. East Asia's share of total Soviet commitments amounts to 13 percent,

but virtually all of that aid ($1.1 billion) was committed
to Indonesia prior to the overthrow of President Sukarno
in 1965. The remainder of the military extensions for the
period since 1955 ($620 million) has been directed to Af-
rican countries, mainly (65 percent) to Algeria. No known
military aid extensions have been provided through 1972
to Latin American countries, except for Cuba. (See Table
A.10.)

Delivery of Communist arms assistance to the less developed countries has historically proceeded at a pace far
exceeding utilization of economic assistance. Consequently, the ratio of drawings to extensions is significantly
higher than the corresponding drawings' ratio of economic
aid, which is estimated at less than 50 percent.

As part of the Soviet military assistance program,
approximately 2,600 military personnel from more than a
dozen less developed countries were undergoing training
in the USSR in 1972. This brings the approximate total
of all such personnel who have received Soviet "in-house"
training since 1955 to 28,000. Moreover, nearly 9,500
Soviet military personnel were present in the following
LDCs for a period of one month or more during 1972:

Country	Number of Military Personnel
Afghanistan	200
Algeria	1,000
Egypt	5,500*
India	200
Iraq	500
Somalia	400
Sudan	100
Syria	1,100
Yemen (Aden)	200
Yemen (Sana)	100
Other	150
Total	9,450

---

*This number does not include an estimated 7,500 So-
viet military personnel who were assigned to Soviet operational units in Egypt. These troops were withdrawn
at Egypt's request in mid-1972, along with most Soviet
military advisers and technicians.

TABLE A.10

Soviet Military Aid Extended to Less Developed
Countries, 1955–72
(in millions of U.S. dollars)

Total	8,475
Africa	620
Algeria	400
Burundi	negligible
Congo	15
Equatorial Guinea	negligible
Ghana	10
Guinea	25
Mali	5
Morocco	15
Nigeria	15
Sierra Leone	negligible
Somalia	55
Sudan	65
Tanzania	5
Uganda	10
East Asia	1,115
Burma	negligible
Cambodia	10
Indonesia	1,100
Laos	5
Near East and South Asia	6,740
Afghanistan	455
Bangladesh	--
Cyprus	25
Egypt	2,700
India	1,200
Iran	500
Iraq	1,000
Lebanon	3
Maldives	negligible
Pakistan	40
Sri Lanka	2
Syria	715
Yemen (Aden)	25
Yemen (Sana)	75

TRADE

Value

Communist Trade with the LDCs
Rose Less Than 5 Percent in 1971*

The total trade turnover (exports plus imports) of
the Communist countries with the less developed countries
in 1971 increased less than 5 percent--from $5.9 billion
to $6.2 billion--compared to a 9 percent increase in 1970.
(See Figure A.2 and Tables A.11 and A.12.)

About 70 percent ($200 million) of this small 1971
increase was recorded by the Soviet Union whose turnover
with the LDCs increased by approximately 8 percent, compared to a growth rate of 13 percent in the previous year.
Unlike 1970 when China's trade with the LDCs declined
fractionally, in 1971 China's trade turnover with those
countries rose by $127 million, an increase of nearly 16
percent. The trade turnover of the East European countries, on the other hand, increased in dollar value by
less than $14 million or 0.6 percent, compared to a 7 per-
cent rise in 1970.

Trade turnover of the LDCs with the remaining Communist countries[†] declined sharply from $176 million in
1970 to $120 million in 1971, a decrease of more than 30
percent in a single year. Most of this decrease was accounted for by a fall-off in imports from Cuba.

On an overall share basis of Communist country trade
with the LDCs, the Soviet Union provided just over 45 percent of total Communist exports and imports, and the East
Europeans provided just under 38 percent. China's share
rose slightly to 15 percent, and the other remaining Communist countries accounted for only 2 percent of the
total.

The Soviet Union's trade turnover with the LDCs increased in 1971 by about $200 million, compared to a $300
million increase in 1970. Most ($162 million) of this
increment was achieved in the Near East and South Asian
region and specifically as the result of increased Soviet-
Egyptian trade levels, stepped-up imports of gas from

---

*The most recent year for which comprehensive trade
data are available.

[†]Albania, Cuba, Mongolia, North Korea, and North
Vietnam (see footnote c, Table A.11).

Iran, and aid-related exports to Iraq. The remainder of
the increment was accounted for by trade with African
countries, largely the result of economic aid and deliveries to Guinea and expanded purchases of cocoa from the
Ivory Coast and Nigeria. On the other hand, a 50 percent
increase ($45 million) in Soviet trade with Lain American
countries in 1971--attributed to Soviet purchases of zinc
and tin from Bolivia, corn from Mexico, and coffee and
corn from Brazil--offset a $45 million trade decline with
the East Asian region resulting from a decline in rubber
purchases from Malaysia.

With regard to the trade of the East European countries with the LDCs, the marginal increase of only $14
million was primarily attributable to a $25 million de-
cline in trade with the Near East and South Asia--mainly
in decreased exports to Lebanon and Turkey--and a $15
million decrease in trade with East Asia (Malaysia and
Singapore). These declines contrasted sharply with a $33
million increase in trade with Latin America, principally
Brazil, and a very modest increase of $11 million with
the African countries.

Chinese-LDC trade, which experiences considerable
annual fluctuation, increased by over $127 million, or
more than 15 percent over 1970. This increase was accounted for in Africa where the value of exchanges rose
about 70 percent--concentrated in trade with Sudan, Tanzania, and Zambia--and in Latin America where the Chinese
made relatively substantial purchases from Chile and Peru.
Decreases in trade levels, on the other hand, were noted
with Indonesia and Malaysia in East Asia, and with Sri
Lanka in the Near East and South Asian region.

Direction of Trade, Balances, and Relative Shares

Like Aid, Most Trade with the
Near East and South Asia

As the major recipient of the Communist aid programs,
the Near East and South Asian region accounted for approximately 63 percent of total exports of Communist
countries to LDCs in 1971, and nearly 56 percent of their
imports from all LDCs. As in the past, Egypt and India
were the two largest single trading partners of the Communist countries in the region; combined they accounted
for nearly one-half of that area's LDC-Communist country
trade turnover. Following the Near East and South Asian

TABLE A.11

Total Communist Country Exports to and Imports from
Selected Less Developed Countries,[a] 1970-71
(in millions of U.S. dollars)[b]

Area and Country	Exports		Imports		Total Turnover	
	1970	1971	1970	1971	1970	1971
Total[c]	3,200.4	3,319.7	2,702.8	2,869.3	5,903.2	6,189.0
Africa	556.7	639.9	418.1	531.2	974.8	1,171.1
Algeria	93.0	79.0	94.2	110.5	187.2	189.5
Angola	0.3	0.3	1.7	1.9	2.0	2.2
Cameroon	5.1	6.3	8.6	4.9	13.7	11.2
Central African Republic	--	1.6	--	--	--	1.6
Chad	1.1	0.9	0	--	1.1	0.9
Congo	2.4	6.2[d]	2.3	1.7[d]	4.7	7.9
Dahomey	2.0	2.3[d]	n*	1.0	2.0	3.3
Equatorial Guinea	--	1.0	--	--	--	1.0
Ethiopia	9.4	8.2	2.0	4.3	11.4	12.5
Gabon	n*	--	1.5	--	1.5	--
Ghana	25.7	24.9[e]	49.7	10.8[e]	75.4	35.7
Guinea	12.4	34.7	3.3	5.6	15.7	40.3
Ivory Coast	5.6	5.0[d]	3.9	15.9	9.5	20.9
Kenya	12.4	17.4	4.8	9.2	17.2	26.6
Liberia	4.3	1.5[d]	n*	--	4.3	1.5
Libya	58.9[d]	57.2[d]	0.7	0.7[e]	59.6	57.9
Malagasy Republic	0.3	0.2	0.9	18.8	1.2	19.0
Mali	9.0	3.4	2.0	2.0	11.0	5.4
Mauritania	0.4	0.6	n*	n*	0.4	0.6
Morocco	87.5	74.2	57.0	71.0	144.5	145.2
Mozambique	0.2	--	0.1	--	0.3	--
Niger	n*	--	n*	--	n*	--
Nigeria	62.9	79.6	33.5	53.2	96.4	132.8
Senegal	6.5	9.3	0.3	4.7[d]	6.8	14.0
Sierra Leone	13.4	11.6[d]	0.3	--	13.7	11.6
Somalia	3.1	7.5	0.9	2.8	4.0	10.3
Sudan	67.4	80.2	85.1	107.2	152.5	187.4
Tanzania	42.0	90.5	12.1	16.4	54.1	106.9
Togo	4.2	4.3	3.1	5.7	7.3	10.0
Tunisia	20.2	21.8	18.1	25.9	38.3	47.7
Uganda	5.2	8.8	18.3	7.0	23.5	15.8
Upper Volta	0.3	--	--	--	0.3	--
Zambia	1.5[d]	1.5[d]	13.8[d]	50.0[d]	15.3	51.5
Europe	118.4	122.5	113.0	101.7	231.4	224.2
Malta	8.2	9.6	0.2	0.5	8.4	10.1
Portugal	8.3	21.7	7.8	6.7	16.1	28.4
Spain	101.9	91.2	105.0	94.5	206.9	185.7
East Asia	319.8	287.9	273.4	195.7	593.2	483.6
Burma	4.7[f]	21.4	1.6	3.6	6.3	25.0
Cambodia	12.2[d]	1.3	6.3[d]	--	18.5	1.3
Indonesia	55.1	50.3	34.5[d]	18.6[d]	89.6	68.9
Malaysia	82.2[d]	50.2	167.4	121.8	249.6	172.0
Singapore	155.1	154.9	60.9	45.0	216.0	199.9
Thailand	10.6	9.8	2.7	6.7	13.3	16.5
Latin America	150.5	176.9	341.5	437.0	492.0	613.9
Argentina	21.0	20.1	80.3	78.5	101.3	98.6
Bolivia	n*	n*	3.4	10.0	3.4	10.0
Brazil	57.8	102.5	126.7	175.2	184.5	277.7
Chile	4.4[d]	8.8[d]	8.4	17.3[d]	12.8	26.1
Colombia	18.1	11.7[e]	31.7	25.8	49.8	37.5
Costa Rica	1.1	1.2	7.3	3.6	8.4	4.8
Ecuador	6.7	3.2	9.0	13.3	15.7	16.5
El Salvador	0.1	0.1	6.3	0.5	6.4	0.6
Guyana	0.2	--	n*	--	0.2	--
Honduras	0.8	1.6	1.2	0.8	2.0	2.4

Area and Country	Exports 1970	Exports 1971	Imports 1970	Imports 1971	Total Turnover 1970	Total Turnover 1971
Jamaica	0.1	n*	0.8	2.6	0.9	2.6
Mexico	6.8	7.0	4.0	19.5^d	10.8	26.5
Nicaragua	0.1	--	n*	--	0.1	--
Peru	2.2	4.3	33.0	80.8	35.2	85.1
Uruguay	8.4	4.0	29.1	9.6	37.5	13.6
Venezuela	22.8^d	12.3	0.2^d	n*	23.0	12.3
Near East and South Asia	2,054.4	2,092.5	1,556.7	1,603.7	3,611.1	3,696.2
Afghanistan	44.0	53.3	35.3	39.6	79.3	92.9
Bahrain	8.6	8.5^d	--	--	8.6	8.5
Cyprus	15.3	17.0	11.5	11.7	26.8	28.7
Egypt	515.7	545.9^d	481.2	497.5^d	996.9	1,043.4
Greece	100.4	106.2	106.9	84.3	207.3	190.5
India	282.8	288.9	409.1	432.6	691.9	721.5
Iran	264.1	246.9	114.1	155.2	378.2	402.1
Iraq	139.0	227.0	22.1	23.8	161.1	250.8
Israel	33.2	32.3	20.1	17.5	53.3	49.8
Jordan	22.0	17.3	1.2	0.5	23.2	17.8
Kuwait	52.0	59.5^f	2.4^d	0.8	54.4	60.3
Lebanon	69.2^d	55.8^d	11.0^d	7.3	80.2	63.1
Nepal	2.8	2.7^d	0.7	3.1^d	3.5	5.8
Pakistan	133.9	119.6	126.9	120.4	260.8	240.0
Saudi Arabia	14.4	21.1^d	0	--	14.4	21.1
Sri Lanka	73.3	46.9^d	70.2	59.8^d	143.5	106.7
Syria	114.0	102.7	56.7	62.3	170.7	165.0
Turkey	136.3	125.5	85.4	86.6	221.7	212.1
Yemen (Aden)	13.9	7.4^d	0.7	n*	14.6	7.4
Yemen (Sana)	19.6	8.0	1.1	0.5^d	20.7	8.5

*n = negligible.

[a]Data for the USSR are from the official Soviet Trade Yearbook. For other Communist countries, data are from official trade statistics of the LDCs. The data for the USSR and other Communist countries are not completely compatible because Soviet data exclude freight and insurance costs, while exports from other Communist countries include these costs, although they are excluded from other Communist countries' imports.

A leader entry (--) indicates that no trade data are known, although some trade may have taken place.

[b]Converted at official exchange rates.

[c]Components may not add to the totals shown because of rounding. Total figures include the foreign trade of the USSR, East Europe, and China (see Table A.13), as well as the estimated trade with the LDCs of Albania, Cuba, Mongolia, North Korea, and North Vietnam in millions of U.S. dollars as follows:

Area and Country	Exports 1970	Exports 1971	Imports 1970	Imports 1971	Total Turnover 1970	Total Turnover 1971
Albania	0.9	3.1	2.4	1.1	3.3	4.2
Cuba	95.0	54.1	54.1	41.6	149.1	95.7
Mongolia	0.2	n*	n*	0.1	0.2	0.1
North Korea	6.5	9.0	8.9	7.9	15.4	16.9
North Vietnam	7.2	2.6	1.3	0.6	8.5	3.2

[d]Estimated in part.

[e]Some partial-year data.

[f]Includes some estimation and some partial-year data.

TABLE A.12

Soviet, East European, and Chinese Exports to and Imports from Selected Less Developed Countries,[a] 1970-71
(in millions of U.S. dollars)[b]

Area and Country	USSR Exports		USSR Imports		East Europe Exports		East Europe Imports		China Exports		China Imports	
	1970	1971	1970	1971	1970	1971	1970	1971	1970	1971	1970	1971
Total	1,292.4	1,380.2	1,298.8	1,412.5	1,243.4	1,288.2	1,081.8	1,050.7	554.8	582.6	255.5	354.8
Africa												
Algeria	216.4	225.6	225.9	251.6	189.3	200.2	122.5	122.9	138.8	192.9	65.0	152.9
Angola	69.4	58.4	62.0	77.8	11.2	15.4	23.2	23.1	12.4	5.2	9.0	10.4
Cameroon	--	--	--	--	0.3	0.3	1.7	1.9	0	n*	0	--
Central African Republic	0.7	1.6	7.7	4.1	2.6	2.3	0.8	0.8	1.6	2.1	0.1	n*
Chad	--	--	--	--	0.5	--	--	--	--	--	--	--
Congo	0.9	4.7	0.8	0.7	--	--	--	--	0.6	0.9	0	1.0[c]
Dahomey	0.8	1.1	--	1.0	--	--	--	--	1.5	1.5[c]	1.5	--
Equatorial Guinea	--	1.0	--	--	--	--	--	--	1.2	1.2[c]	0	--
Ethiopia	1.4	1.4	0.9	3.2	5.4	4.6	0.4	0.5	--	--	--	--
Gabon	--	--	44.2	7.7	n*	--	1.5	--	2.6	2.2	0.7	0.6
Ghana	11.0	14.1	3.3	5.6	8.0	5.8[d]	3.1	1.3[d]	0	--	0	--
Guinea	12.4	34.7	1.7	12.4	--	--	--	--	6.7	5.0[d]	2.4	1.8[d]
Ivory Coast	0.4	1.3	0.4	2.4	4.2	2.7	2.2	3.5	--	--	--	--
Kenya	1.6	1.3	--	--	7.4	12.1	2.7	4.3	1.0	1.0[c]	n*	--
Liberia	--	--	--	--	2.8	--	--	--	3.4	4.0	1.7	2.5
Libya	14.3	9.9	--	--	34.0	40.0[c]	0.7	0.7[d]	1.5	1.5[c]	n*	--
Malagasy Republic	n*	n*	0.7	1.0	0.3	0.2	0.2	0.4	10.6[c]	7.3	0	0
Mali	5.2	2.6	1.9	2.0	0.6	--	0.1	--	--	--	--	--
Mauritania	0.4	0.1	n*	--	--	--	--	--	3.2	0.5	0	--
Morocco	36.1	31.3	19.6	21.0	28.1	16.3	25.5	27.7	11.0	11.9	7.2	18.5
Mozambique	--	--	--	--	0.2	--	0.1	--	--	--	0	--
Niger	--	--	--	--	--	--	--	--	n*	--	n*	--
Nigeria	12.1	17.4	22.6	45.6	31.1	33.9	9.7	7.1	19.7	28.3	1.2	0.5
Senegal	1.3	1.0	n*	n*	0.7	2.1	0.3	0.3	4.5	6.2	n*	4.4[c]
Sierra Leone	1.8	2.6	--	--	8.8	9.0[c]	0.3	--	2.8	--	--	--

Somalia	1.8	2.6	--	--	8.8	9.0[c]	0.3	2.8	--	--	--
Sudan	36.1	22.3	49.9	52.2	19.7	28.4	18.0	11.6	23.2	17.2	31.7
Tanzania	1.2	0.7	0.8	1.8	3.7	5.7	3.1	37.1	84.1	8.2	11.8
Togo	1.3	2.0	3.1	4.9	1.3	1.0	0.8	1.6	1.3	0	--
Tunisia	3.4	4.0	2.9	7.0	16.6	17.4	18.6	0.2	0.3	0	0.3
Uganda	1.2	4.3	3.1	n*	1.7	2.5	13.7	2.3	2.0	1.5	1.4
Upper Volta	--	--	--	--	0.1	--	--	0.2	--	--	--
Zambia	--	--	--	--	--	--	--	1.5[c]	1.5[c]	13.8[c]	50.0[c]
Europe	9.4	13.5	6.3	10.2	70.3	76.9	69.5	2.3	3.3	0.6	0.6
Malta	0.8	2.4	n*	0.2	6.1	5.5	0.1	1.1	1.1	0.1	--
Portugal	--	--	--	--	7.8	21.5	7.8	0.3	0.2	n*	n*
Spain	8.6	11.1	6.3	10.0	56.4	49.9	61.6	0.9	2.0	0.5	0.6
East Asia	19.4	24.2	158.3	108.1	36.9	31.9	55.7	229.8	222.6	53.0	39.2
Burma	3.3	3.6	1.6	2.0	--	5.2[d]	--	1.4	12.6[c]	0	1.6
Cambodia	0.3	0.1	1.6	--	3.8[c]	--	0.3[c]	8.1	1.2	3.7	--
Indonesia	5.0	11.2	27.8	11.2	9.6	7.9	1.7	40.5	31.2	5.0[c]	5.0[c]
Malaysia	1.8	1.7	123.3	86.2	3.9[c]	3.8	22.4	53.9	44.7	21.6	17.4
Singapore	6.1	4.9	3.2	4.1	12.0	8.0	29.5	125.3	132.9	22.7	15.2
Thailand	2.9	2.8	0.9	4.6	7.6	7.0	1.8	n*	--	n*	--
Latin America	8.7	14.7	78.8	116.3	137.7	155.5	250.9	4.0	6.1	3.8	50.4
Argentina	1.9	2.1	31.3	33.8	18.2	17.0	46.4	0.9	1.0	2.5	6.5
Bolivia	n*	n*	3.4	10.0	--	--	--	--	--	--	--
Brazil	2.7	2.2	23.1	46.3	55.1	99.7	102.3	n*	0.6	1.3	--
Chile	0.6	7.8	0.3	0.9	3.3[c]	0.2	0.4	0.5	1.0[c]	0	16.0[c]
Colombia	1.7	1.2	10.4	4.8	16.3	10.5[d]	21.3	0.1	n*	n*	--
Costa Rica	0	--	6.9	2.4	1.0	1.1	0.4	0.1	0.1	0	--
Ecuador	C.1	n*	0.8	3.7	6.6	3.2	8.2	--	--	--	0.4
El Salvador	--	--	--	--	0.1	0.1	6.3	n*	n*	0	--
Guyana	--	--	--	--	n*	--	--	0.2	--	n*	--
Honduras	--	--	--	--	0.8	1.6	1.2	0	--	0	--
Jamaica	--	--	0.8	2.6	n*	--	--	0.1	--	--	--
Mexico	0.8	0.8	0.3	10.2	6.0	6.7	3.6	--	--	n*	4.3[c]
Nicaragua	--	--	--	--	0.1	--	n*	n*	--	0	--
Peru	0.1	n*	0.2	0.2	1.9	3.3	32.8	0.2	0.4	n*	23.2
Uruguay	0.9	1.0	1.1	1.4	7.3	2.9	28.0	0.1	0.1	n*	--
Venezuela	--	--	--	--	21.0[c]	9.4	0.2[c]	1.8	2.9	0	0

(continued)

TABLE A.12 (continued)

Area and Country	USSR Exports 1970	USSR Exports 1971	USSR Imports 1970	USSR Imports 1971	East Europe Exports 1970	East Europe Exports 1971	East Europe Imports 1970	East Europe Imports 1971	China Exports 1970	China Exports 1971	China Imports 1970	China Imports 1971
Near East and South Asia	1,038.5	1,102.1	829.4	926.3	809.2	823.7	583.2	554.5	179.9	157.7	133.1	111.7
Afghanistan	40.0	50.3	34.3	38.4	--	--	--	--	4.0	3.0	1.0	1.2
Bahrain	--	--	--	--	--	--	--	--	8.6	8.5c	--	--
Cyprus	4.6	8.1	5.8	5.4	10.7	8.8	5.7	6.3	n*	0.1	n*	--
Egypt	363.2	381.3	310.6	334.1	135.1	145.0c	147.9	133.0c	15.3	15.3	17.7	23.1
Greece	35.2	33.0	34.9	18.9	65.1	72.2	72.0	65.4	0.1	1.0	0	n*
India	135.9	129.2	269.6	284.2	146.9	156.8	138.8	146.5	0	0	0	0
Iran	187.8	154.8	69.1	111.2	74.6	88.5	39.6	38.9	1.7	3.2	4.4	5.1
Iraq	66.0	110.1	4.6	6.1	53.0	97.1	9.5	14.7	20.0	19.6	8.0	3.0
Israel	--	--	--	--	33.2	32.2	20.1	16.2	n*	0.1	n*	1.3
Jordan	7.1	6.6	--	--	10.7	6.3	0.6	0.5	4.2	4.4	0.6	0
Kuwait	10.8	19.3	0.3	0.8	20.8	22.5c	n*	--	20.4	17.7d	2.1c	--
Lebanon	15.2	20.4	4.2	4.0	45.2c	24.9	6.5c	3.3	8.8	10.5c	0.3	--
Nepal	0.8	0.7	0.7	1.1	--	--	--	--	2.0	2.0c	n*	2.0c
Pakistan	35.7	28.7	31.4	38.9	54.7	54.6	54.6	50.5	27.8	35.0	39.3	30.2
Saudi Arabia	6.0	6.0	--	--	8.3	15.0c	--	--	0	0.1	0	--
Sri Lanka	5.6	9.4	13.3	16.1	19.1	10.4	14.6	12.2	48.6	27.1d	42.3	30.3
Syria	46.4	57.7	19.2	29.3	48.9	40.0c	18.9	20.0c	9.8	5.0	15.9	13.0c
Turkey	62.4	76.0	30.1	37.3	73.8	49.4	54.4	47.0	0.1	0.1	0.9	2.3
Yemen (Aden)	4.8	2.4	0.2	n*	4.1	--	n*	--	5.0	5.0c	0.5	n*
Yemen (Sana)	11.1	8.0	1.1	0.3	5.0	--	0	--	3.5	--	0	0.2c

*n = negligible.

a Data for the USSR are from the official Soviet Trade Yearbook. For the other Communist countries, data are from official trade statistics of the LDCs. The data for the USSR and other Communist countries are not completely compatible because Soviet data exclude freight and insurance costs, while exports from the other Communist countries include these costs, although they are excluded from the other Communist countries' imports. A leader entry (--) indicates that no trade data are known, although some trade may have taken place.

b Converted at official exchange rates.

c Estimate.

d Partial-year data.

region, Africa in 1971 accounted for 18 percent of Communist trade with the LDCs, Latin America 9 percent, East Asia almost 7 percent, and the three European countries of Malta, Portugal, and Spain 3 percent.

The total overall balance of all the Communist countries in this trade with the LDCs was favorable in the amount of $450 million in 1971, as compared to $486 million in the previous year. Specifically, China was in surplus by $228 million and the East Europeans by $237 million. The Soviet Union, for the second consecutive year, recorded a deficit which in 1971 amounted to $32 million as compared to $6 million in 1970.

Regionally, the Soviet Union achieved a surplus position of $178 million in the Near East and South Asia, primarily in trade with Egypt, Iran, Iraq, Syria, and Turkey. Surpluses in those countries more than offset the growing Soviet deficit in trade with India. That deficit exceeded $150 million in 1971 as Indian repayments for past economic assistance outstripped deliveries of new Soviet aid. With all other LDC regions the Soviet Union registered a trade deficit in 1971: $26 million in Africa, $84 million in East Asia, and more than $100 million in Latin America. In East Asia the deficit is accounted for in its entirety by rubber purchases from Malaysia, and Latin America sizable deficits were recorded with Argentina, Brazil, and Mexico.

Of the East European overall surplus in trade with the less developed countries, $77 million was accounted for in Africa, primarily in trade with Libya and Nigeria; $10 million in European LDCs (mainly Portugal); and nearly $275 million in the Near East and South Asia. In that region, the East Europeans were in surplus with virtually every country, but more so with Iran and Iraq. Deficit regions were East Asia (Malaysia and Singapore) and Latin America where East European imports outstripped exports by more than $110 million. Argentina, Brazil, and Peru were the major trading partners.

The traditional Chinese-LDC trade surplus was recorded in Africa ($40 million) due to large aid-related exports to Tanzania; East Asia ($193 million, of which $118 million was accounted for by Singapore); and the Near East and South Asia ($47 million). China's only deficit region was Latin America from which imports exceeded exports by $54 million, principally accounted for by Chile and Peru.

Mixed Shift in Shares of Trade

In the aggregate, the less developed countries accounted for 8.7 percent of Communist world trade in 1971.
The share of total Soviet trade in 1971 represented by the
less developed countries was the same as in 1970:   10.6
percent.   The LDC share of East European trade, however,
declined fractionally, while the share of Chinese trade
gained almost two percentage points, as shown below.

Percentage Share of Less Developed Countries
in the Trade of Communist Countries, 1970-71

| | Percent of Total Trade | |
	1970	1971
Soviet Union	10.6	10.6
East Europe	6.1	5.8
China	18.8	20.4

The Communist countries continued in 1971 to account
for only a very small share of the total trade of the less
developed countries. Communist states took roughly 4.7
percent of total LDC exports of $61 billion and accounted
for about 5.2 percent of LDC imports of $64 billion during
the year.   In the case of several LDCs, the importance of
trade with the Communist countries was of far greater significance: combined the Communist states took nearly 59
percent of Egypt's exports, more than 30 percent of Sudan's
and Syria's, and more than 20 percent of India's.   On the
import side, both Egypt and Iraq obtained more than 30 percent of their purchases from Communist countries, and Sudan, Tanzania, and Syria each took over 20 percent.   (See
Table A.13.)

Commodity Composition

Aid Repayments Spur Soviet
Import of LDC Manufactures

Rising economic aid repayments have been an important
impetus to the growth of Soviet imports of manufactured
and semi-manufactured goods from the less developed countries.   Increasingly these goods are coming from Soviet-
assisted plants.   It is estimated that this category of
imports now accounts for one-fifth of Soviet imports from

Percentage Share of the Combined Communist Countries in the Trade of Selected Less Developed Countries,[a] 1970-71

Area and Country	Exports to Communist Countries 1970	1971	Imports from Communist Countries 1970	1971
Africa				
Algeria	8.0	10.5	5.5	5.7
Angola	0.4	0.5	0.1	0.1
Cameroon	3.7	2.3	2.1	2.0
Chad	n.a.	n.a.	1.9	1.5
Ethiopia	1.2	3.1	5.5	4.7
Ghana	10.6	5.9	7.5	6.2[b]
Ivory Coast	0.8	3.1	1.5	0.8
Kenya	2.7	3.6	3.0	3.5
Libya	0.1	0.1[b]	6.9	12.0[b]
Malagasy Republic	0.5	0.1	0.2	0.1
Mali	1.8	2.8	20.9	19.5
Morocco	9.6	13.4	11.5	10.2
Nigeria	2.9	3.1	5.8	5.2
Senegal	0.2	0.2	2.8	4.3
Sierra Leone	0.3	n*	10.7	9.7[b]
Sudan	28.9	32.0	17.7	23.5
Tanzania	5.3	6.1	15.5	26.7
Togo	5.8	13.5	6.6	6.1
Tunisia	9.8	6.7	6.7	6.3
Uganda	7.4	3.0	4.2	3.8
Europe				
Malta	0.5	0.8	5.2	6.1
Portugal	0.8	0.6	0.6	1.2
Spain	2.9	3.2	1.4	1.9
East Asia				
Burma	n.a.	n.a.	n.a.	19.2[b]
Indonesia	1.9	0.7	0.6	1.2

Area and Country	Exports to Communist Countries 1970	1971	Imports from Communist Countries 1970	1971
Malaysia	8.3	6.7	5.7	5.4
Singapore	6.6	4.5	6.3	5.7
Thailand	0.4	1.0	1.4	0.8
Latin America				
Argentina	4.3	4.3	1.3	1.2
Brazil	4.6	n.a.	2.1	n.a.
Chile	0.6	n.a.	0.1	n.a.
Colombia	n.a.	3.0[b]	4.3	2.4[b]
Ecuador	4.1	6.0	2.8	1.2
Mexico	0.3	0.4	0.3	0.3
Peru	3.1	9.0	0.7	0.6
Uruguay	12.2	4.8	3.7	2.1
Near East and South Asia				
Cyprus	10.4	10.0	6.6	7.0
Egypt	59.1	58.7[b]	31.3	30.9[b]
Greece	16.6	13.0	5.2	5.0
India	20.3	20.7	14.9	11.5
Iran	4.6	4.2	11.9	13.3
Iraq	2.0	1.4	26.2	31.0
Israel	2.6	1.8	2.3	1.8
Jordan	4.5	1.8	11.6	6.2
Kuwait	0.1	n.a.	8.0	8.1
Pakistan	17.5	17.7	9.8	12.4
Saudi Arabia	n.a.	n.a.	2.6	2.5[b]
Sri Lanka	20.8	18.5	15.1	15.3
Syria	25.8	35.6	23.8	27.6[b]
Turkey	14.4	12.3	15.2	10.4

*n = negligible.

[a]Data from U.S. Department of Commerce Value Series and the International Monetary Fund and International Bank for Reconstruction and Development's Direction of Trade.

[b]Based on partial-year data.

the LDCs as a whole, and even higher percentages from such countries as India, Egypt, and Iran. Nevertheless, the bulk of Soviet imports still consists of raw materials, such as natural rubber and cotton fiber, and foods--oils, coffee, cocoa, vegetables and fruit, etc.

One-half of Soviet exports to the LDCs consists of machinery and equipment, still largely aid-generated. However, in recent years the aid share has declined while commercial Soviet sales of these goods have risen sharply. This rise reflects the market for replacements and spare parts created by the Soviet aid program as well as, perhaps, some diminution of LDC inhibitions against Soviet goods. Other Soviet exports include ferrous metals, timber, pulp and paper, and petroleum products. Soviet grain exports, however, are now insignificant because of poor Soviet harvests.

East Europe and China

East European exports to the LDCs continued in 1971 to run to machinery and equipment and other manufactures, while imports were mainly agricultural and natural resources. No adequate data are available, however, to estimate more specifically the commodity composition of the trade. Similarly, there are insufficient data on Chinese-LDC trade, but it can be assumed that Chinese exports mainly consisted of food, light manufactures, and equipment in conjunction with Chinese aid projects. Imports by China from the LDCs would be mostly in the raw materials category.

Peking's aid policies toward the African
countries reflect changes in its political outlook, and the priority given to
relations with the continent.

China's growing role in world affairs appears to be
causing a change of emphasis in her trade and aid policies
toward the developing world. Whereas her assistance has
in the past been channeled mainly toward her Asian neighbors, a substantial proportion of it is now going to Af-
rica--particularly to those countries whose views carry
weight internationally. By 1972 (the last year for which
global figures are available), offers to African countries
accounted for almost 40 percent of Chinese aid to Africa,
Asia, the Middle East, and Latin America, compared with
20 percent ten years earlier. In 1962 about 75 percent of
all Chinese aid went to Asia, whose share had fallen to 23
percent by 1972.
China began, in the early 1960s, to provide economic
aid to the newly independent states of sub-Saharan Africa.
Later, her aid-giving capacity was adversely affected by a
variety of considerations--the failure of the Great Leap
Forward, a succession of poor harvests, preoccupation with
the Cultural Revolution and relations with the Soviet
Union. In Africa her position was further impaired by her
involvement with extremist revolutionary movements that
were threatening newly formed governments. Toward the end
of the decade, however, China moved out of isolation; and
since her admission to the United Nations in October 1971,
she has sought to reestablish herself as an influential
member of the international community while also identify-
ing herself as a developing country, thereby claiming a
special understanding of the problems of the Third World.
The widening of China's political horizon has been
accompanied by the expansion of her economic aid program.
Before 1970 her aid to sub-Saharan Africa was worth some
$650 million, only about half of which was taken up by the
recipient countries. From 1970-73 she offered approximately $1,000 million. While the largest single element

This document has been made available without attri-
bution.

in this is a $400 million loan divided equally between Tanzania and Zambia for the construction of the TanZam Railway, the remainder represents a significant overall increase in China's aid program. Soviet offers during this period were in the region of only $10 million.

China has also extended the range of recipient countries. Until 1970 her aid went to 11 countries in sub-Saharan Africa: the Central African Republic, Congo (Brazzaville), Ghana, Guinea, Kenya, Mali, Mauritania, Somalia, Tanzania, Uganda, and Zambia. In the same period the Soviet Union aided 15 countries in the area. In 1971 Ethiopia and Sierra Leone were added to the Chinese list, followed in 1972 by Burundi, Dahomey, the Malagasy Republic, Mauritius, Rwanda, and Togo. Cameroon, Chad, Senegal, and Zaire were included in 1973. The Soviet Union, on the other hand, added only two new countries, the Central African Republic and Equatorial Guinea (both in 1971). The inclusion of Ethiopia, which was offered over $80 million during Emperor Haile Selassie's visit to Peking in October 1971, is an indication that China is now prepared to aid conservative countries in addition to radical ones—like Congo (Brazzaville) and Guinea.

Apart from Tanzania and Zambia, which are an exceptional case in view of the railway project, China's commitments up to 1970 were heaviest in Guinea and Mali, both of which have received new loans although on a reduced scale. In Mali, the decline in relations following the overthrow of President Modibo Keita in 1968 has been arrested; some new projects have been announced and an economic and technical agreement covering the loan of an undisclosed amount for agricultural projects was signed in June 1973. Guinea negotiated agreements for financial and commodity credits at the end of 1972. Total Chinese commitments now stand at about $66 million in Mali and $55 million in Guinea.

In the Congo and Somalia, where her economic stake had previously been about $25 million, China's interests increased substantially after 1970. A financial agreement for a further credit of $24 million was signed with the Congo in January 1973, and a loan for an unspecified amount agreed to during President Ngouabi's visit to Peking in July. Chinese aid to Somalia rose even more sharply with a loan of over $100 million in 1971; China is now undertaking the country's largest single development project—the construction of the Belet Uen-Burao highway. Both these cases represent a special effort by the Chinese in countries where they are in direct rivalry with the Soviet Union.

Countries which have undergone a change of political outlook have also received special attention. Following the replacement of President Tsiranana by a more radical government, China loaned the Malagasy Republic $9 million in 1972 to enable her to pay off debts to South Africa incurred when she was pursuing a policy of dialogue with that country. One of the largest Chinese loans was that made to Zaire, only two months after the establishment of diplomatic relations in November 1972. The loan followed President Mobutu's visit to Peking in January 1973, when China's support for opposition groups came under review, and when Mao Tse-tung was reported to have commented: "I lost much money and arms attempting to overthrow you." In some cases the Chinese have offered economic aid following recognition, even though no formal diplomatic relations exist. This is the position in Gabon, where they have signed a technical assistance agreement for a sugar refinery.

In the past the Chinese have tended to concentrate on small countries, where the return in goodwill is high, and a modest outlay assumes some significance. For instance the $20 million extended to Burundi under the 1972 agreement represented a third more than the total aid she received from all sources in 1969. Rwanda was in a similar position. China has also on occasion provided small grants following natural, and other, disasters--for example the $10 million given to Zambia in May 1973 to offset the effect of the closure of the Rhodesian border. But in view of her own increasingly important role in world affairs, China has begun to pay more attention to influential countries like Zaire and Nigeria. Although no credit has been announced, she signed an economic cooperation agreement with Nigeria in November 1972, and during 1973 Chinese experts advised on agriculture, including the mechanization of rice, wheat, and cotton production. Other initiatives are apparently intended to break down her isolation from the rest of the world, among them the inauguration of a regular air service between Addis Ababa and Peking, despite the small flow of traffic expected. Discussions are being held about a Zaire-China air link.

Most Chinese aid is supplied under terms not very different from those attached to many Western loans. For example, International Development Association (IDA) credits are repayable over 40 years after a ten-year grace period, with an annual service charge of 75 percent; British credits are generally interest-free with maturity over 25 years. Chinese credits sometimes call for repayment over ten years, but 20 years or longer is now usual

and further extensions can sometimes be granted. The
majority specify repayment in the form of goods or convertible currency. These terms are generous compared to
Soviet practice--normally, repayment over 12 years at $2\frac{1}{2}$
percent for economic aid. The local cost of projects
that come under Chinese agreements is usually financed by
the sale of goods imported by the recipient country from
China to generate funds for the purpose.

By means of repayments in kind, as a means of covering local costs, China is able both to gain access to primary produce grown in Africa and to develop markets for
her own consumer goods. Now that she is engaging in big-
power competition for clients, an ability to persuade producer countries to break away from their traditional markets, to promote future markets and to develop client relationships is increasingly important to her. The main
African products in which the Chinese are interested are
minerals such as copper (24,000 tons of which are to be
supplied by Zambia during 1974), zinc, and possibly ura-
nium (from Zaire); and also cotton, sisal palm, groundnut
and seed oils, coffee, cloves, and other spices. China
is an important customer for cotton, sisal, and pyrethrum
which are also bought on a purely commercial basis from
countries where there are no significant aid programs,
such as Kenya.

The Chinese have found that redressing the balance
of trade with African countries is one way of improving
relations. For example trade with Ethiopia had been one
way, since 1971, China has begun to purchase coffee and
oil seeds resulting in a $E5 million balance in favor of
Ethiopia. But this is exceptional, the overall balance
of trade being in China's favor; in 1970 her exports to
Africa were over $70 million more than her imports.

While changes in trading patterns may be advantageous
to both sides, the results of importing Chinese products
to offset local costs of projects have been less easy to
control, particularly in East Africa where the flow of
goods generated by the TanZam Railway is much higher than
elsewhere. Because Chinese consumer goods are relatively
simple, they compete with similar articles produced locally. Such difficulties have been experienced with textiles in Zambia and pharmaceuticals in Tanzania, while
Kenya has complained that the influx of Chinese goods has
seriously affected markets for her newly established industries within the East African Community.

Other snags have been the lack of suitable goods to
import, resulting in some unsaleable ones having to be

written off, and consumer resistance to certain items, like bicycles, which are below the standard of those previously available from the West. This has inhibited some importers from stocking Chinese goods. By April 1972 Zambia had accumulated a short-fall of nearly $46 million in her contribution to the local costs of the TanZam Railway because of buyer resistance. In April 1973 it was announced that all future buying would be channeled through the Zambian National Import and Export Corporation to facilitate Chinese imports into Zambia. A spokesman for the Ministry of Trade and Industry said that while the government would not force businessmen to buy from China, it would do everything possible to encourage extra trade.

Another factor is the rise in the cost of Chinese goods which were at one time marketable because they sold at highly competitive prices. At the Canton international trade fair in May 1973 the price of some textiles was reported to be up by between 110 percent and 200 percent. Many buyers thought that the Chinese claim that the rises were in tune with world trends was unjustified, since there had been no increase in China either in wages or in the price of raw materials. Zambian buyers found that prices in general had risen between 15-70 percent over the previous year.

Probably the greatest drawback is the monopoly of trade which follows the acceptance of any large Chinese aid scheme, involving the financing of local costs by the import of Chinese goods. China now has the lion's share of Tanzania's market, is Mali's second most important supplier, and is improving her position in Zambia. While the recipient country would probably prefer to shop around in world markets, the volume of Chinese goods which it is required to absorb precludes this. Once the trend is established, the Chinese no doubt hope that markets in Africa will provide long-term outlets for exports which are not sufficiently sophisticated to sell in more industrialized countries.

Because of her own stage of development, China's overseas undertakings are, in the main, labor-intensive and do not need much technological expertise. Agriculture, particularly rice-growing, is high on the list. In African countries which previously had diplomatic relations with Taiwan, the Chinese have taken over existing Taiwanese rice projects with little difficulty.

Since 1970 China has greatly extended the scale of her projects. The progress of the TanZam Railway has led to speculation that she might undertake other rail schemes including the modernization of existing lines--a possibility in African countries with long-established rail systems such as Guinea, Mali, Sierra Leone, Congo, Ethiopia, and Uganda. In addition to the Belet Uen-Burao highway in Somalia (1,045 kilometres), China is constructing the Woldia to Werefa road in Ethiopia (300 km); the Serenje to Samfya road in Zambia (264 km) (the Lusaka to Kaomo road [389 km] was completed in 1972); and the Mongomo to Ncue road in the Rio Muni province of Equatorial Guinea (approximately 100 km).

A number of large dams are planned, including the Bouenza Dam in the Congo and the Lagdo Dam in Cameroon. China's current programme in Ghana involves a contribution toward the development of the Dawhenya scheme irrigating 1,200 acres; and the construction of a 50-mile canal from the Volta lake to the Accra plains. At one time the Chinese were also reported to be interested in the Manantali Dam on a major tributary of the River Senegal in Mali, but have not apparently earmarked existing aid funds for this project which is likely to cost some $150 million. A further scheme in the same area--the port at Nouakchott, in Mauritania, involving about $20 million--has not progressed beyond the feasibility study, which was due to be completed by March 1972.

Another initiative which appears to have run into difficulties is the main component in China's aid offer to Mauritius--the building of a new airport. According to local reports, it is doubtful whether the Chinese are capable of supplying the level of technological expertise or the advanced equipment required. There has also been adverse reaction to their demands for payment in cash for imports intended to be sold to finance local costs, and there are fears that Chinese goods will compete with Mauritian products. The island, over 80 percent of whose commerce is in the hands of indigenous Chinese traders, has recently begun to industrialize in an effort to provide a viable alternative to reliance on a one-crop (sugar) economy, and to reduce its serious unemployment problems.

The Soviet Union has tried to exploit African reservations about China's economic campaign by accusing Peking of being largely motivated by self-interest. It claims that the Chinese have used economic aid as a means of obtaining products which they lack, such as copper which they have previously had to buy on the international market, paying either in dollars or sterling. The Chinese are also accused of extending large credit knowing that only a small part can be utilized because they do not

TABLE B.1

Chinese Aid Offers to Sub-Saharan Africa, 1970-73
(in millions of U.S. dollars)

1970		1971		1972		1973	
Country	Amount	Country	Amount	Country	Amount	Country	Amount
Guinea	10	Ethiopia	84	Burundi	20	Cameroon	73
Tanzania	201	Mauritania	20	Dahomey	44	Chad	45
Zambia	201	Somalia	110	Malagasy Republic	9	Congo	24
		Tanzania	1	Mauritius	34	Senegal	45
				Rwanda	22	Zaire	100
				Togo	45		
Totals	412		215		174		287

281

have the capability to undertake projects which African
countries require to improve their industrial capacity,
such as an iron and steel complex or petrochemical industry. Chinese projects are, at best, simple and integrated,
and where they include small-scale industry it is mainly
keyed to agricultural schemes, such as sugar refineries
and other processing plants.

The Soviets also maintain that China carries on trade
with South Africa and Rhodesia--either directly or through
third countries--and has considered opening relations with
Portugal because she buys "valuable strategic raw material"
in Angola and Mozambique. In short, according to a Moscow
Radio report on May 20, 1973, "Peking's so-called new line
contains nothing basically new. Only the methods have
changed, becoming more tractable and intricate. The aims
of the Maoists are the same, however; these are to boost
Maoist prestige, achieve Peking's political hegemony in
Africa and isolate the African countries from their true
friends. . . ."

CONFLICTS IN TRADE UNIONS
David Brombart

American labor has continued a tradition of opposition
to totalitarianism. Basic policies adopted by the American
labor movement, as far back as 1880 when the AFL expressed
public disapproval of Czarist Russia, have not changed.
However, we must admit that in the last few years, the most
firmly held notion of the role and place of free trade
unionism has been increasingly questioned in various continents of the world. The January 1973 meeting in Brussels
of Western European trade union organizations not only has
decided to drop the word "free" from the title of the new
European trade union organization, but the organization has
a clear mandate to open relations with the communist trade
union organizations of Eastern Europe. It is not a coincidence that the primary objective of the Soviet-controlled
WFTU is to call for a Pan-European Trade Union Conference.
The major aim of such an exercise was described in December 1971 by A. Shelepin, President of the Council of Soviet Trade Unions, during a WFTU General Council Meeting
in East Berlin: to "create a single European trade union
organization." The concept of such a conference was
launched by WFTU on the advice of the Soviet trade union
and following an initiative of the Soviet Communist Party
in 1969.

On the continent of Africa the Soviet trade union is
working through their front organization, WFTU. As on
other continents, the WFTU's tactics for infiltrating
trade unions in developing countries are based on an "es-
calade" in actions, in approximately the following way:
contacts, study trips, friendly visits, bilateral relations, support for governmental actions, joint seminars,
common meetings, common conferences, standing committees,
permanent committees, permanent organizational links, and
so on.

They have succeeded in signing successive joint
agreements with one Pan-African trade union organization,
the AATUF. Even the ATUC has not dared to have a similar
working relationship with the ICFTU. It is ironic to see
that such a relationship with all its implications, propaganda, and funds has now been challenged as the OAU has
recently established its own Pan-African organization of
trade union unity.

The majority of the activities of Soviet-controlled
WFTU continues to deal with problems affecting the non-
communist countries where it has only 5 percent membership compared to 95 percent in communist nations, nations
where trade unions are an arm of the party which is also
the government.

When they talk about problems affecting the communist
workers, it is done in a long standing tradition of per-
juries and lies. The Tunisian labor organization, the
UGTT, felt it necessary to invite to their convention last
March representatives of communist countries including the
Soviet Union. "Their embassy was phoning us every day and
we had to invite them."* In his address, the so-called
representative of the Soviet trade union talked about the
increase in productivity of the Soviet workers and new advantages in pensions and wages. A sophisticated trade
unionist commented on how is it that they improved so much
when they have always told us that the Soviets had already
attained a high standard of living! African trade unionists are not duped by communist tactics even when they are
invited to the Soviet Union. A Moroccan trade unionist
mentioned, after returning to Casablanca from a Soviet
trade union convention, "now I will read in 'Le Monde'
what happened in Moscow at the convention. There was no
Arabic translation. When the Rumanian delegate talked,
the French translation was very poor; when the Italian
talked, there was no translation at all!"* More seriously, what has been the Soviet Union's strategy, and therefore WFTU's up to now? After independence, they had developed a strategy based on nonalignment and disaffilia-
tion from international organizations. On the latter, it
was not too difficult for them, as their support for Marxist labor organizations didn't succeed and the number of
WFTU affiliates was minimal in the newly independent African countries. However, in the 1960s they realized that
their policy of nonalignment and international disaffilia-
tion had failed and decided to reaffiliate with organizations in Africa. Such is the case in Nigeria, Dahomey,
Upper Volta, Zaire, the Gambia, Mauritius, Reunion, and
Somalia, not to mention exile trade union groups.

In the 1970s their virulent attacks, particularly on
the AALC, are changing. They are not convinced any more
that the concrete projects of assistance rendered by the

---

*Confidential information from diplomatic sources.

AALC are not worthwhile, and the question is now whether the so-called Soviet trade unions should render similar assistance to African trade unions. Interested as they are in problems affecting the foreign affairs of others, the Soviet trade unions have been very active in gaining active African trade union support, particularly in the ILO. They succeeded in assuring some African trade union support by gaining, for the first time some years ago, a seat in the workers' group of the ILO. Such a move is extremely dangerous as it affects the basis of the tri-partite philosophy of the ILO.

The Chinese trade union movement was revived in April 1973. I will offer the suggestion that it has been revived more because of external pressure than for internal reasons. It has been ironic to see that the governing board of the ILO has accepted communist China as a member without assuring the existence of employers' and workers' organizations. Once again the tri-partite structure of the ILO has been damaged. China's trade union organization was therefore reactivated after five years' discredit partly because they concentrated too much on improving workers' welfare! The trade unions disappeared some years ago because they became linked with the head of state Liu Shao-Shi who was disgraced during the Cultural Revolution. A "People's Daily" editorial of April 15 said that the former leadership "tried to vitiate the militancy of the working class and turn the trade union into a tool for pushing the revisionist line." This is quite similar to the tragic events in the Soviet Union in the years 1917-28 which have been captured so well by Jay B. Sorenson in his book The Life and Death of Russian Trade Unions (New York: Atherton Press, 1969). The "People's Daily" editorial made only scant mention of what is regarded in Western countries as the traditional role of trade unions--to improve the lot of the working class. The editorial went on to state that "The workers should have an even stronger sense of responsibility as masters of the country and should be models in carrying out Chairman Mao's proletarian revolutionary line and in grasping the revolution and promoting production. They must go all out to aim high and achieve greater, faster, better and more economical results in building socialism through self-reliance and hard work."

In Africa we have seen two major phases of Chinese involvement. The period before and after independence when strong support was given to Marxist organizations and in 1964 when Chou En-lai issued his memorable declaration on the policy of China in Africa at the time--

"Africa is ripe for revolution." Now in the 1970s, we can
see a total new approach similar to that of the Soviet
Union's. The emphasis is on relations between states and
not through mass organizations. China is learning quickly
in Africa, particularly after their disastrous experience
in Mali. The way the state-run Chinese enterprises were
managed in Mali during the Keita dictatorship has been one
major element in the new revolution. Workers in the
Chinese-run enterprises revolted against the "management."
Moreover the population soon realized that the products
made by the Chinese were useless. Their cigarettes were
unsmokable though they tried to maintain in their adver-
tisements that the cigarettes called "Afrique" were similar in taste to "Salem's" or that the cigarettes "Frater-
nite" equaled "Kent."

Another more important aspect is the reaction in
Mauritania vis-a-vis AALC assistance in the labor movement.
It is most significant that both the Soviet Union and China
have not developed one single labor institutional project
in Africa. In Mauritania it is the AALC who built a Workers' Education Center. The reaction of Mauritanian trade
unionists was that the Soviet Union and China are not interested in the workers or in a labor movement and are
only providing assistance to the governments.

China has now become a more important factor in Africa than the Soviet Union, which is considered naively
by some Africans as a European nation. I came back in
May 1973 from a head of state conference of the OCAM countries. You are all aware that only three heads of state
ever attended and that this regional organization of
francophone countries is facing a serious crisis. One
significant element is China. The two others are the new
influences being exerted by Libya and other Arabic countries and the search for a new kind of relationship of
the francophone countries with France and the European
communities. China is now giving long-term, interest-
free loans to several African countries in the francophone area. In the case of Togo and Dahomey, these loans
equaled their annual state budgets. This new development
is extremely dangerous and may have an indirect effect on
the labor movement in some countries.

To conclude, the challenge to the West by the Soviet
Union, working through WFTU, and by China, who at the
present time is more involved with students than with
unions, must be viewed in its global aspect of subversion
as well as in their attempts to create sources of grave
and potential tension (the USSR in the UAR, formerly in

Zaire; China in Tanzania and Mauritania, formerly in
Cameroon). We believe that more attempts to infiltrate
the African labor movement will be made. As far as we
are concerned, let me simply repeat the conclusion of a
1959 AFL-CIO Council report on Africa:

> What is important for American labor, is
> the fact that in spite of all the criti-
> cism that may be made of American policy
> and of some of its perhaps inevitable
> drawbacks, American unions still have a
> tremendous reserve of good-will and can
> still have an important role in assisting
> and advising those who are attempting to
> build not only free trade unions but a
> free Africa.

WARREN WEINSTEIN is Associate Professor of Political Science at the State University of New York, Oswego. He was a Fulbright graduate researcher at the Free University of Brussels (1967-68) and a research associate at the Bujumbura Official University in Burundi (1968-69). During 1973, Dr. Weinstein was a consultant to the Carnegie Endowment for International Peace.

Dr. Weinstein has contributed articles to the major U.S. journals on Africa and is a member of the editorial board of <u>African Studies Review,</u> the African Studies Association journal. He is coauthor of <u>The Pattern of African Decolonization</u> and is currently preparing a book on Rwanda and Burundi.

Dr. Weinstein received a Ph.D. from Columbia University in 1970.

VALERIE PLAVE BENNETT is a graduate of the African Studies Center, Boston University, and is a former research associate in the International Development Studies Program of the Fletcher School of Law and Diplomacy. She is a contributor to <u>Politicians and Soldiers in Ghana</u> and <u>Comparative Socialism,</u> and is coauthor of the forthcoming <u>Politics in Francophone Africa.</u>

DAVID BROMBART is Assistant to the Executive Director of the African-American Labor Center, a specialized organization of the AFL-CIO.

After studies in social science, he was active in Belgian politics as Secretary of the Social Democratic Youth Movement. In 1958 he was elected Secretary for Labor Affairs of the World Assembly of Youth, where he served until joining the AALC in 1964.

Mr. Brombart was recipient, in 1971, of the National Order of Dahomey for his contribution to the development of free trade unionism in Africa.

HELEN DESFOSSES is a Research Fellow at the Russian Research Center, Harvard University. She is the author of <u>Soviet Policy toward Black Africa</u> (Praeger, 1972) and numerous articles on Communist relations with the Third World. She is also coeditor of a forthcoming volume on socialism in the Third World (Praeger, 1975).

MOHAMED A. EL-KHAWAS is Professor of African and Middle Eastern History at Federal City College in Washington, D.C. and was chairman of the Department of History and Philosophy from 1969 through 1974. He has been a frequent panelist and speaker on political issues encompassing the United Nations, China, Africa, and the Middle East, and he has written extensively on these and related subjects. Professor El-Khawas received his Ph.D. from the School of Advanced International Studies, Johns Hopkins University, in 1968; in 1971 he was recognized as an "Outstanding Educator of America."

JOHN D. ESSEKS is Associate Professor of Political Science at Northern Illinois University. He was recently a research associate at Harvard University's Russian Research Center. Dr. Esseks is coauthor of Politicians and Soldiers in Ghana, 1966-72 and of A la Recherche de L'Independance Economique. Dr. Esseks received an A.M. and a Ph.D. degree from Harvard University.

MICHAEL H. GLANTZ is on leave from the Department of Government and Law of Lafayette College to work at the National Center for Atmospheric Research in Boulder as a senior postdoctoral fellow. He is engaged in research on the political effects of climatic changes in northern Africa and is editor of the forthcoming Politics of Natural Disaster: The Sahel Drought (Praeger, 1975). Dr. Glantz received his Ph.D. from the University of Pennsylvania in 1970.

THOMAS NSENGA KANZA is a former Cabinet Minister and held ambassadorial posts for the Congo before its independence. He is currently an associate professor at the University of Massachusetts, Boston, and a research fellow at the Center for International Affairs at Harvard University. Dr. Kanza received his advanced degrees at the School of Oriental and African Studies, University of London, and St. Anthony's College, Oxford University.

BRUCE D. LARKIN is Associate Professor of Politics and Fellow of Merrill College at the University of California, Santa Cruz. He has published articles and reviews on China's foreign policy, principally in relation to Africa, and is the author of China and Africa, 1949-1970: The Foreign Policy of the People's Republic of China. Dr. Larkin received an M.A. in East Asian Studies and a Ph.D. in Political Science at Harvard University.

ANGELA STENT has a B.A. from Cambridge University and an MSc. from the London School of Economics. She is currently a teaching fellow and Ph.D. candidate in the Government Department at Harvard University and is associated with the Russian Research Center. Ms. Stent is a regular correspondent for the London _Times_'s Higher Education Supplement and has also published articles in _Change_ Magazine.

GEORGE T. YU is Professor of Political Science at the University of Illinois in Urbana. He is the author of _China's African Policy: A Study of Tanzania_ (Praeger, 1975) and _Party Politics in Republican China: The Kuomintang 1912-1924_. He has written numerous articles and reviews for leading journals in Asian and communist studies. Professor Yu received his doctorate in political science from the University of California, Berkeley.

CHINA'S AFRICAN POLICY: A Study of Tanzania
George T. Yu

SOVIET AND CHINESE INFLUENCE IN THE THIRD
WORLD
edited by Alvin Z. Rubinstein

SOVIET POLICY TOWARD BLACK AFRICA
Helen Desfosses Cohn

TOWARD MULTINATIONAL ECONOMIC COOPERATION
IN AFRICA
B. W. T. Mutharika